Your Life Is
<u>Not</u> A Label

A guide to living fully with
Autism and Asperger's Syndrome
for parents, professionals
and <u>you</u>!

by Jerry Newport

FUTURE HORIZONS INC.

Future Horizons, Inc.
721 W. Abram Street
Arlington, TX 76013

800-489-0727   817-277-0727
817-277-2270 fax

Website: www.FutureHorizons-autism.com
E-mail: info@FutureHorizons-autism.com

ISBN #1-885477-77-5

Acknowledgments

I want to thank my partner, Mary Meinel, my brothers John and Jim, and my departed parents, Floyd and Loved Newport. I also thank my friends throughout life, especially Johnny Aichroth, Steve Lazzaro, Don Shlimbaum, Ken Brier, Mike Novak, Ken Weinman, Bob Scott, Steve Ferguson, Ron Bass, Robert Lawrence, Marti Galovic Palmer, Toby Arenberg, Charlene Wise, Artie Kemper and Ken Brewer, Stephen Shore and Robert Morris.

Some of my chapters have been enhanced by what I have learned from dedicated professionals, Carol Gray, Michael Powers and Reed Martin, J.D. I also must thank Colleen Weick, director of the Minnesota Governors' Council on Developmental Disabilities, for the Partners in Policymaking training program. Without that, I never would have become an advocate and co-founded my first adult support group. I also thank Autism Society of Los Angeles, ASA, ASC-US and other advocacy groups who helped me make the most of my adult life.

Finally, I thank Future Horizons Publishing Company for two reasons: -It was that company which originally helped me learn to make informative and effective presentations. -It was my friends there, especially Wayne Gilpin, who helped me keep focused and recover when life wasn't so great.

Editor's Note

We at Future Horizons are proud to bring Jerry Newport's wit and insights to the printed page as he offers his ideas and caring to people from around the world.

Editing Jerry's sense of humor and thought process was a challenge because of the uniqueness of his style of communicating. We feared that too much editing would dilute the genius that is Jerry. Therefore, unlike a medical or professional offering that we monitor closely, we gave Jerry a free rein to explore ideas and opinions that we felt were important, although we were not always in complete agreement.

Jerry's referrals to autism are always references to both Asperger's and autism. Also, Jerry's natural perspective is that of a man and therefore he speaks from the male view. A female perspective is provided in the two interview chapters. No disrespect to our female friends is intended by Jerry or Future Horizons.

You will note that this book has 23 chapters. Each could be a stand alone mini-book on its own, offering thoughts and counsel on the subject that the chapter title implies. Therefore, other than the foreword or the last chapter, this is one book that you could read front to back, or back to front, or start anywhere in between.

Jerry's ideas will delight you while challenging you to consider options and different perspectives. His sensitivity to his world and those he has met and loved will impress you.

Enjoy the ride--Here's Jerry!

Table of Contents

Foreword

No doubt about it. Jerry Newport is one of the most extraordinary people I know. A brilliant mind, a warm and generous heart, a non-stop sense of humor, and tireless perseverance for his mission to empower those who feel disabled and helpless. When Jerry becomes your friend, you feel you have a friend for life. Remarkable qualities in anyone. Many times more remarkable in one branded by conventional thinking as disabled. And astonishing when one realizes that the disability is Asperger's Syndrome, a form of autism, the condition we have been led to believe must be marked by anti-social, withdrawn behavior.

I met Jerry and Mary while researching a script inspired by their love story. While Asperger's is a far, far higher-functioning condition that the form of autism that afflicted the character in "Rain Man," the idea that two individuals with any form of autism could fall in love, marry and live together was a revelation. It was the beginning of their teaching me of the autistic tendencies in myself (and in us all) and of the continuum that exists between personalities whose behavior sadly is mislabeled "disabled" or "normal."

In the course of working with Jerry on my script, I watched Jerry conduct AGUA meetings and witnessed first hand the tenderness, concern, level of understanding, and most of all his absolute respect for their humanity when dealing with the group members. The range of functioning among the members varies considerably, but to Jerry each was an individual, a valuable human being, and a personal friend. It was obvious what Jerry meant to each of them—how much each life had gained from having Jerry in it.

I have seen Jerry battle through hard times, witnessed his unwillingness to be branded and limited by the expectations of others. Jerry has, through sheer determination, intelligence and guts, found practical ways of dealing with problems and disabilities that would seem insurmountable to others. Jerry's advice is based on real-life experience on what actually works in the real world, as opposed to theories by those who have only observed but never lived through these situations.

Experience, of course, is the best teacher. If you choose to go to the "horse's mouth" for advice, you could find no wiser, kinder, wittier (or more talkative) stallion than my pal, Jerry Newport.

Ron Bass
Screenwriter for "Rain Man"

Introduction

Why Should You Read This Book?

That's a good question! Let me tell you why I feel uniquely qualified to write this book. I am a person with an unusual condition, although I have never thought of it as a disability. My "disability" is Asperger's Syndrome. It is a bewildering condition in which normal-appearing people are great at some things and laughably incompetent at others. You may say that is everyone, but in Asperger's there is a more bizarre mix of peaks and valleys than in most people.

Asperger's Syndrome people are particularly challenged with the nonverbal part of social interaction. They rarely marry and are professionally under-employed, if employed at all. Technically, it is called a disability, but I have always thought of myself as "differently-abled." I felt unusual but didn't have a clue about a name for it until I had stumbled from pothole to pothole for almost forty-one years.

In the spring of 1989, about a year after my mother passed away, I saw "Rain Man." Autistic savant Raymond Babbitt (portrayed by Dustin Hoffman) was enough like me in his talents and also in his obsessions, for me to become active in the autism community. However, walking out of that movie I did not think of myself as autistic, and classically I am not. After all, poor Raymond had to return to his institution in Cincinnati. Outside of a threat from my mother when I was twenty-two to find one for me if I didn't "straighten out," I never came close to such a place.

To make a long story short, my interest in autism led to co-founding an adult support group, getting a diagnosis, marrying an Asperger's peer, divorcing and reconciling. It also made me a frequent lecturer on autism and Asperger's Syndrome support groups, adult issues and advocacy throughout the world.

But that is not my living. I have held many jobs. I do what is available. Sometimes that's public speaking. Other times, it's substitute teaching, pet-sitting or even delivering pizzas. It doesn't matter. My parents taught me, like my two normal brothers, to be proud of any work I did and to do it with attention and respect.

I have lived almost fifty-three years. That is longer than most of the people who ever lived on our planet. I have enough life experience to share what I have learned about life and how to live it to the fullest with my younger peers, disabled people in general, their parents, siblings and friends. My advocacy and traveling has enabled me to learn from many adults, both with my disability and others.

Who should read this book? I have written it as if I speak directly to a person with a developmental disability. Certainly people from my own community, autism, will find it most useful. Also their parents, teachers, siblings and friends will find that this book highlights many issues for the person with the disability.

Within and without my autism community, there is a spectrum of potential. In other words, some readers will feel that they won't ever be able to try every possibility in this book. I intend it to be more of a catalogue of possibilities rather than an unrealistic formula for all. Each reader should use what he can and not compete with his peers.

Others may feel more like me. They have milder forms of disabilities, never had a debilitating childhood label, but also never got some services that were needed. They went through much of life feeling inexplicably estranged from the "normals" with whom they visually blend. These people may find that some of this book was already accomplished ages ago. But not all of it. Not by a long shot.

The truth is that for all people with disabilities, the theoretical threshold for achievement is raised to a new level when someone, along with a herd of peers, passes that prejudicial barrier. This happens because of improvements in diagnosis that facilitate earlier assistance, as well as improvements in the assistance.

More acceptance helps, too. "Problem-free" normals are slowly learning that there are other ways to live. People born different can accomplish the most when the aim is not to normalize but to simply help the person make the best of his unique set of talents and challenges,

Since I got involved with the autism/Asperger's community in 1991, I have learned from adults with every type of disability. I have discovered that as adults, what we share, the common experience of growing up feeling different and feeling devalued by that experience, is far more important than our labels.

That is why I recommend my book to people with any disability, and the important people in their lives. I honestly believe that when most of us are adults, we have already learned many coping strategies for living. In many cases, We have learned how to compensate in areas where we are lacking, and to accept permanent assistance in areas where it must happen. That is not the big adult issue.

The biggest barrier for adults with autism or other disabilities is not our condition; it is our state of well-being or rather the lack of that state. Poor self-esteem is the greatest cause of our self-defeating attitude. That results from how we grew up, what we heard said about us, the way we were teased or made fun of and other unpleasant experiences.

It results from well-meaning people who want to shelter us from disappointment. In many cases, this also denies us the necessary survival skills that are learned when one fails.

Failure is part of life. It may inspire another more successful attempt. It may mean accepting one's limitations and striving in a more practical direction. But to be denied the excitement and intensity of experimenting with dreams and chasing them until one finds the right dreams to chase, is to be denied the right to life itself.

This process begets an adult who mentally and physically, with reasonable support, can live in society, work and have relationships in the community. But he fails to because he lacks self-esteem and belief in his potential. By the time we are adults, too many of us acquire an attitude of inferiority and "learned dependency."

This is the disabled adult paradigm: I can never be normal.

We are told, by inference, that only normal people are loveable, happy or successful. Therefore, I can never be happy, loveable or successful. Therefore, I can't love myself or anyone like me. We honestly think that "normal" people are better and that we have to settle for less. We don't realize that even, with some handicaps, we individually have tremendous power over the quality of our lives and the direction in which we grow.

Let me quote an old Buddhist story. A man was at a lake, catching many fish. Another man, very hungry, walked up and asked the lucky fisherman for a fish to eat. The fisherman replied, "I am sorry, I have a use for every fish I have caught but I can give you something far more valuable than any fish in this pile."

Then the fisherman gave the hungry man a pole.

More than anything else, this book is about poles--practical insights on all phases of life for those of us who, diagnosed or not, feel quite different from normal people. I hope this book finds a lot of readers and not just because that means more money to buy fish. Nobody is rich enough to give fish away to all of those who would gladly eat them. But if you want to learn to fish the seas of life, you will see that poles rule these pages.

The most significant lesson anyone ever shared with me did not come from another person with autism. It came, instead, from a young man who has cerebral palsy. His name is Michael Long. Michael is the Consumer Coordinator for the Department of Developmental Services of the State of California. I first met Mike in the fall of 1992 as a member of a Partners in Policy-making training class.

The purpose of this class was to teach a group of forty-seven parents, consumers and professionals representing the spectrum of developmental challenges how to share, coalesce and constructively form new public policies. As one of our first speakers, Michael spoke about how he, a fellow consumer, and DDC could help us accomplish our goal.

Michael impressed me that first day, but that was only the beginning. Less than a year later, he really blew my mind. By then I had helped a team from University of Southern California produce a training film in self-advocacy. We wanted a peer to introduce the film, and Michael Long was the choice. This is what Michael shared at the beginning of our film:

"When I was born, the doctor told my parents that I would not walk or talk. My parents (smiling) believed in me. One day in second grade I asked a classmate to marry me. My teacher came over to me and said, 'Mike, do you have a couple of minutes?' I said, 'Sure.'

"My teacher asked me, 'Mike, do you know what marriage is all about.'

"No,' I said.

"She said, 'Well, it's about love and commitment and being responsible and able to have your own job.'

"Wow! That is a big job,' I replied.

My teacher then said, 'It is a big job, Mike, and I need to tell you that your IQ is too low, you are too mentally retarded and you will never, ever be able to get married.'"

Michael finished the story with, "Twenty-two years later, I walked into a People First Self-Advocacy Meeting and met the person of my life. Her name was Halle. We began dating and six months later on July 18th, 1993, I realized my second grade dream and got married."

"Now I have a wife. I have a life. I have a home and a real job. If I had listened to my second grade teacher, where would I be today?"

You may read this as a parent, a sibling, teacher, friend or advocate. Maybe you spend much of your time trying to lobby, advocate and insure that the person for whom you read this book will be surrounded by the best services available. I commend you for that but I must tell you that services are always vulnerable to political winds. The greatest private array of services and assistants that you acquire for your child can vanish at the stroke of a bureaucrat's pen.

But you can teach your child to accept and love himself, do for himself as much as he can and use good judgment in deciding when he needs help and who should help him. That is his forever.

The greatest service that you can perform for anyone, normal or disabled, is to teach that person to love himself as he is, make the most of every opportunity and never settle for less than his best effort or the best of interactions with his associates. That is what Michael Long learned as a child and it is why he is the inspiration that he is today.

My book is for everyone who ever knew or will have to know the pain that seven-year-old Michael Long survived and overcame. He and his parents were wise enough to know what you must learn: Your life is not a label. You, or the person you try to help by reading my book, were not born to fail on schedule.

Instead, you were born just as much in the image of the creator as anyone else. Just read the Old Testament, and even if you don't believe in God, you can see that an entire chapter is dedicated to numbers. If that isn't autistic enough, how about the part about how to build the Ark, who can get on it and how many of each kind can board it? How about that temper, turning people into pillars of salt? If that God, real or not, didn't have some autistic moments, what was it? By the way, have you ever noticed how all of the planets spin?

Similarly, when one's god seems insensitive, blind, unhearing or lacking any other ability we would assume in a deity, that is his/her reflection of every human disability. Therefore, all people are God's children, disabled or not. The Bible says, we are measured by how we treat the "least" or most needy of us. In that case, perhaps God tests "humanity" with an occasional earthly walk in the body of a disabled person.

Failing on schedule is not your mission. You have the same mission as every "normal" person. You have to learn what you can do well and work hardest at what you can't. I don't want to mislead anyone. You are probably more affected by your condition than I ever was. Or you are reading this book in order to help such a person.

Once I understood how the way I felt about myself was defeating me, I battled that and guess what? I became a much happier person and still have Asperger's Syndrome. I make the most of life, and my original condition is not the big deal it used to be. That's because I finally accepted myself and got on with my life.

You have to care. If you don't, who else will? This book contains progressive chapters about all phases of living fully with autism, Asperger's Syndrome and any disability. Some people need help to read it. What I share is best shared with pictures of what I describe. The economics of publishing doesn't allow that. But you should look for ways to make the contents easier to absorb by using pictures wherever possible. For example, you can get photos of the actual buses that your community uses to help a person prepare to ride the local transit system. You can hang a map of the routes on a wall in your home. That is the way many of my peers learn.

Now, it is time to me to share with you what has helped me reach the point where I live as fully as I possibly can. You can't be a lot of things you may like to be, but if you find the right path and love yourself enough, you can be a success. Living fully is not just a personal choice. Living fully is a personal, moral responsibility.

Jerry Newport

"Jerry, if you don't act like you care about yourself, why should anyone else care?"

- anonymous college friend

You Must be Your Own Best Friend

I have great news for every reader of this book. No matter how bad things are, or will get, there will always be one person around who knows you as well as possible and should always be there for you. Would you like to meet this permanently loyal, wonderful person? It's easy. Just look in the mirror! Now, if this book is being read to a blind person, I apologize for that statement.

The support group that I helped start in 1993 actually has a member who is blind and autistic. But to my friend, Andy Edelman and other such readers, I guarantee that even if he can't see himself in a mirror, my point is the same: All of us must be, for ourselves, the best friend that we can possibly have. After all, if you don't care about yourself, why should anyone else care?

I used to feel sorry for myself and wanted to be like other people. It seems foolish now. I made a big mistake. I took for granted many things that I should have been thankful for. I wanted to be a person that I wasn't meant to be. I didn't like myself because I failed to live up to those wishes. I tried to be what I thought everyone else wanted me to be, instead of working to become the best "me" possible.

Life is much better today, now that I know better. But you may struggle with doubts about yourself. We need to retrace a road to help you think more positively about who are you are and

1

how much the world needs you. It isn't easy but it is possible. It is necessary if you want to live as fully as you can.

Almost thirty years ago, I drove a taxi in San Diego. I hated myself for being a college graduate, driving a taxi. I felt that I was a total loser. I couldn't understand why other cabbies, some of them even more educated than me, had families, girlfriends and everything else I thought that only money could buy. Didn't these people know that they were just a bunch of worthless cabdrivers? How could they be happy?

The inspiration for this book first came to me in 1974 when I was attending a union meeting. After our union election, many of Yellow Cab's five hundred veteran drivers came to hear the new president. They were a complete spectrum of humanity: ex-sailors; other World War II, Korea and Vietnam war veterans; students; renegades; ex-members of every profession imaginable. One driver even showed up in his Boy Scout uniform. I learned that night that like most of the saner parts of humanity, these men and women didn't let a job define who they were.

Those people did their jobs and went home to spend the rest of the week doing anything they wanted with whomever and wherever. That night I began to see the value of accepting what life offers at the time, making the best of it and moving always ahead. Today I am happy to see that some people from that room full of Yellow Cab's finest, and a few who had already moved on before, have become: teachers, an antique dealer, a print shop owner, a software executive and a United States Congressman.

You never know just where life will place you, but wherever you are you must take full advantage of every opportunity. Learn that no matter how far back of the starting line you were born, you will cross the finish line of your life as a winner.

Before I found out about autism and began the journey of reflection that led to my diagnosis with Asperger's Syndrome, I often asked "Why me?" while not knowing just what kind of "different" I was. I searched through lots of philosophies and religions, trying to find a perfect approach to my world, to make up for what I thought I lacked.

It's a simple principle, "Just do the right thing." If you do something right the first time, you don't have to correct it or lie about what you did if you can't change it. If you know the right way to do something, it is foolish to do it any other way. This book is dedicated to help you do, personally, the right thing, all of the time: Love and accept yourself as you are meant to be.

I will list some principles that help me keep on a positive track. I will list them without details. Just read them and let them sink in for a couple of minutes:

1. You are your own best friend, but you are sometimes your worst enemy.
2. You must accept full responsibility for your actions.
3. Nobody will live your life for you.
4. You don't have to be normal.

Let's go over these points in more detail:

Point One is: You are your own best friend but sometimes, you are your own worst enemy.

That should be self-explanatory. You can't expect anyone else to put your interests at the top of his list. If they do that, they short-change themselves. Conversely, imagine yourself waking up every day with the needs of someone or something else, not yours, as your main concern. That happens to many who are in unhealthy marriages or other relationships. It stinks.

Maybe this sounds selfish to you. I think it sounds practical. If you learn to love yourself, seek what really motivates you, and do it in such a way that you can be happy without endangering or hurting others, what can be better? This is often referred to as "enlightened self-interest." In other words, the people who are most able to help others are those who learn to help themselves.

As far as being your own worst enemy, you are capable of judging your actions more harshly than others would. You can talk yourself out of doing things that are fun or would help you progress in life.

In the extreme, as happens far too often in general and especially to people with tough situations, you can even end your own life. Where is the good in that?

Point Two: You must accept responsibility for your own actions.

This is what makes the difference between civilization and barbarism. This is the difference between the whole planet becoming the "Jerry Springer Show" or populated by the idiots on "Judge Judy" versus a planet populated by imperfect, yet good people, who try their best to live responsible, fulfilling lives.

Let's suppose you get angry, living in your group home, and break some furniture or a window. You **can** do it. But don't expect me, a working, tax-paying peer, to pay for your loss of self-control. I have enough bills to pay without paying for some screw-up that you can learn to avoid.

That doesn't mean that if you do something destructive out of anger, that you don't have reasons. I know all about the abuse that many of us live with on a daily basis and we all have to unite and stop it everywhere. The danger is that your anger can be a trap that you never escape. It's not that I do not have sympathy for you. However, I do you no good if all I do is pay for the damage your anger caused and not help you learn better ways to channel your anger into constructive action.

Breaking windows is not the answer. The real answer is to understand why we get angry and do something constructive about the cause. If you need to just let some energy go, take a lap around the block, punch a pillow, or lift a barbell. You'll get your anger out and feel better for not having blown it and hurt something or yourself.

If you can identify the source of your feeling, share that with somebody. Try to control and work with the feeling, rather than be controlled by it. In too many instances, people like you and me are excused from responsibility for our actions by a "normal" society that thinks we are inferior and can't be held accountable to the same rules. It may seem like an easy way out, but it is a dead end for life. I can assure you that if you want to live where you choose, have friends, even a partner, a job and a real life, then you must accept responsibility for what you do.

What if you broke a window in a group home and the cost of fixing it was taken out of your next SSDI check? That might be the last window you'd break. Being responsible for your actions may seem harder, but the reward is this: You get credit for all of the good things that you do. Most of the time, you will do the right thing.

Thus, the gain of becoming fully responsible for what you do, instead of blaming it on some condition, is the chance for a much fuller, freer, happier life.

Point Three: Nobody will live your life for you.

Take a look at something you would like to change in your life. Suppose you want to learn how to do something. Can anyone else do that for you? What if you want a firmer body? Who will do your exercises? Maybe you met somebody with whom you would like to socialize. Who will ask that person out? Sure, people do get "set up" but that's only for the first time. After that, you have to follow through. You should get help when you need it, but the best teacher can't teach a student who doesn't listen. The best equipment in the gym can't jump into a person's arms and make him exercise. The best food can't force its way into a fat person's body and drive out all of the junk food. In the end, you have to love yourself enough to do the wisest things you can do.

All of us need help in something. That's why many of us hire someone to fix a car or figure out an income tax form. But we all have to do as much on our own as we can. **Learned dependency is a huge barrier to a naturally disabled person**. If the assisting person helps you eventually learn to do things for yourself, when possible, that is great. But if he does that, he has to find someone else to help.

Some people can take that risk and some can't. It's just human nature to protect your job, so if you do require assistance, make sure that it is only what you absolutely need and always look for ways to improve your self-reliance skills. I know too many autistic adults, smart and capable, who wake up and their first thought is "Where is my staff person?" The first thought should be, "What can I do on my own before I even need help?" The more you think like that, no matter what your challenge is, the more of a life will be in your grasp.

Point Four: You don't have to be normal.

I envy people with more visible disabilities. I mean, the trouble with any variation of autism is that we really don't look any different from normal people. It's not usually a physical difference as much as it is a difference in our brains and how we are "wired." That causes a lot of well-meaning people to try to make us normal. The result is a lot of wasted effort, trying to ram a square peg into a round hole by any means necessary.

I am still not normal. There are days when I feel really high-functioning. There are even days I feel more in command of my life than other people. But it doesn't last for long. Reminders always come, of where I started and where part of me will always be. A memorable reminder happened at a local health spa. I got there early and had a great workout. It seemed like I could do every exercise more times and with higher weight than ever before. I topped it off with some laps in the pool and some time in the sauna. I then decided to take a quick shower before changing my clothes. I walked out of the sauna in front of a huge room full of other folks, turned on a sprinkler and relaxed in the spray. I relaxed so much that without thinking, I let my swim trunks slide completely off!

"Hey!!" The shout woke me up and I immediately saw my error. I bent down, hurried my trunks back on and rushed out of the pool area. I didn't want anyone to see me. I was so embarrassed that I went to the health club at night for a couple of weeks, hoping people would forget what happened. I guess they did, but I didn't. It was the old me again, so absorbed in one activity that I lost track of where I was and how people would react to what I did.

If that had happened to me as a kid, it would have taken a lot longer to recover. I have accepted that I am not ever going to be normal. So what? I have a job, friends, and a wife who isn't normal either. We enjoy living with fourteen parrots and other pets. We wouldn't have it any other way!

Many people would not want a home in an area that is home to as many trucks as our neighborhood. It has a mix of houses and light industry, so many trucks park here. It is also near the railroad tracks where as many as one hundred cars pulled by up to five engines, go through. I know that because I asked the train's engineer. There are so many wheels, moving in perfect unison. What could be a higher-functioning neighborhood than this?

Chasing an impossible goal is a sure way to life-long misery. You must strive to know who you are, what you can do, and what you need help with and use that knowledge to be the best person you can be. Some of that may even seem normal, but I can promise you that if you become the best person you can be, you will be too happy being you to worry about being "normal."

Autism Public Enemy Number One: STRESS

Stress is a leading cause of death. Stress is an incredible modern drain on how one feels about himself, about coping with living in general. I am convinced, after a decade of intimate association with disabled people of all types, that stress and its cousins, anxiety and anger, are huge and destructive parts of the disability equation. Stress keeps us on unequal footing in a world in which we are a minority. For my peers with autism, stress is an even bigger part of daily life.

Stress controlled me from birth. I wouldn't even let my mother hug me. I can't imagine what my unspoken thoughts were. There I was happily spinning in the womb, and then after a lot of contracting, I slid out into the cold air. First thing: The doctor slapped me. Then somebody wanted to hug me. Sure. But of course, it was all my fault, right?

As far back as I could remember, I was like a little bird on a wire, ready to flee from the next embarrassment at a moment's notice. No matter how hard I tried to obey all of the rules, spoken by parents with frustration and siblings with sarcasm, I knew I would eventually screw up and tread water in another sea of laughter.

That, mind you, was life with so-called high-functioning autism. I never had a diagnosis or spent a day in special-education, never had a label other than eccentric, odd, nerd or just socially inept. I guess I looked fine, in control most of the time, on the outside. But inside, I was usually tense and very angry about life.

So, my stress, and perhaps yours, came from many sources: frustration, neurological overload, and social humiliation to name a few. Whatever the source, it was there. It is still there, but I have a much better grip on it now. The coping strategy is part physical and part mental. I picked up the physical part earlier and recently have added the mental part. They are both important.

The most important part is mental. By the time we are adults, whether we have been "busted"/diagnosed or not, we have heard enough messages and had enough experiences to know that the world we live in is not exactly tailored for us. We keep hearing that we are out of sync with it because the majority of people who tell us that find it easier to assume that than give us any credence. Majority rules, right or wrong.

There is nothing more frustrating than the lifelong accumulation of scars that result from trying to be like normal people and failing daily. It is especially hard when your disability is invisible like mine. I spent almost forty-one years trying to be some kind of normal person that I was never meant to be. Once I learned about autism, I realized that I was never going to be normal and decided to be as good a person as I was meant to be and to heck with what anyone calls it or me.

That is what I call a state of autistic or disability wellness. It means that I accept myself as I am. I believe that I have a right to be in society. I believe that my experiences and feelings are valid. I believe that I have something to share with peers and I can gain from what they share with me. I don't care about being normal. I care about gaining enough understanding of a world in which I am a minority to get a maximum of what I want from it while sacrificing as little of my natural essence as possible. In that sense, my value system is no different than that of any healthy normal person.

I didn't just come up with this on my own. After seeing "Rain Man" in 1989, I began to read about autism. There was not much in the way of personal accounts. The ones available were written by people who had accomplished much but were trying to convince themselves that they had recovered from autism. They had been brainwashed like me. They thought that the best they could hope for was to achieve something called normal and no longer be themselves. I didn't see the possibility of that. I still don't. I am, compared to the most celebrated cases, far closer to normal, but I still am not. Considering how billions of normal people have messed up my planet, I don't want to be normal. Human is enough.

When my self-discovery began, I fantasized about living on a planet of people like me. But I decided that I had to learn to negotiate better with the majority of Earth's residents. In 1992, I joined the board of directors of the Autism Society of Los Angeles. My goal was to start a support group for adult peers. My idea was shuffled around various committees. None of the board members thought it could happen. After all, we were hopelessly anti-social, right? We had no social empathy. What if we had a group and our autism just rubbed off on each other and made us worse? That is the kind of ignorance I had to just walk by. I knew better. At least I hoped I did. The support group eventually happened in spite of them. A couple of other ASA chapters held a conference in the spring of 1993 and invited me to try to use the last hour to organize a county wide support group.

Fourteen of us showed up that first day and decided to meet a month later. We began having regular meetings, hosted occasionally by families but always run by ourselves. The results were amusing. At our second meeting, after two hours, people practically bolted out of the home. They were so intimidated by their own autism and the prospect of being in a room full of autistic people (professionals probably warned them of the

11

dangers of such prolonged association) that conversation was difficult to encourage. It took a few key people like the very structured but determined Geneva Wulf, an Asperger's grandmother, to force a meeting to happen.

By June, our third meeting, things had lightened up. A new reason was Marshall Weeks, a young man who just refuses to be unhappy. This was the first appearance of a gangly, angular hybrid of Jim Carrey and Steve Martin. Marshall is happy to be himself. He walks and looks like a pool table on feet, all angles and grins. At times, he will stand in the middle of a room and happily mutter to himself. Most of the time, he is "with" the rest of us. But it was Marshall's totally uninhibited presence that lit up the room.

Since then, our group, which named itself AGUA (Adult Gathering, United and Autistic) has maintained a monthly comfort zone for a group of over one hundred people in Los Angeles county. I know of no other regular group that better proves what other peers of mine have opined in e-mail and at conferences: There is a culture of autism. When a critical mass of people with this condition is assembled and allowed to interract, share and exist on its own terms, there is a uniquely shared common understanding based on experience and shared beliefs about the surrounding world; an autistic culture.

Within this culture, we share what we have individually learned about living as a minority on earth, usually without comparison or judgment about who is trying or who isn't. Nobody at a meeting has to apologize for how he was born, yet that is not a blank ticket to act out anger or be obnoxious. There is a shared civility that allows unique humor, such as the time that somebody said, "You know, you'd be a great guy if you weren't so autistic!"

This book has another chapter in which we will return to this group, further explore its development and learn how similar groups are now growing in other places. I just want to share another early development. Once we had relaxed as a group and gotten past the fear of each other, we shared what we were reading about ourselves, from publications about autism. This resulted in vigorous debates over whether we should be cured, etc.; debates that just showed that we are diversely autistic. One person shared an essay by a psychology graduate student named Jim Sinclair.

Jim's essay, titled "Don't Mourn for Us" is a remarkable and uplifting elevation of how we can look at ourselves. Written to be read by "normals," Jim's essay says that we are who we are meant to be. It says that we gain nothing by mourning the child who did not arrive. Jim's essay was one of the most significant writings that I have ever read.

The bottom line is this: You can't mourn the person that every one else expected you to be, who never arrived. The stork didn't go to the wrong address. You were born the person who you were meant to be. If that is not in line with the definition of "normal", so be it. What is important is to accept yourself as someone who has a unique set of virtues, talents, needs and preferences. Do that and you can stop hating yourself for never becoming the person who everyone else wants you to become.

They don't do that out of spite. They honestly think that their way of living is the only way and that you can't possibly be happy any other way. It is more out of misguided compassion and ignorance but the result is the same. In the name of making you happier, you are challenged to somehow sacrifice your basic nature and become who they, not you, want you to be.

You are different and always will be. So were Helen Keller and FDR. So is Stephen Hawking. Your mission is to find what makes you happy, what makes your life vital, exciting and meaningful and find a compromise between those ideals and what the majority of the world wants from you. In that, you are no better or worse off than anyone else. Everyone is good and lousy at some things. Everyone has limitations. Everyone has days when it just seems to make no sense at all.

Adopting and embracing an attitude that as you were born, you are just as "okay" as everyone else, no matter what the differences seem to be, is very liberating. It will relieve a lot of the psychological stress that you feel and also the hopeless feeling of lack of fulfillment that often engulfs us. If you learn not to want what isn't meant for you to have, then you can redirect your efforts to getting what is achievable, enjoy those victories and stop missing what you shouldn't be wanting. You are the state of the art you. There will never be another you as good as you. Accept it. Celebrate it. Relax. You are OK!!

However, knowing that you are "OK" does not place you on an autistic pedestal or any other kind of disability pedestal, from where you can feel free to refuse to make any compromises. In all likelihood that will make you totally unemployable and totally dependent on society's charity, while expecting people like me, who find a reasonable middle ground of living, to pay taxes to keep you on your pedestal.

Your recognition that you are "OK" does mean that you don't have to surrender to the majority. You can negotiate with the "normal" world, without the impossible and self-devaluing intent of seeming more normal. It means you, like all humans, should negotiate how you relate to the world and reach a workable compromise between your needs and the world's. You can't have everything the exactly way you want it. Nobody can. But you can have a lot of what you really need.

That attitude can relieve a lot of stress, but not all of it. Some stress is from overworked senses and nerves. It mounts up and paralyzes the best of us, especially us autistic people who, on a good day, can juggle one orange. I have always had trouble when too many demands are put on my attention. It results in things just not getting done. Worse yet, it can result in total spiritual stagnation.

Stress has a cousin called anxiety. When one is constantly stressed out, the next escalation is anxiety, a tendency to have doubts about literally everything, short and long term. I had a bad case of that last year. I remember talking to Temple Grandin about it. I told her that to relieve my anxiety, I was taking Ativan. Her response, as usual for Temple, was direct and correct:

"Jerry, you need to get that *&^p out of your system. There isn't any good medication for anxiety. I handle mine with exercise and that is the only thing that will work for you." That was in the winter of 1999. It took me almost another year before I heeded my friend's advice. I needed help from another friend. You could say that a little parrot told me.

Shayna is a Goffin's cockatoo. After Mary and I separated, he migrated between Tucson and Los Angeles, our shared-custody winged child. He was with me, in October of 2000, when my world was crashing on me like never before. I reached a dead end. I was lonely, overweight, depressed, hated my job and took medication for depression, anxiety and high blood pressure. I had missed so many days that I had to either quit or stop being absent. I chose neither. Thankfully, I was given a temporary leave of absence, up to a year if needed, to figure things out.

Actually, Shayna's shift with me began shortly after the leave began. Whatever inclination I had to stay in bed, now relieved of work, quickly vanished. This bird insists on sleeping with me, on my shoulder. He gets up with the sun and once he is up, I do not sleep any more. I had to wonder what I could do at 5:00 a.m. Then, I remembered. The Bally's Health Club opened at 5:00 a.m.

15

It was a perfect solution. After feeding and playing a little with my cockatoo, I headed for the gym. Within days, I felt completely better. I soon stopped taking the medications, tapering off in a month. Thanks to the exercise, my depression disappeared, anxiety likewise and my blood pressure went down, even though my weight went up once my appetite returned in the absence of Prozac.

Reflecting on the past, it made sense. I was never a good athlete but always got exercise. It helped me settle down, improved my focus and my grades improved every year. Most of my really good life periods have been when exercise was a regular part of life. The best kind is that which allows us to do what is natural for us, repetitive activities. To be autistic is to stim if nothing else. Why not stim on swimming, running, rowing, walking, weight lifting or modern dance and be autistic and get healthier at the same time? Stimming is something people force many of us to give up. It is integral in us and should be redirected, not punished or extinguished. I never did well at team sports. Too much confusion. But there are plenty of individual ways to work up a good sweat.

It need not be in a sport. I met a young fellow in 1990 who was a graduate of a local high school. Tom was bi-polar, as was, probably, his chain-smoking mom. He wisely chose to attend a local junior college and enrolled in a modern dance class. It completely changed his life. I imagine that he is still bi-polar but he is no longer a bi-polar bear. I only have heard good things about him since. The last time I heard, Tom was self-employed in the computer field.

Modern dance helped him feel more integrated, much as other more conventional exercise does for me. Yet, I have found that having a total state of mental and physical wellness is not something that you can absolutely measure in terms of body fat, cholesterol or alpha waves. It is a feeling I have now, that took me a lifetime to find. It is a feeling that I am capable of having as good a life as I wish, as long as I accept who I am and live it on my terms, in reasoned harmony with the rest of the world.

Wellness is something that you, too, can have. It starts with total acceptance of yourself as you came into the world. It involves a healthy mental and physical daily discipline. If you feel wellness, you wake up knowing that living is a good idea, period. You look forward to a new day with confidence and self-esteem. Wellness is a popular subject for good reason. You will find resources on it listed in the appendix. I highly recommend that you add this philosophy to your world view.

YOUR LIFE IS NOT A LABEL

"Time has come today...." Chambers Brothers, 1968

So Much Time, So Little To Do With It

It is time to talk about what changes with each second, time. Most of us waste more of it than the life spans of the majority of humans and animals who have lived. But we often say we don't have enough of it. I am over 1.6 billion seconds old. People who are born today may live more than three billion seconds. For a guy who once lacked the patience to count to fifty, that seems like enough seconds of life to me!

Time is precious and getting more so. Gone is the world where people, normal or not, lived their entire lives within a few miles of their birthplace and possibly could actually remember everyone who they ever met. Today, we all are exposed to more people, ideas and visual experiences in one day, to remember them all. College students today talk casually of possibly having several careers, living in different countries and even expect to have different partners. It wears me out just to listen to them.

For me and my peers, time is not easy to manage. As most people who work in early assistance programs know, structure and scheduling helps a lot. The problem is that we become super-dependent on this and most of us are not taught how to design schedules and structures for ourselves. The sad result is people like me getting to be over fifty before finally acquiring self-discipline. Far worse, many of my adult peers lack the kind of self-managing independence they need to work and have a life beyond life. It doesn't have to be that way. No matter how young you are, you can learn how to schedule your time and make the best use of it.

There are two basic kinds of time. One is a lot easier for us to cope with than the other. The easier kind of time is scheduled time. That is the part of each day that you can do by habit. Suppose you are still in elementary school, high school or college. Scheduled time is what you spend, sleeping, eating, grooming yourself, going to and from school, doing chores, and maybe homework.

Schedules are like a group of rules for a certain period of time: Between 7:30 a.m. and 3:00 p.m., I go to school. I catch the bus home at 3:10 p.m. etc. When I was really young, the way to survive was to obey the rules, period. One year, Easter was coming. I had no idea what Easter meant. All I knew was there was this basket in my room with some fake grass, candy eggs and a chocolate bunny. I knew when Easter Sunday would come and it wasn't going to be soon enough. I decided to break a rule and eat the Easter bunny. I nibbled off its feet first, then with each day, ate a little more until by Easter morning, the only thing left was his ears.

I heard Dad walking up the stairs. I propped the ears up behind an egg and hoped he wouldn't notice. He walked in the room and said, "Happy Easter." Then, he saw the Easter basket. He smiled, picked up the ears, ate them and walked out. That was a close call. I rarely tried breaking a rule. We had lots of rules. Back then, we lived in a place with a front door and a back door. The rule for us was to come in and out via the back door, so the front entrance didn't get dirty. One weekend, Dad was on a trip. My older brothers Jim and John loved to debate anything. They usually tried to win by getting me to pick a side.

My mom got tired of it and said, "If you boys don't stop this carrying on, I will just quit and walk out the front door." Silence followed until I, about three, said "No, Mom. Go out the back door." I know that happened because it appeared in my mom's essays from her creative writing class that she attended even in her eighties. So, like many of you, I developed an early dependency on rules and rules of time: schedules.

For us with autism, especially, scheduled time adds a lot of needed security. It becomes something dependable. When I was young, the world seemed unpredictable, full of too many demands on my senses. Life was like being in an ocean, constantly treading water and I was the one who took three years of swimming class before I put my face in the water! Knowing my schedules made life manageable. The schedules were sets of rules for what to do with that amount of time. I learned that the best way to avoid misery was to obey all rules! Rules and schedules appeared in my ocean like little ice floes. I jumped on them whenever possible. Today, there are enough of those in life's ocean that I don't have to tread water too long before I find something to grab onto.

If you are in elementary school, this may not seem like a big deal. I can promise you that as you get older, the issue of what you do with your time when it is not scheduled will be a big deal. The kind of time, that is not automatically scheduled is called "free time." That seems like a funny way to describe it to me. If you don't make proper use of your free time, the consequences are very expensive.

The amount of free time varies at different times in our life. In your early life, most of your time is scheduled, from when you wake up to when you get home from school. But not all of it is scheduled. In high school, you may have a "study period." This is usually a period when you and other students are in a classroom and are supposed to use it to do homework. How you use that time is your choice. I did not waste it and as a result, I brought less homework home than most of my classmates.

In some schools, physical education is very scheduled and the entire period is devoted to some activity that all of the people do. It was not that way in mine. In the spring, we were let loose on the playing fields, given some balls and other equipment, and left to our own decisions on who played what game. This, for people like us, is chaos. If you are stuck in that kind of gym class environment, your best option might be to just walk some laps around the track, run them if you want, or get in the middle of the least confusing game. I say that, because being in the middle of a game is the best way to avoid bullies. But we will talk more about those people in another chapter.

Before you graduate from high school, your biggest block of free time is after school. It is different now, for many of you, than it was for me. I was always in a club, managing a team or on a team, so I rarely got home much earlier than dinner. Most schools have lots of different after-school activities. If there is something in which you have an interest, check it out. I made most of my friends in such activities, rather than in the classrooms. If you are old enough to work legally, a part-time job after school or on weekends is a very good option and you can learn more about that in chapter sixteen.

Eventually you go home, and that is where it is different today. My parents were both teachers, so we had a common schedule. We ate dinner together, my parents, two brothers and I, almost every evening during the week. Today many of you have parents who work different schedules. It is rare today that families can survive without both parents working. Also, many of you only have one parent.

You may come home to find yourself with only a TV and your siblings. How you spend the late afternoon and evening is up to you. If you are like many people in school, your options boil down to one: watching television.

Now, I am not going to lecture you on that. I am going to say that this is not your only option. You also don't have to watch the same channel every time, even if being autistic makes that more comforting. There are lots of channels. There is always something on that is worthwhile and something that is probably as gross and disgusting as you desire.

Here are some other options for your after-school time:

- Check up on your pet and/or garden.
- Do homework.
- Listen to the radio. Use your imagination while listening.
- Read a book for the fun of it.
- Learn something new every day: just one new word of a foreign language, or how to cook a new food. It will add up to something if you make it a habit!
- Spend time with a friend.
- Participate in a sport or club.
- Do something to make life easier for your parents. Mow the lawn. Dry the dishes. Volunteer to help out.

On weekends, you can be a bored couch potato, or you can:

- Go out by yourself, if you don't have a date.
- Go out on a date.
- Visit an interesting place like a museum.
- Do something with your family or friends.
- Go to a religious ceremony of your choice.
- Play with your pets.
- Do homework.
- Help around the house.
- Go to a real-live concert or sporting event.
- Work at a part-time job.
- Go to a poetry reading or an amateur play.

It's up to you. I am just showing you that you have more than one choice. The more you use your brain to make wise choices about your time, the more control you will have over your life.

You won't be in grade school forever. You will graduate or they will kick you out because you are too old to go anymore. I think most of you will graduate, and that is a great thing to celebrate.

But that also means that somebody isn't automatically scheduling your life for you!!

You will either go to college or to a junior college or look for a job. I hope you will do one or both of those things, because if you plan to just sit at home and be a couch potato, you may as well stop reading because I am obviously wasting your time. If you take the book back to the store, maybe they will refund your money and somebody else can read this book. That way, we won't waste part of another tree to make another book.

Either way you look at it, life will be different after high school.

If you don't go to college and get a job instead, then you will have to decide what to do when you aren't at work. That will revolve around the alternatives that I already listed. If you are working, you will eventually find out that you aren't making enough money to have everything you want since jobs that pay well often require more than a high school education.

So, if you are working, why not find some free time to go to school part-time? That will take care of some of that free time. It will also give you a chance to learn something to become a more valuable employee and move you closer to a job that you want but aren't yet trained enough to do.

Another nice thing about school, beyond high school, is that the students aren't usually as snotty. They don't waste as much time picking on each other and teasing. There will always be some idiots no matter where you go to school, but after middle school, there are fewer and fewer idiots left, each year. For one thing, in college, students pay to go, or their parents are paying. There is something about not getting something for free (like high school) and having to pay for it, that makes people take it more seriously and spend less time being idiots.

You may wind up in college full time with no job. In that case, there is a big difference between college and high school. In college, you spend less time in classrooms. But, you have more homework, and obviously, more free time to do it. You have to decide when, where and what to study.

I used to study at the campus library because it was quiet. If you need to look up something for an assignment, you're already at the library. If you do that, be sure to leave when it is still safe to walk to your car or the bus and make sure the bus is still running. If you are female, it is wise to walk with someone you know. Most colleges have escort service at night. These are people who you can trust, who will walk with you to your car or a safe place to get a bus or wait for someone to pick you up.

The other thing I can share about studying is that you will probably have one subject that requires lots of time, one that requires little effort, and the rest will be in-between. The best rule for study is to spend time on the hardest subject first. Get that out of the way and then it is downhill. However, if you are having a bad day, then start with an easier, enjoyable subject to get going.

Remember at college your education is much more independent. It is up to <u>you</u> entirely. It is easy to fall behind if you waste this new-found, free time that you never had in high school. You have to keep up a habit of studying at least some time, every day.

You will get older eventually and either graduate from college or reach a point where your main activity is your job and you aren't in school. I think it is a good thing to keep going to school as long as you wish, because there are lots of things that you can learn without them having anything to do with your career, but maybe you will reach a time when you just want to concentrate on your work and the rest of your life.

So, let's look ahead (for most readers) at a time when you are in your twenties or older and the main activity is work. Even at work, the quality of what you do depends a lot on your ability to manage your time. The better jobs belong to people who don't need someone looking over their shoulder ever minute. Very often, you will be better paid if you can be trusted to do a good job on your own.

This has been an overview of the element of time in your life. I can tell you, as one who has met many an adult peer, that the issue of time management (in most cases, the adult inability to make such decisions easily) is a huge issue. It prevents many people with autism from having jobs or succeeding in college. So they sit around in group homes, paralyzed by their own isolation, frustration and anger.

That is no way to live. You will be an adult possibly 80% of your life. I am tired of meeting peers who are wasting their lives. It doesn't happen because they aren't smart enough to work. It doesn't happen because nobody wants to be a friend. It happens because they don't know how to manage their time. It happens because they are so angry with themselves for being who they are (and not accepting who they are and living with it) that they are literally paralyzed into perpetual, angry isolation. It need not be that way, but no matter how young you are now, you must prepare to be old enough that you will have to decide whether to use your time wisely or waste it.

You can start now by just looking, not too far ahead, maybe just this evening or tomorrow. Get a sheet of paper and write down what you will do, each hour that you are awake. Some of it you already know. The important part is the time that is yours to decide. Now, challenge yourself to really use that time. If this was the last day of your life, what would you do? Tell your parents and others who help you that you want to learn how to do this.

You may think that you are too young to think about this. I can assure you that you aren't. I wish someone had encouraged me to learn how to manage my time. When I graduated from college, my grades were too low for advanced degrees, and I had no idea what to do. It took me over twenty-five years, almost 800 million seconds, to learn. That is a lot of wasted time. Don't let it happen to you.

YOUR LIFE IS NOT A LABEL

"I was a great student! I liked sixth grade so much, I stayed in it for six years."

Al Capone

Schools of Hard Knocks

Much of the first quarter of your life is spent in school. It was the happiest time of my life in many ways and also provided some of the saddest moments.

The bottom line is this: You must go to school. This chapter is intended to share some survival skills I learned at each level. They helped me and will help you, too. The day comes in every child's life when he is rudely awakened to the truth: he is not the sun. The rest of the world does not revolve around him, his every need and tantrum. He can't sit in his universe, a room of his house forever. He is taken, often kicking, screaming and crying, to a room full of age peers who have lost their universes. If you can read this, it's all in the past. And guess what? Some of those normal kids act worse on their first day of school than we do!

I don't remember how I reacted to nursery school or kindergarten. I remember first grade. Jim, my unusually sociable middle brother, entered fourth grade on the same day. We were taken to a new school in our new hometown, Wingamhauppauge Elementary School. I met the principal, Mr. Babcock, my future scoutmaster--another big, scary adult, but nice. I felt more comfortable upon entering my classroom. The clock on the wall was made by IBM. It said so in the middle of it. I was a bit hyper and I took the opportunity to look at the clock and say "IBM" as often as I could each day, walking off my excess steam in the hallway.

Right away, I saw that some other kids were ahead of me. The music teacher came in and they all knew some songs. I didn't know any of them. But they were easy to sing. There were happy faces all around me, singing "Oh, where have you been, Billy Boy, Billy Boy...," so that looked like fun. It was. I quickly found out an important lesson. If you want to survive in school and in life, be a part of what's going on. Singing is one of the easiest activities. If you have trouble talking, then singing will help you get better at talking. There's so much noise going on that it doesn't matter how you sound. Just open your mouth and have fun. Most of the time, you have to be quiet!

There are some good strategies to help you get the most out of your school years. They are important because we get more overwhelmed by classroom activity than normal peers. **Rule number one: Sit in the front row or as close to it as you can.** That works because the teacher notices students who are close to her. It also works because the teacher wants her class to look good if somebody just walks into the room. She will pay extra attention to make sure that the most visible desks and the students occupying them look appropriate.

This helps for another reason. Some kids may decide to pull tricks on you if you are a new student or seem a little unaware. It is harder to do that to you if you are closer to the teacher. I should have mentioned this before but if you take a school bus, you are better off sitting as close to the front of the bus as you can. The same principal applies here. The further away you sit from the driver, the easier it is for other kids to mess with you. Some kids intentionally sit in the back of the school bus so they can smoke or do other things that they aren't supposed to do.

Rule number two: Keep your hands off of anyone else's desk, body or property. Someone may bump into you accidentally, getting in line or on the playground. That is okay. A teacher might even tell you to hold someone else's hand as part of a lesson. That is okay. But at other times, you should respect other people by not touching their desk, property or them.

Rule number three: Only food belongs in your mouth. Pencils, crayons, lunch tickets, erasers and anything that is not food, including scabs, fingers or what you scrape out of your nose, don't belong in your mouth. What you put in your mouth is your business, but to put in anything but food is not safe or healthy.

Rule number four: Obey the rules. The easiest way to stay out of trouble is to just obey the rules of your classroom. They are usually simple. There is a time to be at your class in the morning. There is a place to go when the teacher says it is time to line up. You don't run in the hallways. You don't scream at other kids. This stuff sounds a lot easier to me now than it did in first grade.

Why all of these dumb rules? Here is the truth. Most of the world is not full of people like us. It is never going to give us all that we want. Nobody gets to do everything that he wants to do every time. Even normal people have to obey rules. I am not telling you not to be who you are. I am asking you to understand that if you make some compromises by following the rules that everyone obeys, you will have enough freedom and time to celebrate your unique self.

The main thing to understand is that you are not sitting in your room at home anymore. The teacher is a big person like your mother or father, but the teacher is not one of your parents. He has to divide his attention between you and the rest of the class. It is not like at home. You have to share the teacher with the rest of the class. SHARE is a scary, new word. The sooner you learn to share, the more comfortable you will be in the school.

31

You are in a school full of rooms full of people like you. You all have one job. Your job is to learn so you can grow up and be a GOOD big person instead of being one of the big people who winds up in jail because he breaks the rules that big people live by. You are part of a team that has that common goal. You can't be a good part of that team if you are off in your own world.

I don't for a moment discount the joy and comfort of my private space. It is just a question of when you can retreat to it. School is just not the place to do it. Now, you may already be in a class with a smaller number of students. It could be any one of a number of variations from the regular classroom. All of the rules will still work.

Depending on your needs, there may be another adult working with you, in addition to the teacher. This person is called an aide. Some disabled students will always need an aide at school, because of physical problems. The aide may even go to the bathroom to help some students and to protect the student from people who would take advantage of him.

Aides can help you a lot but you have to help them do that. You need to communicate with them. If you are not talking, I encourage you to try to talk no matter how difficult. It doesn't matter how slowly the words come out. There is a huge difference between slow talk and no talk. You will feel nervous trying. So did I at first. I was into my forties before I was finally able to comfortably enter group conversations. But if you keep trying, talking gets easier.

Some people find that singing doesn't seem like talking. It makes it easier for them to talk. Others find that slowly reading printed words from a book helps them. If either of these works, please try. If you talk, it will be much easier for you to make friends and survive in school. One reason that disabled students get in trouble is that if they can't talk and get upset, they kick, bite, scratch or do something else in order to communicate. Talking is much better. Raise your hand and say, "I need some attention. Something is bothering me."

There are other ways to communicate. I am not an expert in any of them but I know that some disabled students use sign language, point to pictures or even type what they want to say onto a keyboard that says it for them. If you learn to print or write, do that. **One way or another, you must learn to communicate!** If you are not talking and are in school, it is not too late and I can't stress how helpful it will be if you do learn to talk.

I have noticed that many of my young peers seem very anxious when they try to talk. Don't worry about "sounding right." It is okay to make mistakes in talking and everything else you try to do at school. Nobody is perfect.

In your early school years, especially if you are autistic, you will have a hard time sitting still all day. There will be a temptation to rock in your seat, hum or do other repetitive things that help you relax. This is distracting to other students and the less you can do it, the better. But many of you will need to do this occasionally. There are some relaxing activities you can do at recess, when you are in a play area. Swings are fun and so are see-saws. It is best to use them when an aide or adult is present. Make sure you can use them safely.

I am fifty-three and still do repetitive things every day as I have always done. I count cars on railroad trains and like to measure the height of our sunflowers. I love to just walk into the aviary and see how quickly I can count all of our birds. In youth, I was obsessed with knowing the facts about the world around me, how many people were in a room, how big things were, how fast certain animals could run. I used my obsessive curiosity to build bonds with other kids. I guess that by showing curiosity about my world in a way that I could share with them, I was "socially stimming." In most classes, I was usually the one who helped keep things in order, especially in the library.

In general, you need a daily way to deal with your internal stress. You can do this by sharing your hobbies and interests with classmates when you can, and you can do it by making sure your body gets enough exercise. Your autistic body, in comparison to most of your peers, is really overloaded when you are young. It will seem as if there is too much activity around you for you to keep track of. Eventually, you may be exposed to team sports. They are confusing not only because of the rules but because of the many people moving about. It is not easy for us to keep track of all of that and know what to do.

However, you are much better off doing something physical, especially when you are young. Your body needs to get rid of as much excess energy as possible. It will help you relax and concentrate better in your classroom.

Some of your nervous habits, like picking your nose or chewing nails, will be easier to manage if you get daily exercise. Also, you will look and feel better about yourself. It is hard enough being a student with any disability. It is even harder if you are fat or just look like an easy target for playground bullies. It doesn't have to be that way.

If you are not in a regular gym class, you will be involved in some physical activity. I urge you to make the most of it. After school, there are some great individual physical activities. Swimming is one. It is repetitive and is a great conditioner. The hardest part for me was putting my face in the water. It is easy to say now, but trust me because the water won't hurt you at all. It is much easier to swim once you allow your face to be in the water.

Another great activity is a self-defense class. This is also very repetitive and encourages fitness and self-discipline. You will learn things that, hopefully, you will never have to use to defend yourself. But it is good to know them because not everyone in school or life is someone who you can trust. It is good to know how to act if you are in a dangerous situation. I took some self-defense classes as an adult and was amazed at how much better and safer I felt by learning some simple strategies, I also learned how to walk in a way that discouraged people from picking on me in the first place.

Many special needs people tell me that when school is over, they are tired of a day's effort at "acting normal." I sympathize with you completely. Too much homework is a bummer. Too many parents dump their kids into all kinds of "busy therapy" after school. Swimming, scouting, clubs, self-defense and time with your garden or pets are the exception.

All of them are fun and will help you do the most important thing that most of you need to do as young students: **RELAX**. It will seem at times like so much is going on in the world that it is about to eat you up. It won't.

One big thing to understand is that it is okay to make mistakes. Nobody gets through school without making mistakes.

You will make lots of them. It is much better to make mistakes and learn from them than to never try anything. Sure, if you do that, you'll have everything under control. You'll never make a mistake, but you will spend your life with no friends, no job and no independence at all.

Just take a look at successful people. Mark McGwire doesn't get a hit almost three times as often as he gets one. Who cares? His hits go places and bring in lots of runners with them! Allan

Iverson misses lots of shots. He is also the shortest MVP in NBA history because he makes a lot of shots and even when he misses, he makes extra people guard him and creates opportunities for his teammates.

The best writers misspell words. People make mistakes on national TV on quiz shows. Mistakes are an important part of life, so relax and stop trying to control your world because you are sick and tired of always being corrected and don't want to ever make a mistake again. True, your parents and aides may need to lighten up and also give you credit specifically for what you do right, but they mean well. Even God made a mistake.

That is why he invented the rainbow to promise us that there will never be a great flood again. If God can make a mistake, so can you!!

Hobbies and interests often allow us more room for errors. With that in mind, after-school activities are especially helpful. One of these is scouting for boys and girls. The groups are much smaller and there is a lot of variety to what you do, arts and crafts, nature, etc. I made my first school friend, Johnny Aichroth, in my Cub Scout pack.

There are also leagues for various sports. Team sports are confusing, but even though I was never good in any of them, I enjoyed baseball and soccer. There are also individual sports like gymnastics, running, and swimming. We "stim" a lot anyway. Why not socialize the stimming with a healthy exercise?

Many of you will learn how to use a computer at school or at home. This is very attractive to us because we can control what we watch or do on it. Control is a big thing for us, especially when young! You can learn a lot from a computer. Many of us learn better from pictures than from hearing words. You can also use your computer to make a friend. Invite a classmate to come home and play with you with your computer. Show him how to do something and SHARE the computer. Let him use the mouse, too. Don't expect him to stand around and watch you use your computer.

One last tip on learning. **If there is a way to find a picture of something that is hard for you to learn, ask your aide or teacher to make one available.** You can also use your natural visual bent to make it easier to master the physical layout of your school. You can start with your own classroom. Make a model of it at home. Draw a map of your class with all of the desks, labeled after each classmate who sits there. To do that, you have to learn the name of every classmate. If you only learn one name a day, you will learn them all. People would much rather hear the sound of their name than "hey, you!!"

This is really a good thing to learn. After you finish the map of your classroom, expand the project. Make a map of the whole school. Label every room by the class, grade, teacher and activity. This will require some curiosity and research. But the end result is that you will really know how to move around your school and the teachers will all know that you are a student who is there to get something out of school. No way can you lose on this activity!!

I never had to do this. I have a very good visual memory, but one of my hobbies was collecting maps. My father helped me write a letter, in second grade, to the secretaries of state of each of the states. In 1955, there were only forty-eight of them. I asked each person to mail me a map of his state. In a couple of months, I had maps of every state. It was really fun to look at them and imagine myself visiting all of the neat places, the Grand Canyon, Natural Bridge, etc. The funniest thing happened when my family went on vacation trips. I was put in charge of the map, and I often knew what exit we should use, without even looking at the map. That amused my father.

You may not have much luck making friends in your early years, but that is not unusual, and there are a lot of normal kids who don't either. I had one great friend and that is one more than many of you will have in third grade, but I was hardly popular. It is easier for me to say this than for you to know, but if you are a good friend to yourself and make the most of your chances to learn and be a good citizen at school, you will have friends eventually.

The key is starting off with good habits. Learning the rules, especially the social ones, will help you. You will get older. You will reach a point when school changes again in its structure. Middle school usually begins in sixth grade or sometimes later. Here, you may not stay in the same class for the whole day. You will have more than one teacher. Depending on the subject, you will move from class to class. Needless to say, the habit of map-making and planning in advance will help you adjust to middle school.

One part of middle school demands special attention: bullies. You know when you meet a bully. It is not a nice experience. It usually means someone says something insulting about you. Worse, the person may hit you or cause you to drop your books. If this happens to you, you need to know how to handle it. Bullying is not acceptable behavior. Bullies are children who are out of control, people who lack self-esteem.

If you are bullied, the smartest thing to do is not to ignore the bully. You need to look at the jerk in the eye, say something once, and move away to a safer area. A teacher can help you decide what to say, usually something like, "I heard what you said, and I don't have to listen to that." Say it once and walk away from the bully immediately.

Walk in the direction of other students, a teacher or playground staff person. How you walk is important. Don't run like a scared chicken. Walk deliberately with a direction in mind until you are in a place where the bully can't do anything to you.

Once the incident is over, you report it to a teacher. Make a full report of who did it, what he said and did, where and when it happened. Tell the teacher that you need help to avoid this from happening again. Most bullies will keep bullying as long as they can get away with it. They are even worse if you ignore them.

You also need to tell your parents so they can make sure that the school does something to protect you in the future. Now, some parents don't get it. They may say, "Well, if you didn't wear such geeky clothes or space out looking at the fishbowl in the library, you wouldn't get picked on." They are wrong.

I don't care how unusual you behave or look. Nobody has a right to pick on you!

There are other things you can do. If a bully does things to you at certain times or places, maybe you can change your habits or at least know where to head once the bullying starts and you need to avoid it. You can keep reporting the incidents. The one thing you don't want to do is attack the bully. I say that because these cowards often have friends watching, who will rush to their aid if you start a fight. Secondly, modern bullies can sneak weapons into any school and no fighter I know is a match for a gun or knife.

It is not easy to walk away from hurtful people, but it is smarter. If this problem happens enough, your parents need to come to school and meet with the teacher. In some schools, assemblies are called to talk about bullying. Some schools have student teams where the better students look out to protect kids who are targets.

One thing you also have to do is not react to every kind of ordinary kidding as if it is bullying. If you do something funny in class or on the playground and people laugh, that is not bullying. When you go to the playground and the other children play and make lots of noise that confuses you, that is not bullying.

That may sound illogical but some children who are frequent victims of bullies do become overly sensitive to stuff that other children just laugh off.

A bully is somebody who uses speech or physical force to make you feel threatened and uncomfortable and obviously enjoys his power over you. A bully sometimes has no rational reason to be one, and you can't reason with a bully because he is not thinking. All he wants is to cause you pain. Sometimes, this is because someone who is larger causes him pain. It is bad learned behavior.

There is another strategy, especially on the playground. Be a part of the action. Games may confuse you but you will earn more respect if you take part in a "stupid" game than if you just wander around the sideline, your autistic head looking all over the place. You may as well walk around with a sign over your head saying, "Pick on him. He's out of it."

It is a lot harder for a bully to walk into a crowd and pick on someone. Other kids might care less about you but they won't like the bully's actions. Bullies are predators. Like hawks, they look for the birds who fly at the edge of the flock. They are easier birds to pick on than the ones in the middle of the flock. So, stay close to other people, especially people who are your friends. Find some safer place than a bully-populated playground, to do your "stimming" and other autistic stuff. There's time for that at home.

Middle school is also a fun time. You will find more clubs, a band or even sports if you want to try them. These are great places to make friends because you have a common interest. I made early friends in these activities. You will also notice some classmates start to do social things as couples. This is not easy to watch if you feel left out but be patient. Plenty of normal children don't date until they are older, either.

As for the bullies, the best thing about middle school is that it doesn't last forever. Many of the worst bullies will be gone once you are in high school and I never heard of them in college. If they try that stuff at that age, they just wind up in jail! So when you get to high school and that sick bully is no longer around, he's probably quit school, is in jail or both, already. Too bad. Karma happens. Better him than you. However, things may get so bad for you that you don't want to go to school, period. Some schools will not respond to your needs. Some teachers are not sensitive to the bullying issue. You and your family have to work together if it comes to this. You can go to another public school maybe. It would give you a fresh start. You might be able to go to a private school. In private schools, parents have to pay for their children to go there and behavior is often better.

You also can be home-schooled. That means you stay at home and do your learning at home. Mary home-schooled her sons when they lived in New York. It kept them away from the gangs and other bad influences. Home schooling has one big plus: it means no bullies. It also means no classmates, clubs, teams and chances to grow other than mentally.

I have mixed feelings about home-schooling. If you want a life in your community, you must function socially as an adult. Home-schooling does not foster social growth. It retards it. If you are going to be home-schooled, then you must have group

41

activities after regular school hours. Just reading the books and passing the tests will not be enough.

However, some school districts are acting quickly enough and I think that home-schooling may be the best way for some of us to survive our middle-school years. A recent report stated that almost two percent of students below college age (or about a million students) are now being home-schooled.

I believe this should only happen if you and your family have exhausted your options within your current school. If you are home-schooled, there is another advantage.

Once you qualify, you can take classes at a local junior college. You can pass the equivalency test for a high school diploma, called the GED and go back to classes in a local junior college. Now, you may feel a little younger than some of the people there, but bullies are not a big problem at any colleges. People in college are more tolerant of differences among us, and I was much happier there than in high school.

I wish I could make it easier for you, but middle school was no picnic for me. It is a lot worse today. There is one great truth about it: it's not forever.

More Hard Knocks

I rushed you through Middle School. That wasn't my favorite time. Most people in my class began "pairing up." I didn't know how to get started. In fact, I never had a date until I was seventeen, entering my senior year in high school. I was considered a late starter, but at least I started. That wasn't so unusual then, but today it would be.

High school is where a lot of stuff starts in earnest, not just dating. Future athletes finally get a chance to show off on a high school team. The top musicians sound like someone who might sing on an album or at least play an instrument on one. Most of the people don't get that far, musically or athletically, but they have a lot of fun trying.

Other fun things happen. There are lots of clubs. You can be as good a chess player, poet, artist, writer or anything you want. Just find a club for it. Time on a team or a club beats the heck out of spending your time after school in front of the TV set. By now, you may have a favorite subject and begin feeling some success in it. I remember in my senior year finally opening a calculus book. It felt like, "Wow! I'm doing big time math now."

High school was a very happy time for me. I was a lousy athlete, but I was pretty well liked despite social awkwardness. People saw my other qualities. Sure, I still got lost in my own space. I remember, in social studies, we had a quiz and corrected each other's quizzes. When we reached a certain question and I knew I missed it, I loudly said, "Oh, S...!!" My class got a big kick out of that.

But, I had an interest in the school world around me. It meant writing articles on our teams for the student newsletter. It also meant managing and keeping statistics for the basketball team. It meant senior band and track and cross country teams. I never really earned a letter in sports although the coach felt so sorry for me because I worked so hard in cross country that he gave me a letter. It wasn't important. It was the daily exercise that helped me settle down, focus and be a better student each year. I was thirteenth in my class at the end of ninth grade and graduated second out of 180. Letter or not, the exercise paid off in the classroom, big time! Of course, there was the math team, but everyone expected that out of me.

What I am saying is that there has to be something by now that interests you, so find people who share that interest. If you like fast cars, there's probably an auto mechanics club. If you like science, I'm sure there's a science club. If you like cooking, you might be the only man in the cooking or future home economics club, but so what? Some people will think that's weird, and others will think it's cool.

I will tell you one thing about cooking. I wish I had been in such a club. It will sure spruce up your bachelor life. Most of the famous chefs in the world are men, like Wolfgang Puck! I don't hear them complain about lacking women! Any man who can invite a date to his place and cook up a good dinner is way ahead socially. So, if some guys think you don't belong in the home economics club with their girlfriends, don't worry about what they think. Do what you like to do and find people to do it with. That's always cool.

Of course, there's the social stuff. By now, some people are dating all of the time. I don't have to waste time on the safe sex lecture. You'll hear that one every year. Most of you are miles away from any sex, safe or not! Now, here's a math problem for you: In most high schools, about ten percent of the girls get the attention from at least a third of the boys or more. If that is true, then the other ninety percent of the girls are getting attention from, at most, two-thirds of the men. Do the math; if you want to find a girl to date, who are your best chances, the cheerleaders and campus queens who are chased by tons of boys, or the other girls?

Of course, I didn't understand it either, but it's true. It is amazing how many nice high school girls don't have a date on a typical weekend. You can be the person to rescue one of them. Just find something that you want to do and ask one of these girls to do it with you, something simple like a game or a movie or maybe just a cup of coffee. Trust me, asking someone out the first time is major-league scary. But the scarier alternative is to never get used to that risk taking and wait until you are a lot older to try it.

I discovered this finally in college but it is not as hard as we think. Our trouble is the incredible amount of worry and obsessing we do about even trying. It takes a lot less effort to just try it and get it over with. If the person says, "yes", that's good. If not, you tried, and there are other people to ask. Don't insist on just one person. Nobody's that great. The main thing is timing. Unless it's a big event like a prom, a few days in advance is soon enough to call or ask. You should ask when the time is convenient for the other person. Don't call in the middle of dinner or at her part-time job, if she has one.

I used a simple drill. I would call a girl up and first thing, say, "This is Jerry, is ----- there?" Of course, if she answered the phone, I would know her voice usually. I would not waste much time. It is okay to spend a little time on "small talk." but not too much. For example, if you know the person had a test, you can ask how it went. Then, I would tell the person what I wanted to do, saying something like, "There's a good movie at the State Theater on Friday night...*Dr. Zhivago*. Can I pick you up at your dormitory at 6:30?" I made it easy to say "yes." I sounded like I knew what I wanted to do and people like to hear that confidence.

So the person either accepted the invitation or not. No problem. If nobody wanted to go to the movie with me, I went anyway, enjoyed it and saved the money that I would have spent on a date. At least I had the experience and another thing to talk about with people in the future. If the person said "yes," I made sure that I was on time, knew how to get wherever we went, left enough time to park and knew the physical layout of the place, including where the bathrooms and emergency exits were. I also knew the safest way to get to the car, home, or wherever we were going.

Sooner or later someone will say "yes." You have your first date and no matter what happens, a second date is a lot easier to get than the first one! Here's another tip: If you don't have a date, which is most of the time for us at that age, go out and do things anyway. There's no law that says you have to stay at home just because you don't have a date. Movies and restaurants and ballparks will take your money anyway. Besides, you might go to an art gallery and find some single, opposite sex member looking at the same painting you like. Opportunity! Just share that interest. Ask the other person why he/she likes the painting. Or maybe it's the book you both notice while walking through a bookstore.

This is probably hard to grasp. It is natural for us to want a predictable, guaranteed social situation, as if we can just fill out a social profile and order the perfect person. The whole thing about social stuff is that you really can't predict the best happenings. Most of the happiest couples I have ever known tell me that they weren't looking for anything when they met each other. They just had something to share and each person was comfortable with himself.

The biggest barrier for most disabled (and especially autistic) people is self-consciousness. The only way I see to battle that is to keep gaining exposure to all kinds of social environments and activities until you can relax and enjoy them. Sitting in your room alone, obsessing on some girl instead of contacting her, then asking her out and either hearing "yes" or "no" will get you nowhere. Life is for the living. Learning to live means taking risks. That means giving up enough of your autistic wish to control every moment, enough to give someone else a chance to be a part of the next moment.

Too many of us, by the time we are teenagers or young adults, are frozen with fear of making errors. You must accept that when it comes to social stuff especially, everyone makes a fool of himself sooner or later. When people feel really attracted to someone, they don't always think so clearly. "They lose their heads" is the saying. You don't have to worry about looking silly because you will have lots of company. But I promise you that the earlier you start trying, the sooner you will gain some confidence and enjoy some dating.

Remember too, that a lot of the "ladies' men" among your peers aren't nearly as confident as they say they are. All of us are probably scared to death when we make the first attempt to have a date. There is nothing wrong with asking your friends for advice. Just trying will earn you some respect from some people because they will remember how difficult it was for them at first.

One thing is true, and we get into this in detail in another chapter: you don't have to reinvent the wheel on every social occasion. Once you know how much time it takes to get ready for a date, you plan for that time. Once you know how to get in and out of different places, you know. Once you have been to a movie theater, you know where the popcorn is, where to line up for tickets or how to get them ahead of time. The more experience you have, the easier it gets. Instead of burning up your nervous brain cells on what you already know, you can use them to relax and even have a good time!

Some of you are girls. It seems easier to be a boy because traditionally boys are the ones who get to ask girls to do things. However, things have lightened up a bit since 1966, when I graduated from high school. Today it is okay for girls to ask boys to do things. In fact, Mary, who is now my wife, called me up before we had our first date. It helps if you think a boy is interested in you but is too shy to do anything. Since I am not a girl, I can't give you a lot of advice on this, but I do know that girls who want to date don't have to stand around and wait to be asked.

Also, if a weekend comes up and you don't have a date, you can still do something enjoyable on your own or with other girls. The only thing I should mention is that if some boys accept your invitation, they may get the mistaken idea that you are "fast" or "easy" and no details are needed on that. So just remember, if you do go out and like the other person, you don't have to do everything in one night! This is especially true if you are a girl. Guys seldom want a second date with a girl if she is "easy" on the first date and lets them do anything sexual. It is much wiser to take your time. That's another lesson I wish someone had taught me.

One thing I should add about dating is that you don't have to do it the same way that "normals" do. I have spent time in a cool coffee shop, watching the fans, with an autistic companion. You can spend an hour walking through a parking lot, examining and factoring license numbers. Or you can take turns reading street signs backwards. The whole purpose of a date is to have fun together. Depending on your "disability," you may think of completely new ways to have mutual fun, so don't let normal people decide your dating options for you. Do what you want to do and with the company you want. That is cool, normal or not.

Dating is not the only high school activity. It just seems that way at times. Your schoolwork is still the most important thing. Once you are in your last couple of years, it is time to think about what you will do after high school. College is almost required now for people who want any kind of a decent job. If you can, having a part-time job while in high school is a good idea. It means some money to do things, takes pressure off your parents, and teaches you to use your time more wisely. It also helps you learn good work habits. Finally, having a part-time job looks great on any college application!

If you want to go to college, then it pays to think about where to go and what you would study. Guidance counselors can help you with that exploration. My high school had a day every year where a lot of local colleges sent representatives to my school to talk to juniors and seniors. Often, the representatives were former students from my high school. There are tests, like the SAT and National Merit Scholarship exam, that help colleges decide who to accept. If you want a higher score, there are ways to study for those.

To find the right college, you have to make some realistic assessments of yourself. Will you be comfortable living away from home? Will you need some assistance on a daily basis to get through college? If that is the case, you need to see what kind of services for disabled students are available at any college you consider. You should also see if the college has counselors for disabled students. Of course, you should want to know if the college has good teachers in the subjects you want to specialize in. I think that if you can go to a school away from home, you should have a roommate. It is a good experience to share a living space with an age-peer. But if you really need to have your own room, that can usually be arranged.

The reason that I suggest having roommates is that for most of my life, I have been better off when I had company. I also

49

think that learning to share socially is far better, especially for people like us, than always insisting on everything following our rules. The biggest barrier to my adult peers, socially and professionally, is inflexibility. If you never learn to share and be considerate of others, how do you gain the flexibility that you need to have jobs and a social existence? You can learn a lot from books, but not everything.

I hope you don't make the mistake I made about college. I went to Michigan for one reason: to get away from my family and everyone who knew me. For a while that escape was cool, but when things didn't go well and I lost my direction, I was too far away from my roots for people to notice. You will be better off if you go to a school that is not so far away from home.

This is why I feel this way. I was a lot more independent than most of you at college age, but a big, far-away school was too much for me. College is different in some big ways. You are on your own a lot more. There is nobody around to make sure that you go to school, do your homework, do your laundry, eat or do anything. You have to be "self-managing," and most new students will struggle with some aspect of that. The big challenge is that you have tremendous freedom and many choices to make on what to do with your time.

You don't spend nearly as much time in class once you get to college. You are expected to study a lot more. A typical college class will cover more information in half a year than you would in a year of a high school class in the same subject. The big thing you have to handle is making those daily decisions. Going to class is easy. Once you have the schedule and know where the classrooms are, you just go to each class at the correct time. But the challenge is when you don't have a class, determining how to spend your time. What you do then makes all of the difference. There is no mom or dad around to keep you focused. You can study. You can goof off, watch TV with people in your dormitory, go out, drink beer, or whatever.

Self-discipline is the big factor. Most of us are heavily dependent on schedules. High school is a lot easier in that way since the entire day is usually scheduled. College, and the rest of your life, require a lot more of your initiative. You have to make your own schedule. You have to decide when to study, when to party, when to hangout, when to eat, sleep and everything else. Master this and your ship can go anywhere. Fail to master this and you will spend your life unemployed, alone, and breaking furniture in the group home or institution of your choice. Sounds like a pretty obvious choice to me!

That is not the only difference between college and anything you have experienced before. You can be miles away from your family or anyone who knows you well. Many of us have low self-esteem, if any, at age eighteen. Most autistic students I have met are fine academically but quite behind socially. They may seem like they are doing fine, especially in a structured class setting, but they really aren't.

Things may go well for a while at college, but can go downhill in a hurry. That happened to me at Michigan. The first year was fine. My grades were good, partly because the fraternity I joined made me attend classes or do pushups as a penalty for skipping. But once I was an active member it was assumed that I would set my own direction. I didn't.

By this time, the original three sections of my honors math class had been narrowed to one. I was still there because I had an "A" in the second semester of my freshman honors math class. But in my sophomore year, the competition discouraged me. I was used to studying other subjects but never had to study math before! It suddenly was no longer fun and I began to lose interest. But I had nothing to replace that lifelong talent.

I was in deep trouble and had no clue. In a smaller college, closer to home and my family, somebody would have noticed. Somebody would have said, "Okay, pure math is not your goal, but what about physics? You have two A's in that. You like sports. Maybe you can help design better equipment or running shoes. What about applied math? Accounting?" There would have been something to which to shift my focus. But in a college far away, with minimal counseling and the available distractions of the sixties, I found drugs and other hobbies. My grades and my future went downhill with each semester. I did the minimum to earn a degree and it meant nothing to me. It took almost twenty years of menial jobs before I finally wound up with anything that used my natural skills.

That's my story. And, even though at eighteen I had less autism to deal with than most of you. I strongly recommend that our people start college closer to home while they get used to the overall college experience.

There are some other options to consider. If you have a strong desire for a certain career, a college may have a co-op program, where you work for a company one semester, go to college the next and alternate until you graduate with the proper training and already have an employer who has known you for years.

College is challenging because you are expected to choose classes that prepare you for work. Once you have a career goal, it is up to you to find out which classes are appropriate If you can get a summer job that is relative to that goal, you will be wise to do it. My oldest brother majored in accounting and worked in the accounting department for an aircraft plant for three years. That was a big plus for him.

If you eventually go away to school, there are living options available besides a dormitory. Older students are usually allowed to live in their own apartments. Some of you may prefer that independence. Another option, sharing an apartment with a roommate, is usually cheaper not just because the rent is less, but also because you are sharing food and other costs, too. Some students rent a house out together, as I did in my last year. Others live in co-operative housing, where everyone takes turns with cleaning up, shopping and other household duties.

My main concern for those of you who go away to college is to avoid an isolated situation. That is why I prefer situations with roommates, housing cooperatives or even social organizations like fraternities and sororities. If you explore the "Greek" system, do it slowly. Typical new members make a decision to join a fraternity after a brief whirlwind week called "rush" week. The name is no accident. You pay a few one-hour visits at different houses, meet a bunch of people on a very superficial basis, and then are asked for a commitment to live with those people for the remainder of your college years.

That is not a wise way to decide. Even if you are away at school as a freshman, take my advice and in year one, concentrate on your academics and getting to know your college. The same is true for all of the other options available. There are countless clubs and organizations in colleges. These are great places to make friends. But you have at least four years to explore those options. Your first job is to get decent grades. In your spare time, you can opt for "open rush" where you get to visit a fraternity house during the school year with no pressure for a decision to join. But remember, if you don't make your grades, you won't have a chance to be in a fraternity, sorority or a club. If you make your grades on the other hand, the smart houses will have room for a new member who is a proven upperclassman.

If you decide to try out the Greek houses, don't be afraid to ask questions. A good house should have a house grade point average above the campus average. It should have an up-to-date exam file, a great resource for studying. Some houses even have a mentor program, a way that you can talk to alumni who are in the profession of your choice when you are an upperclassman. Some fraternities also have scholarships available. You should ask about the time commitment required of new members. It does take time to be a member but it was worth it for me. But that is a personal choice. The ironic thing about the Greek houses is that most people join them for one reason (social) and stay in them to be part of all of the other common activities. I can't tell you if this is good for you. That is something you can decide for yourself.

College does not last forever. I thought it would. If you are getting really good grades, you may get a scholarship for graduate school. But many of you will end up working after your first college degree. It is a good idea to pick a professional goal as early as you can so that the courses you take will lead you to a job.

It takes more than good grades to get a job but grades are the most important thing, especially in classes that pertain to a job. If, for example, you want to be an accountant, C's in accounting are not going to help you nearly as much as A's. Once you are a senior, your college should have a placement center that helps you find work in the profession you seek. You will have to be interviewed. A good college will help you prepare for that. There isn't time to tell you about that here.

I want to close the two chapters on schools with this thought: you should never stop learning. You can always gain something by learning more, about your profession, about your world and about life in general. Every course doesn't have to be something designed to advance you professionally. If you just want to learn more about anything—cooking, dancing, sailing, or anything that interests you—keep your mind open and find a way to learn wherever you are.

Not only will your mind and world expand, you never know who else with the same interests may wind up in a class with you. I wish I had planned better when I was in college, but this was and still is true: the positive atmosphere of a college campus is infectiously hopeful. People like you, who are there to improve their lives, will surround you. It's like an academic health club. It beats the heck out of any singles bar in the world.

YOUR LIFE IS NOT A LABEL

"If I known I would live this long, I would have taken better care of myself."

Mickey Mantle

It's Your Body

I was given a reasonably functional body, short on coordination but big enough. But my boyhood hero Mickey Mantle could approach the plate from either side, crouch low with a mountain range of muscles rippling up his spine, the arms of a boxer and legs of an Olympic level sprinter, and strike fear in the heart of pitchers. They threw the ball and prayed that it wasn't hit back at them.

Athletes like Mickey Mantle are born, not made. But for all of his natural physical gifts, this Hall-of-Fame, New York Yankee centerfielder only lived to be sixty-four. Most of us will live longer. His drinking did him in and that is only one of the more popular ways that some of us hasten our exit to the great stim room in the sky. According to Mickey, "I would have been a greater hitter if I didn't have to swing at three balls."

I do not write this as a role model. I myself am working on my weight. For most of my life, it was not a problem. Temple Grandin says that anxiety and stress are dimensions of adult life that are increased for people with autism. I think that may apply to other disabilities, too. The only way to counteract this is to pay even more attention to stress-reducing activities. My favorite stress-reducing activity is compulsive eating. It was my father's act, too, along with smoking, until a heart attack and adult-onset diabetes forced him to change his lifestyle.

You are stuck in your body. It is the one place you can't move from. Some Indians—fakirs, I think they call themselves—

claim that their spirits can leave their bodies, but the only time a spirit ever left my body was when I drank too much and threw up. Your body is what you put into it. Imagine your body as a car. Your car runs on a certain kind of fuel. You don't feed your car potato chips, candy, booze and drugs and get very far. But many of us do that to our bodies and expect them to go on forever. Bodies last a lot longer than the average car. It is a miracle.

I am not going to lecture you about diet because I am still working on that issue. But I can mention some danger in the area of excessive consumption. It is popular for young people, usually men, to engage in competitions to see how much or how quickly they can drink. In organizations like fraternities, it is called "chugging" when a person tries to swallow a mug of beer as fast as possible.

I was a new future member of a fraternity at Michigan in the fall of 1966. My first chugging experience was on the night before my German midterm. I was what they call a pledge. A pledge is a student who promises to become a member with full rights and privileges of a fraternity after a probationary period of a semester or two. During this time, he must have acceptable grades and perform duties for his chosen fraternity, usually work sessions or coming to the house occasionally to answer phones.

That is not bad. I liked the structure and was eager to please. I was not allowed to skip classes either. There was always a member of Delta Chi walking by my classroom, before or after, to make sure that Pledge Newport was in school. Result: a 3.1 GPA in my first semester at Michigan.

The chugging was another story. I joined the majority of our house in the basement, singing rowdy versions of the school songs, and then we began chugging.

I am not a drinker, but that did not stop me from downing enough beer in a short time to wake up the next morning with an incredible hangover. I had a test at 8 a.m. My "C" on that midterm was a gift of God, who must have had an angel take the test for me. I knew what Mickey Mantle spoke of. It is hard to fill out a blue book when there are five of them on your table.

That is not the worst of it College students have died from excessive drinking. It is dangerous and not funny. Also, some of you may be taking medication. Much medication is specific in the warning: "Do not consume alcohol." That is not some Moral Majority admonition. It is because when medication is in your system, it can combine with anything else in your system, including alcohol. Sometimes, the effect of the medication and alcohol are multiplied by their interaction. When that happens, the body in which that happens is in big trouble. It can faint, stop breathing and shut down.

It can die.

It can happen to people strong enough to toss you like a Frisbee or play for your football team! It can happen to anyone.

There are smarter ways to earn acceptance from people. This is very important to understand. Many of you may not make your first friends until you are in college or out of high school. You have to understand that they may not always show good judgment. If you are autistic, people may assume that you can be taken advantage of, that you will do something to please them even if it is dangerous.

It is not easy to resist such pressure, but it is necessary to do so. The stakes are way too high. You have no business drinking too much anyway, and doing it while you are taking medication is just plain crazy. No real friends will insist that you do this, and if they do, just excuse yourself. Hopefully, when they become sober, they will come to their senses and stop pushing you in the wrong direction.

Another popular source of abuse is drugs. I am guilty of that. I am not one of those people who bored you in high school with the "Practice Safe Sex" and "Just Say No" videos. It never seemed to me like any of those people had ever had any fun, and the only reason they showed us those movies was to keep us from having any fun either, even if the movies made sense.

I had fun; sometimes too much. I explored drugs at the end of my second year at Michigan. First, it was a couple of times smoking pot. Then, I decided to elevate the experiment. I took a bus to San Francisco in May of 1968. My mission was plain: to meet some hippies who would help me get high on LSD.

It is a miracle that I survived that day. I proceeded in classically clueless fashion. I took a bus to downtown San Francisco. Getting off, I looked out of place already with my Michigan college jacket and crewcut. But I had a mission. I walked out of the Greyhound station and immediately noticed a young girl in classical hippie garb, long hair and a fringe jacket. She was selling the "Berkeley Barb," a radical newspaper in 1968. I decided, of course without knowing her at all, that she would be my LSD connection. A little gypsy and an acid queen, for sure.

I walked up to her and said, "Hello, my name is Jerry."

She: "I'm Mary." (different Mary than my wife)

Me: "Do you know where I can get some LSD?"

She: (puzzled, looking me over) "You don't look at all like someone who would ask me a question like that. Are you sure you're not a narc?" ("Narc" was slang for a narcotics cop.)

Me: "No, I'm just a tourist, from Michigan. I heard this was the place to get high, so I'm here...."

I am not proud of this day but share it to show that at age nineteen, for all of my good grades and outwardly normal collegiate appearance, I was clueless, in a classic Asperger's way. There was no conversational foreplay. I was determined to accomplish my goal, and having spied a likely accomplice, was not about to waste any time. She had ten newspapers left to sell; so I gave her five dollars, and she happily gave away the papers.

Haight-Ashbury Mary escorted me back to her apartment, shared by her boyfriend and a fellow named Don, who must have had a few too many LSD experiences, Don sat in the nude on his mattress, giggling to himself.

But not to worry, I scored six tabs of what was billed as LSD and promptly swallowed one. I sat back and waited for God-knows-what to happen. It was subtle at first, but then the walls began to change shape, while the voice of Jim Morrison sang, *"When you're strange, faces come out in the rain...."*

I was feeling pretty good by then and walked to the upstairs window to survey the hilly neighborhood. A little orange VW drove by, making sounds like it was underwater, bubbling downhill. Not the usual acoustic effects. In the background, a band called *Traffic* sang, *"Dear Mr. Fantasy, play me a tune, something to make us all happy..."*

Me: "What's that music?

Them: "*Traffic.*"

Me: I'm watching traffic. What's the music?

Them: "*Traffic.*"

That conversational loop lasted a while until I think Mary may have gotten the hint that her new drug customer had worn out his welcome. She asked me if I wanted to see a park, and I docilely obliged. We went to a park and saw people with pet rats all looking as high as I felt, if not higher. I decided to get some coffee and walked into a coffee shop. This was the straw that finally broke the camel's back.

No sooner had we sat down than the opening of *Pin Ball Wizard* came roaring on the local radio station.

Me: "Who's playing that song?"

Mary: "The *Who* is playing that song!"

Me: "Who's playing that song?"

I am not sure if I ever got it, but soon my new connection had excused herself. I grabbed a ride on a trolley, looked up at a clear blue sky that looked as if it was nailed to the rooftops, hung off the side, and rode back down towards the bus station. It was a very high-functioning day; too much for my own good. Ironic thing is, most people in my generation who used drugs, took them to get "screwed up" for a while. To me, I felt more normal when the common denominator was a drug experience. If a group of people got high, it was perfectly natural for all of us to stare for hours at a *Jefferson Airplane* "White Rabbit" poster, play "Inna Godda DaVida" forty-six times in a row, order a pizza and fuss over the pizza like it had come from outer space, do something else a ridiculous number of times, or focus on a detail. It was chemically-induced group perseveration.

I guess I did LSD maybe a dozen times during the next two years. It was a popular thing to do in that era. Within weeks after my first experience, I acquired the bell bottoms, long hair and wardrobe to go with my new hobby. I looked no different than a few thousand other students at Michigan, but there was a big difference. Drugs were an occasional escape for them, only. Most of them cut their hair, typed out a resume, and played the corporate game in short order once the college party was over.

For me it was a mixed blessing, but more negative than positive. I enjoyed making friends. I made pot a daily habit and it is easy to make new friends when you have pot to share, not that the friends will be there when you need some pot.

The other side of the coin was a gradual loss in my direction. I began living more from day to day, high to high, with no thought about what I would do when college was over. I had such a great visual memory that I didn't have to take LSD very often. I just instantly replayed the trips in my brain, like a video! That part of autism was very economical.

But in the long run, it didn't do me any good. I think even occasional LSD use made me more likely to have extreme emotional reactions and more vulnerable to depression. It probably helped trigger my first two suicide attempts, even after I stopped using it. I found it harder to concentrate when I wasn't "tripping." My grades were higher before my first drug experience than after. The worst thing was, I had already lost interest in theoretical math in my second year of school and this new hobby gave me an excuse to avoid facing that.

Ordinarily, that would not have been a big deal. Lots of people switch their majors in college. I could have changed from pure math, which is what the future math professors take, to something more practical—like applied math, computer programming or physics. I just needed some guidance.

Physics was my best subject; I always had A's in it. I like sports, and in the seventies, I could have wound up testing running shoes for Nike! But my feet were ten feet off the ground.

I didn't change my major. I did the minimum to get by and wound up with grades too low for graduate school and no idea at all what to do in the work world that I was forced to join.

Looking back, I know it was a terrible mistake. LSD was an illegal "street drug," as are heroin, Ectasy, marijuana and other drugs. The reason that certain drugs are illegal is their unpredictable, dangerous effects on people in general. The other problem with street drugs is that you have no guarantee that you are buying what you think you are buying. Most of these drugs are so powerful that you are consuming the actual chemical, combined with something called a "buffering compound", to help it have the shape of a pill or a tablet. Once again, there is no guarantee that the buffering compound is any safer than the illegal drug itself.

On top of this, don't forget that many of you are already taking medication for your condition. You have no idea what adding another drug to your system will do. In the case of a legal drug, at least you can ask your pharmacist if it is safe to have both in your body at once. But if one drug is illegal, it will be hard to get an answer without admitting that you are thinking of breaking the law.

Now, I am not going to give you the infamous "Just Say No" speech about illegal drugs. I have been there myself, and I know that it is usually harder to say no that one might think. You may be thinking of "getting high" to gain social approval. In that case, just do me a favor and ask yourself if that is the only way that you can gain friends. I doubt it.

Another common reason for using illegal drugs is that it is considered a temporary escape from reality. There are many other ways to escape reality for a while. That is why people go to movies, amusement parks, and other entertainment places. You can escape without putting something in your body that could do permanent damage.

A healthy urge to occasionally "cut loose" and escape is normal. What is not normal is the way I felt about myself when I began experimenting with drugs. I didn't like myself. When I was "high," I felt better, a lot better. But it never lasted. When the experience was over, I was left with the same problems that I had temporarily escaped. In addition, the drugs seemed to leave me less capable of coping with my life than before I began taking them. So the next time I felt really down about things, I would get high again. That is a familiar cycle with drug use.

If that sounds like you, then it is a very good idea to take a good hard look at what bothers you about your life, because I can guarantee you that drugs will not solve any of those problems. Drugs will just give you another problem. If you have a good friend, therapist or counselor, this is a good time to talk to such a person about what you are thinking of doing. With help, I am sure that you can get the advice and support you need to work on the obstacles in your life. You can also find ways to escape that are socially acceptable and are not as dangerous as drugs. Remember, you only get one body, and if you put something into it that does permanent damage, you are stuck in that body forever.

Legal drugs, like alcohol, may also be dangerous if you take certain medications. Usually, the prescription bottle will have a warning if it is not safe to use with alcohol, but you should check to make sure, even if it is legal for you to drink. Also, even if it is safe for you to drink, remember not to overdo it. This is not easy for many of you. I was luckier than many peers. I had some friends in high school and many of you don't. But there are better ways to make friends than to risk your health.

I hope this doesn't sound like I don't want you to have any fun. I do. I also want you to be alive long enough to tell young people about all of the fun you had when you were young or even middle-aged like me! But you can't do that if you get drunk and

65

die in an auto accident, can you? So remember, know your limits. Have fun but don't go overboard. Don't let someone talk you into overindulgence just to look cool.

Funerals are never cool.

~~~

Another thing we need to talk about for your body is food. We know much more today than in earlier times. My father, whose idea of a workout was to lift a glass of beer to his lips, probably thought the four basic food groups were fast, frozen, Chinese and Italian. Pretty funny, huh? Well, my father didn't even live to see me graduate from college. He died almost thirty-two years ago at the age of sixty-one.

Nobody lives forever, but sixty-one is young. Most of you should live into your eighties and beyond. The food you eat will have a lot to do with that. I am not just talking about living a long life. The life should have quality as well as length. I mean, Jesus Christ (33), Mozart (35) and Joan of Arc (19) accomplished a lot in short lives, but they were exceptions. You can live a lot longer and have energy for doing fun things when you are older.

One problem for people with autism is certain food cravings. I like foods with salt and that seems common in our support group.

Dumb joke: What do you call twenty bags of potato chips? Answer: an autistic pot luck.

Too much salt is bad for your blood pressure. Too little and you can get dehydrated, but there is salt in just about every food, so very few people don't get enough salt in their diets.

Diet is mainly a question of balance. If you are eating a lot more of one kind of food, whether it's meat, fruit, vegetables or grains, you probably need to have more balance in what you eat. If you are overweight or feel like you are tired most of the time, it is probably your diet, and a good dietician can help you find a better one.

Smoking? I smoked for nine years and am happy to say that I haven't smoked since 1986. It is a dirty, expensive habit, and my father paid the price for forty years of smoking. It would have been nice to have him around another twenty years or more. My father was just months away from dying when I smoked one of my first cigarettes in front of him. The look on his face said it all as he as watched me start the habit that killed him.

I have just a couple more things to say about your body.

The first is that nobody stays healthy forever. It may not seem like you need to think about this when you are young, but health insurance is something that everyone should have. Not everyone in our country does and that is not right. If you get a job, it is an even better job if you have health insurance. That makes it much cheaper to make sure all is right with your body.

You should have an annual checkup by a doctor. As you get older, other checks should be made to make sure that you don't have cancer of the colon or other problems. If detected early, these can be dealt with before they shorten your life drastically. It is especially important for women to make sure they don't have breast cancer. It takes little time to have these tests done and the potential gain is well worth it.

The last area is the need for daily physical activity. This was not a problem in previous times when most people lived on farms or did physical labor. It is a big problem today. There is a big epidemic of obesity in our country. Obesity is when your body fat is more than thirty percent of your weight. I am in that category right now, but I promise you that by the time this book is done, I won't be! Obesity has lots of side effects, none of them good. It can lead to diabetes, high blood pressure and other health problems, including heart disease.

Some people are naturally overweight because of inherited genes, but even they can keep obesity in check through a good diet and daily exercise.

You may not like team sports. I was no good at any of them either, but there are many individual exercises: walking, running, swimming, rowing, weightlifting to name just a few. If you haven't been doing this and are overweight already, introduce this activity gradually and only after you talk to a doctor.

Much of this may just seem like common sense. But to an alarming number of Americans it isn't. Look around and you will see many of them ignore common sense when it comes to their health. Your parents may look like couch potatoes now, but if you look at a photo of them at your age, I'll bet most of them weren't. If you're young and already fat, you are heading in a seriously wrong direction.

Don't kid yourself. Mother Nature is not happy with what she sees in our society. You are not supposed to get heavier with age. Your heart is weaker and you should get LIGHTER to help it do its work. Too many people have let their bodies and health go in the wrong direction and will pay the price.

Remember, you can get evicted from your apartment, but you are stuck in your body forever. As long as you are living in that body, think of it as your house and make sure it is in the best condition that you can manage.

"Hello!!"

Shayna, my eight-year-old Goffin's cockatoo,
thousands of times since 1996

Pets —They Love You For Who You Are

My family has had pets as long as I remember. My mother and father grew up in farm areas and loved all animals. I have had pet goldfish, hamsters, turtles, dogs, cats, rabbits, parakeets, cockatiels, a cockatoo and a lovebird. I have no favorites. They were all wonderful. None of them cared if I had a label or not. They wanted my attention and returned it unconditionally.

That is a priceless experience to have on a daily basis. Recent research shows that pets are also therapeutic. People who have pets live longer and happier. The most important finding is that in the first years of life, the brain connections of growing infants respond to contact, hugging, stroking and petting. These are the important neural connections that help people make sense of their world and not feel overwhelmed by it. Needless to say, my peers with autism can use as many of those connections as we can get!!

Pets have been particularly helpful to me. I resisted touch as a baby. The first thing I did after I was born was push my mother away. She gave up on hugging me. I was even difficult to hold. I have to wonder how much worse off I would have been if there had not been contact with our pets. For some reason, I never minded contact with them. If anything, I preferred it to human contact. Maybe it was because I wasn't afraid that they would hug me too hard.

The first pet in my recorded history was a crow named "Blackey." I don't remember him. My oldest brother John found him in the backyard of our home in Lockport, near Buffalo, New York. John was a Boy Scout and interested in nature. He adopted Blackey and fed him milk and bread. The crow grew up to be a family pet. John also taught him to talk. The crow lived in a cage, right outside of the room that contained my crib. My first word, "Hello," came after I heard it many times from Blackey. Years later when I had trouble conversing, the family joke was that after all, I learned to talk from a crow.

Pets have made a great difference in the lives of my peers. I have noticed that peers of mine who have pets now had pets as children, usually have more empathy, are less rigid, have better self-esteem and socialization than those who never had pets.

That is my observation and I would bet that a scientific long-term study would support it. As an adult, I have to credit my birds, which Mary also loves, with helping us come together.

When we divorced, our cockatoo Shayna migrated between us and became a common bond which helped us get back together. My fourteen parrots, dog and cat have helped me finally accept more loving touch from humans, too. When I'm at home, usually on the computer, I never know when a parrot will land on my head, or when the dog and cat will come by for a fix of affection. This gradual acceptance, by me, of accidental animal contact has made it a lot easier for humans to love me as well!

Pets are desirable. First decide at what age pets should be introduced and then what pets are appropriate.

The pet must not be endangered by exposure to a child who doesn't know his own strength and can injure or kill a pet accidentally during a tantrum.

The child should not be exposed to any pet or possible germ infection until the child is aware of the dangers. Knowing how to avoid the pet or defend himself if the pet is out of control is important for safety.

Families may have pets before the children come. An animal like a pit bull dog or an African Grey parrot must not be allowed in the same area as a baby or toddler. I know that both of these animals and others can be great pets, but they can lose their temper and wreak havoc on little, defenseless children.

A daughter of my friend had a wonderful, jealous Amazon parrot who attacked her baby. Both survived but it could have been much worse. It was heartbreaking, but she wisely found another home for her parrot.

Suitable, durable pets can be safely introduced when a child is old enough to know that they are other living things with feelings and bodies of their own. You must remember that many disabled children get over-stimulated, have tantrums and don't know their own strength. They lack social empathy at that stage because they are too busy keeping an even keel to show it. They might punish a pet because they don't know better. For that reason, I don't recommend fragile hamsters, parakeets, gerbils, turtles and the like for this age group.

Instead, I suggest durable pets: cats, dogs and guinea pigs are good examples. The best way to start is to contact your local Humane Society. Their personnel have a mission to find good homes for animals. They can help you and your child find a good match. There are also books and videos available on care, feeding and even breeding of most pets. Spaying for dogs and cats is a humane way to prevent the eventual problem of too many animals.

There are other benefits to an appropriate pet besides the daily exchange of unconditional acceptance. If you get involved in the pet's feeding and grooming, it can help you see the value in your own grooming and good diet. The amount of time you spend with a pet is far more constructive than time spent on mental junk food like television. It also leads to other interests.

I had a hutch of rabbits, all named Peter, in the backyard. In the spring, we grew lettuce. It was fed to grateful rabbits. That led to an interest in gardening, which I follow today with daily watering of sunflowers, gourds and cactus.

You must remember that a pet is not a person. A pet will not always do what you want it to do. You can't spank it or punish it. If it pees in the wrong spot, make sure there is a right place available and just clean up after it. You must feed the pet every day. The canned and processed food is not enough. All pets like some fresh, real food, too! The pet store can tell you what to offer, in addition to prepared foods. Can you imagine yourself eating the same little pellets every day? What behaviorist designed those diets for pets?! At least he isn't "curing" our kids.

You should clean your pet's living space at least a couple of times a week. This is especially important for smaller animals like parakeets. They are very sensitive to mites and other pests which grow in unclean areas. Water must be replaced every day and you should remove any lettuce or other fresh food once the pet is no longer eating it.

You may want to be able to play with your pet any time that you wish, but until you know what you are doing and until you absolutely know that you can control your temper and not hurt your pet unfairly, you should not be able to take a pet out of a cage without supervision. Having a pet is a privilege and a blessing, and you need to earn that privilege.

I tell you this because while I loved my pets, I didn't always use good judgment. For example, I used to put a hamster on a record player. I changed the speed from 33 rpm to 45 rpm and then 78 rpm. Then, I put the hamster on the floor to watch him "walk funny." It was not funny to Hammy the Hamster. At first, he eagerly greeted me when I opened the cage door and offered him a raisin but soon, he tried to escape whenever he could, to avoid the record player.

None, absolutely none of this is acceptable. The word, "pet" means to stroke and treat in a loving way. Unloving behavior toward a defenseless, dependent animal is not appropriate. You don't deserve a pet until you can learn to treat them with love and respect. That is the greatest purpose of allowing you to have a pet, to learn empathy and affection. If you don't "get it," that's your problem, not the pet's. Responsible parents will not let you abuse animals. Having autism or any disability is no excuse for that!

If you have a problem treating your pet nicely, maybe it is not the right pet for you. Or look at what you are doing. Imagine yourself as the pet and ask yourself, if you were a parakeet, would you want some big person pulling your tail feathers? Why are you doing this? Maybe somebody is teasing you at school. Be a real person and deal with that. Don't make a poor pet into your victim and become a bully, too.

All of this may sound like more work, in homes where parents already have less time than they did a generation ago. I believe that the benefits justify the time invested. I have seen the difference in my adult peers of people who grew up with pets and those who didn't. It is not totally consistent, but I have noticed better social adjustment, more empathy and less rigidity in those who had pets and have them as adults. Lack of empathy, poor social adjustment and rigidity are the biggest reasons why so many adults wind up wasting the majority of their lives.

There are other kinds of pets. You can start a connection with animals by visiting a park to feed birds or squirrels there. That can be done anytime you wish and you don't have to clean up after the animals. It is not the same as having a pet, but it is a start that can prepare you for a pet.

Another option is "green pets:" a garden. The child can exercise his need for order by planting neat little rows of seeds and watering at regular intervals. He can stretch an obsession into a fun hobby by measuring the heights of plants as they grow each day.

One way or another; green, furred or feathered, you should have a pet in your life. Here's a review of what you and your family should know so that you have the best chance to share your unconditional love with a pet who will be happy to give it back:

1. Learn about possible pets. Visit pet stores and your local humane society. Adopt a pet and save an animal's life. Read books and watch tapes about how to properly feed, house and care for your new companion.

2. Avoid small, vulnerable animals as a first pet. You must develop knowledge of your own strength and your tolerance for accidental pain from pet contact. Once you have those attributes, you may be ready for a smaller pet. Dogs, cats, rabbits and guinea pigs are the best first pets.

3. Feed your pet fresh, clean food every day. Don't just feed the packaged pet food. Learn what fresh foods are good for your pet and don't feed any new food unless you know it is good for your pet. For example, you might like a piece of chocolate birthday cake but it is not good for parrots and other birds at all. It is poisonous.

4. Never tease or punish a pet. That is cruel and unfair. Imagine how you would feel if someone did that to you.

5. Be aware of environmental concerns. Teflon, nonstick pans emit a gas, when heated, that kills birds. If you want pet birds, get rid of the Teflon. If the teflon is more important, have some other kind of pet. If you bring branches in from outside trees for your animals, wash them off in case they have been sprayed with pesticides.

6. If your pet lives in a cage, keep it clean. Always make sure the pet is safely in his cage, with enough fresh food, before you leave home.

7. Do not mix pets who are natural enemies.

If you follow these rules, you and your pets should have many happy hours and years together. In addition, when you visit a zoo or feed outdoor animals, you will feel happy that their neighbors (your pets) would be proud to introduce their big friend (you) to the animals of the wild kingdom.

My love of animals has expanded as an adult. I became a whale watcher in 1997 and am qualified to volunteer on whale watch boats. I help other people identify whales and other marine life. I also went to Hawaii's Sea Life Park for a special program called a "Dolphin Encounter." [*Editor's note: See the cover.*] I had a two-hour session, along with four other adults, with a mature dolphin. Each of us stroked it, swam with it and got towed by its flipper.

When I left the dolphin behind in the water, I was so lost in the pleasure of the experience that I didn't want to talk to anyone. But as usual, that was hard to explain to normal people, who just don't get it and insist on us joining their world for "our own good." I tolerated some comments and questions and finally found a spot where I could relax, close my eyes and celebrate the dolphin time without the threat of neuro-typical intrusion.

Pets belong in your life. A connection with animals or plants helps you connect in a healthy way to the world in general. I remember a recent walk on the beach at Santa Monica. It is not the same beach I saw in 1968. There are no little hermit crabs, seashells or other life. It is a dead beach in comparison. The pelicans and seagulls look miserable and exist from eating french fries and discarded fish polluted by mercury and other city chemicals, a poor substitute for their former natural diet. If you go just a few hundred miles south into Mexico, you will see how pelicans and seagulls are supposed to look!

It is said that people with autism are handicapped in this way: we resist change. In the name of progress, the rest of humanity's lack of empathy is ruining nature and people in general. Maybe we need more autism, not less of it. Only a neuro-typical idiot would accept the death of a beach.

Rain in Your Brain?

Famous last words. I remember my father that when I was in third grade. By then, I was a town curiosity, a boy who could walk into a wall but could do things in his head that amazed everyone. My dad, God bless him, was wrong, but considering all of the other, unappreciated things he did, I give him an "A" in fatherhood, not an "F."

You may be in a similar position. If you have any kind of autism condition, you are much more likely to have what is known as a "savant skill," "special skill" or "splinter skill," depending on the level of ignorance in the person describing it. This means that at least ten percent of us in the autism community can do one thing much better than we do most things. In "normal" people, this is simply called a talent or ability. I have no idea why those words can't apply to us, too.

Phrases like "savant skill," "splinter skill," etc. are descriptive words for our "talents," invented by the same people who preach inclusion for us. Now tell me that makes sense. But we need to understand these terms because they are still being used, although there is no real need to use them.

The term "savant" is the present participle of the French infinitive "savoir," the verb for "to know." A "savant" is simply "knowing." In the purest sense that is a perfect description of why someone like Stephen Wiltshire can look at a scene, turn around, and sketch it in great detail. He made no effort to acquire that talent. It is just there.

In the artistic sense, Stephen Wiltshire is truly "knowing." Similarly, I never asked for my ability to read at age two, repeat music upon one hearing at age five, or my most famous ability to do numerical calculations in my head at age seven. In those ways, I made no effort. I simply do it. My wife Mary paints without even looking at a canvas and composes music without looking at the paper. It just happens with no effort.

Other examples abound. Dustin Hoffman personally witnessed the amazing memory of Kim Peek, a savant (though not autistic). Similarly, Peter Guthrie also influenced his acting, as did Joe Sullivan, an autistic savant like Peter, with specialties in calculation and drawing. Temple Grandin, who coached Mr. Hoffman, has a remarkably detailed visual memory and the ability to use it to design and even test intricate feedlot systems in her head. Most people buy spreadsheet packages from Microsoft. People like Temple Grandin, Kim Peek and I are born with them in their heads.

If it only stopped there, that special label would have been fine, but I guess that our "experts" were so intimidated by skills that some of us had (and they obviously didn't) that they needed a word to describe this that wouldn't be so glamorous. In fact, "splinter skill" is a downright dehumanizing term. Splinters come off wood. People with autism may not be the most expressive folks around, but they are not made of wood. Enough wasted on that.

I guess that "special skill" is much better, but again, why use it at all? It carries with it a hidden reminder, perhaps to soothe the experts, that such people are more often found in "special classes" and we needn't be afraid of them.

Regardless of which words are used, the experts screwed up again in their attempt to categorize us talented freaks (as they see us).   They expanded the terms to include people who actually make an effort to develop a skill to an unusual degree.

In that group, belong most of the people known as "calendar Savants" or "calendar calculators." All of those calendar calculators/savants whom I know, memorized the fourteen calendar patterns that occur in a twenty-eight-year cycle. Some also account for the fact that the "00" years like 1900 and 0100 are leap years only when the year is a multiple of 400. The majority don't know this and are usually off by a consistent number of days once asked to find the weekday for a date which is not in the century that they learned their skill in.

Now, I know how to do that little trick in any century and could teach you, but so what? If you don't have such a skill, you may think that if you had, it would make your life easier but I know better.

For a while, it was fun, having my elementary school classmates show me off to every new student. But one day in third grade, that changed forever. I was on the playground when the usual scene developed. Some new kid appeared in front of me and I heard one of my friends say, "Here's Newport, just give him a couple of numbers and watch what happens."

I did a few simple multiplications and then noticed someone off to my side, pointing to me and with his right index finger, pointing at his ear and making circular motions. The signal was obvious: Newport's great at this, but he's really crazy. From then on, I just tolerated the attention. If the best thing I could ever do was be the next "math genius," I would submit as long as it paid well and required minimal effort.

There is a big difference between being an effortless natural at anything and working to hone an interest into a skill that might not be there in the first place. If our professionals really want to understand us savants or whatever we are, they need to understand that not all of us who are labeled that way are cut from the same cloth. Without making the distinction between those who perform their skills with little or no conscious effort and those who practiced an interest into a skill of high degree, their MRIs and PET Scans will be a waste of time and precious research money.

You are better off if you have an interest in something and work at it. I was nearing five when my brothers took me along to a movie. It was a comedy with Dean Martin and Jerry Lewis. I didn't like Jerry's screaming voice and the laughter it inspired, anymore than I like people laughing at the tantrums of Donald Duck. Too close to home, I guess. I walked out of the theater to the lobby, pretending I had to pee. I didn't. I waited there until John and Jim found me and wondered why I did that.

But I learned that people who made people laugh could be popular and I did want to be popular. That fueled a lifelong interest in humor. I watched the TV "funny men and women" like Gracie Allen. I learned that if you took too long to say a joke, the audience would either expect more of a joke than you could deliver or just give up waiting. I learned that if you just said something funny and didn't act as if it was, it would get more laughter.

I remember Donna Williams mentioning something about trying humor on stage. Maybe autism is just a form of "Gracie Allen Syndrome." I think that what was funny about Donna was probably not what she said, but how she said it. One comedian told me this way: "Comics say funny things, but comedians say things funny." My version is this: "Like the gynecologist said, It's all in the delivery." I am much more of a comedian today than the comic I struggled to be in school, with hopelessly long, invented or memorized jokes. But it took lots of effort. My genuine interest in something at which I had no natural talent has made this a very enjoyable pastime. A sense of humor can help anyone get by the potholes of life with a lot more happiness.

〰〰 〰〰

After third grade, I literally hung around in an intellectual holding pattern until eighth grade, when enough peers caught up to me to be in an Algebra class. Unlike other math prodigies who learned more advanced subjects on their own, I just let my talent entertain people and kicked back on that. I occasionally played with numbers in my head for the fun of it and in that sense, I "knew" a lot of number theory and even calculus although I couldn't prove it. My method of analysis was to just pour a can of numerical Lincoln Logs onto a mental desk and push them around until an interesting pattern emerged. My method of deduction, which would never pass muster in college, was this: "If it works every time you try it, it must work all of the time."

It took no effort to win the county math contest in seventh grade. But once I reached algebra, it was different. I competed against people a year older and didn't reach the county's top again until a senior, when my competition had graduated and the only one to beat me was a junior.

But no matter, everyone around me was convinced that I would go on to be a great math genius even though there were subtle signs to the contrary.

There was a national math contest sponsored by the Mathematical Association of America and the Society of Actuaries. I took it during my last three years and was tops in my school every year. The funny thing was that in my sophomore year my score would have been unusually high for my tenth grade peers, possibly among the top five or ten in the nation. But the next year, I had literally the same score and in my senior year, the same. Nobody noticed because it was always the best in the school.

I understand why now. The test was about half composed of concrete questions which I answered easily and quickly. But the other half was more abstract and I ran into the same wall every year. Others, some of whom wound up in my math classes at University of Michigan, scaled that same wall. But, having hardly ever cracked a book, I went to Michigan, confident that "if only I had tried," I would still be on top of the heap.

That notion quickly faded upon my arrival in Ann Arbor. A friend invited me to his dormitory. That was Bob Kundus who was from Warren, Ohio, and a proud saxophonist in the famous Warren G. Harding Marching Band from the alma mater of football hero Paul Warfield. He was also an honors chemistry major and we met a year before at a National Science Foundation summer program. We were now in the same honors math section. I went to Frost House (named for the poet, a writer in residence once at Michigan) and before long, was introduced to the mathematical "new kid in town."

He was an age-peer named Bob Scott. Not only had he won the Michigan State math contest, Bob had taken a graduate level class in topology in summer school and aced it. He was so ahead of us that he was placed in the sophomore honors math section, and after only one week, the class was in awe of him. It was totally unnerving to stand in a room with the smartest of Michigan's freshmen, watching them worship Bob and totally ignore me. I was not about to multiply any numbers for anyone!

I could not rationalize away the superiority of this fellow's intellect. He just had it and was a nice guy, to boot. He loved what he did and his focus was relentless until he solved a problem. Later that year, he took a national math contest, the Putnam, and finished eleventh individually. I have to wonder if some of the Michigan mathematics department faculty could have done that! The Putnam is all about abstractions and is not the turf that favors us mere mental multipliers.

It was so discouraging that I temporarily blew off math until I woke up to getting a "D" on our first quiz. That put me too far in the hole to get an "A," but I aced enough of the rest of the class to salvage a "B."

Second semester was better. I got an "A" and had almost the top grade in the final. But my second year just yielded two more "B's" and a warning from the honors department: either get some "A's" real soon or be dropped from the program.

As I headed into my junior year, the abstractions finally got to me. The second year had been linear algebra, more abstract than the calculus of year one. The first part of my junior year basically got my group through the undergraduate math requirements. After this, we would be free to take graduate level math for a year and a half and explore what we would do in graduate school. It was assumed that all of us in that section would not stop with a mere bachelor's degree.

I remember that by then, my math peers already had some direction. Tom Goodwin, a neighbor in the Sigma Nu house across the street, had two fraternity brothers who headed into actuarial studies. But not me. After almost five thousand days of being a math celebrity, I had no clue what to do with it and with a couple of exceptions, my math grades dropped until graduation. A bad combination: poor academic timing and no direction.

I graduated with a degree that meant nothing to me. My mom tried to steer me to at least a sane temporary vocation, like teaching math, but I lacked the self-confidence to be a teacher like she and my father, now deceased, had been. Interviews for math-related jobs were a joke. Having no long view, apparent interest or focus to offer, no on-site test scores could make up for that.

The result was almost two decades of wandering the wilderness, driving a taxi and doing other menial work. It wasn't until 1999 when I joined the American Mathematical Association on a lark, that I picked up one of its monthly publications and actually enjoyed some of the problems so much that I spent hours on them, not minutes. That was totally new to me. It only happened because I was settled down and integrated enough to appreciate my ability and not just use it as an occasional, short-sighted stim.

I want to go back to graduate school and got a Ph.D. in applied mathematics. I already have some ideas of how to use it, mainly in designing exercise equipment and other assistive technology for people with disabilities. It is just different now. My attitude towards math is much more practical. I think, in a whole, my way of thinking is just different than when I was young.

Sorry to be so long-winded, but to me, this whole experience of being so misunderstood and misdirected cost me a lot of time. I see other parents making the same mistake, whether it's with kids who can spell or memorize maps, or any other special skill, thinking the skill is alone is enough. The assumption was that I would become a mathematician. I would have been better off applying my numerical skill to something like accounting.

My father wasn't totally clueless on that. Once while giving me a ride home from Little League, he shared with me a story he must have heard of in New York City where he took classes at Cooper Union. A fellow had recently been found dead in the subway system, where he lived. But he was not just any derelict.

This fellow was such a math prodigy that he had a Ph.D. from Harvard. But his father pushed him relentlessly in math, with no attention to his social development. He just dropped out.

Decades later, Dr. Bernard Rimland confirmed this story for me.

The poor fellow was named Boris Sides. He was never able to get a job in math. The only paper he even attempted to publish after his Ph.D. was an algorithm to ride the entire New York Subway System on one transfer. He died in obscurity, and with teary eyes, my father told me that Boris's last words, in effect, damned his father. My father's message was clear: he did not ever want to push me that way and wanted me, in his words, to learn the "liberal arts" and be a well-rounded person.

My father died, probably thinking that I hated him. But I never really did. I do appreciate his efforts to help me become better rounded. He introduced me to science fiction, encouraging me to be a better writer so I could share the ideas that he assumed would someday emerge. Who knows? Maybe I will prove him right, eventually. By the same token, he watched me finish last in every cross country and track race for four years because he wanted me to enjoy that part of life and learn that one is not always victorious. He was dead right on that one!

So, the moral of the story is this: If you have such a talent, don't take the people around you (probably making a big fuss over whatever you can do) too seriously.

If you enjoy doing whatever it is, great, and if you really like it, you may someday use it to make a living at something. If you don't really like that skill, never asked to have it, and just perform when prodded to, then tell people know how you feel. Maybe they can help you use that skill in a way that you would enjoy. In any event, no matter how spectacular the skill, you can't let your parents or teachers overlook the other ways in which you must grow. Talent, even great talent, is not enough.

This is where I have to give my father some credit. He taught me about sports statistics. Soon after Dad knew what I could do in my head, he introduced me to batting averages, earned run averages, win/loss percentages, etc. Knowing how to do those instantly gave me a way into "guy talk" which at the grade school and high school level, often degenerates into sports gossip. I could go to a ballpark, watch them post the batting average of a player and then adjust it up or down, depending on whether he got a hit and how many at-bats he had previously. That was fun to do and it had a social value.

I still play with that. Only now it's when I go to a horse race track and compute the payoffs for win, place and show once the race is over. I like to announce them before they are posted and am usually right. So, if you have an unusual skill, you can possibly use it to gain some common ground with your classmates. If you like to draw, maybe you could draw some of your peers. If you do, do it in a flattering way!

If you are good in some academic activity that most people aren't, you can help some of your peers. I did that with math and people were nicer to me in return. My mother was a math teacher and didn't have time to tutor all of the students whose parents wanted to hire her. She sent me out to tutor some of the older girls and they made me a friend in return. It was the first meaningful friendship I had with girls.

So talent is a good thing to have, but you have no need to feel envious of those who can do these things effortlessly. I think it is better to work and develop a skill at something that just plain interests you. There is no reason why we are interested or not interested, naturally, in some things. It just happens. In romance, when two people are just interested in each other the minute that they meet, like love at first sight, they call that "chemistry." I have to admit that chemistry was not my best subject!

Take baseball, for example. There have been millions of ballplayers since we first started professional baseball. Most of them never got near the major leagues. But many were so talented, when young, that they were considered to be "naturals." Guess who has the most hits in his lifetime? Pete Rose, who by his own description, was not the most talented player, not even on his own team. His hard work earned him the nickname, "Charlie Hustle." Pete was a cab fare of mine once, in San Diego in 1976. I was moved by his intense interest in baseball. I know he got in trouble for gambling, but we never criticized Raymond Babbitt for that, did we?

I sometimes wanted to just wake up and suddenly have no talent with numbers or with any of the other natural gifts. But now, I am glad to have them. It is fun to read faster than most people. It is fun to listen to memorized music for hours with no need of CD players or to replay movies with no DVD device. It's also a lot cheaper!

You may not always get the kind of attention that you want from your unusual skill, but I don't think that you need to follow my earlier life example and run away from it. It might not be in the way your parents or friends see the future, but if you have a gift, it could lead you to a practical career some day. If it does, you will be very lucky, because I can assure you that a job that includes use of something that you love to do, or are naturally good at, is a lot more fun than most jobs.

On the other hand, if you aren't a natural, the grass is not necessarily greener for those who are. The important thing for you is to take a look at some of the things that you just like to do, even if you aren't a genius at them, and see where that interest might someday lead. For example, if you like to just line things up, right now, that habit of lining up all of the items in the bathroom might drive your family nuts. But someday, you can put all of the books in order in a public library, or keep track of the inventory for a warehouse and make good money at it!

The bottom line, my peers, is this: find your passion.

I know your life is tough but there is probably at least one legal, moral thing that you like to do so much that you would do if for free. Find that thing and find a way to work somewhere doing something that uses that interest. That works for normal people, too! My middle brother Jim and I used to stay up all night watching monster movies. Jim was artistically talented and decided that someday he would be a movie director. He loves movies so much that he worked on some movies for little pay but got experience. Jim has done this for over three decades, and even if he still has not directed a movie, he has traveled all over the world, is a very interesting person and has a passion for living.

That's a good place to close this chapter. Find your passion. Having that in your life will always help you out of the tunnels of despair and depression that all humans wander into. Life is not meant to be lived indifferently. Given a choice between a passion—a genuine interest—and a skill that's dumped in my lap, I'll take the passion any day. Lucky for me that after over fifty years, math now fits the bill in both dimensions. I hope the same thing happens for you.

"The best way to help the poor is to not be one of them."
                                                        Reverend Ike

It's Your Money

It's time to talk about something very important: money.

The *Beatles* said, "money can't buy me love." I am not sure about that, even though I'm a big *Beatles* fan. Money can buy you a lot of things that make it easier to show your love for others. At any rate, to live a full life, you need to understand what money is, its importance and how to make sure that you don't waste your money.

Money is what you use when you go to a store and want something. If you want to have that something and don't care how you get it, you steal it. If you don't want to wind up in jail, you pay the cashier for the item with money. Money is usually either in metal, called coins, or in paper, called currency. Either way, paying money for items and services, rather than stealing, is the much smarter way to get things that you want.

Most of you knew that. I didn't always. I guess I was six when I first learned about money. We were in a store and I saw a cuckoo clock on the wall. I saw the little bird come out. That was neat. I walked over and waited for it to come out again. My father saw me and walked over. I asked him when the little bird would come out and make his funny noise again and he told me. I soon knew how many cuckoos the clock would make each day. I decided that we needed a cuckoo clock and told my father that I wanted one.

That's when I learned about money. I kind of knew there was something out there that people used to get things but this made it clearer. Up until then, my closest concept of money was my school lunch ticket. I knew I could use this to eat every day and it got punched to make sure I didn't eat an extra lunch. Until I saw the cuckoo clock, much of my view of economy had been shaped by a visit to a store in New York that had a big electric train set. The set was so big that the tracks ran from floor to floor of the store and the trains carried messages from one department to another. To me, that train symbolized the whole thing about working and getting what you wanted. The world was run like a train, and if everyone took care of his section of track, the train would always bring back enough of whatever was needed for everyone.

Simple. Not correct, but not bad for a first grader.

The next exposure to pseudo-money came when I discovered my mother saving stamps that the store gave her for shopping. I found out that if she had enough books of stamps, she could get things. I wanted to get a blue towel. I began to help her collect stamps by collecting discarded shopping receipts from people who didn't collect stamps. I turned them into the store and got the stamps.

Problem was, when I finally collected enough stamps to get the blue towel, we went to the stamp redemption center and they only had green towels. That was a good color but not as good as blue, which reminded me of fish and the ocean. I was very upset until I discovered the cuckoo clock hanging on a wall of the stamp redemption center.

I had to have that cuckoo clock. If you have even a drop of autism in you, you don't simply want something. You MUST HAVE IT. I wanted that cuckoo clock bad enough to learn about money and how much money it would take to get it. Once I knew that, I began doing things around the house to earn the money. Eventually, I had my cuckoo clock and learned a valuable lesson in the process.

You should know two things about money: how to get it and what to do with it once you have it. Working is the most common way to get money but not the only way. If you are too young to work, maybe your parents give you some money from time to time. This is called an allowance. If you get an allowance, it is good to understand what is expected of you in return. If you are supposed to do something to help, like wash dishes, mow the lawn or feed the pets, that is a good chance to do something to the best of your ability and practice for when you get a job.

Saving some of your money is a great habit. If you can get a savings account at a bank, you can save some of your money every month safely. Depending on the source of some of these public assistance programs, there are limits as to how much you can have in a savings account. If you reach that limit, you need to spend the money instead. That is okay. You can spend it on things that you need.

Another advantage of a savings account is that if you save your money for a long enough period of time, it will actually increase. Interest is the money you get from a bank for keeping your money in it. Saving on a regular basis is a good way to make sure that you have money when you need it, whether it's to buy gifts for someone's birthday or to take a vacation when you want to take it.

That was my first exposure to saving.

My father's bank had something called a "Christmas Club" for people to save a certain amount, every week. That way, he always had enough money when the holidays came. We also had a glass bottle in the shape of a bear, where all of our pennies went. This was called the "travel fund." In the fifties, with gas less than twenty cents a gallon, that bear actually held the gas money for many of our family trips. If you do save money, the rate of interest should always be as high as you can find. That will make a big difference in how fast the money grows over a period of years.

There are other sources of money, ones that frequently are used by people with disabilities. This money usually comes from the social security system and is called SSDI, or social security disability income. The theory behind this income is that people with disabilities need some assistance to make up for not earning as much as normal people. In general, income like this is called entitlement income because it is the legal right of a person with a disability to have it. He is entitled to it.

It is smart to accept this income when you are old enough to qualify. However, you must make sure that you don't waste it. This money is usually paid to people at the same time each month and people who know that may try to get you to be a "nice guy" and spend your money on them. That happens a lot in group homes or other places where support staff are underpaid and manipulate people like us into giving up our money, buying them lunches, presents or going to the movies. This is not something that you have to do to get someone who is hired to help you do his job correctly. It's your money, not his.

The wiser that you are with the money you have, the more the people who really belong in your life will respect you. If someone keeps trying to have you spend your money for him and you don't want to, that person does not belong in your life. If he is a support staff person, you need to tell him to stop asking you to spend money or you will report him. If he is a classmate or somebody else, he is not a friend, no matter what he says.

If you are a parent or a friend of a disabled person, this is not pleasant news but this is the way it often is. I know some wonderful staff and some who are not so wonderful. I have seen support staff walk up to consumers, who just got their SSDI check and DEMAND some, if not all of it for themselves. In one classic case, the victim's mother found out about it and got mad at her son. I don't know if the staff person ever stopped bullying his way into that money, but the autistic victim was so upset with himself and his inability to say no that he banged his head against the wall so much he had a solid layer of scar tissue on his forehead. That stinks.

You'd think the mother would have chewed out the staff member, but the "social deficit" so celebrated in every diagnostic description of autism must be inherited, eh? I will gladly support higher pay for good staff people, but people who extort money from my peers belong on the unemployment line, if not jail.

It is hard to say no, but sometimes you have to for your own good. If you let some of these bullies have a little, they will just raise the demand until they have everything you get.

So, suppose you get a monthly check like that and you know enough to not give it away. What do you do now? I guess you spend it on things that you would like to have. Maybe you would like to go to a few movies or go bowling. Maybe you want some new clothes. Maybe, maybe, maybe.... There is no end to what you can do if you spend your money wisely.

Entitlement income is a mixed blessing for those of us who get it. We would be foolish not to accept it. It is our money. It all comes from taxes, some of which are paid by working people with disabilities too, as well as by us when we work, so it is not a handout. It is okay for us to have it. Other forms of public assistance are not directly paid to you but are just as good as money. Examples of this are the section eight program which helps people with low income pay rent, as well as medical insurance programs for low income people. As you get older, you need to know what you are eligible for. If this is confusing, it is something that your advocate or case manager should know and explain to you as it applies to your life.

I said that income is a mixed blessing. Here's why: usually, the amount you can get from various forms of entitlement income is lowered as you start to work and make more than a minimum amount of money per month. I can see some sense in this, but I think the reduction is too quick. What bothers me more is that certain entitlement programs stop if you save more than a certain amount of money. They force you to spend money instead of saving it and that is just stupid.

I have been a part of support circles. These are monthly meetings of people who help a person with a disability discuss current issues in his life. The whole mess with entitlement income is so bad that I have seen entire meetings taken up by the accounting process, rather than on the ultimate goal of the consumer becoming more independent. We need to change that but not in this chapter.

Another source of money is inheritance. This is when someone dies and leaves you money. Or someone may set up a trust fund, money, for you while he is still alive. This money may be paid to you directly but is usually put in a trust. If that is the case, you probably need the approval of a trustee to spend any of it. The trustee may have instructions to spend the money for certain purposes only. In some trusts, you may get complete control of the money if you reach a certain age or satisfy other conditions.

If you suddenly wind up with a lot of money available, you need to fight the impulse to waste it all. You have to look at your needs, short and long term and see how to best use that money. A trustee can be a valuable aide to this process. If there is no trustee, you should find a Certified Public Accountant. These people understand money and help people get the most out of it. Depending on how much money is inherited, you may want to look at permanent solutions for some issues, like buying a place to live. You may also have to pay taxes on this money. I am not saying you shouldn't have some fun with it but don't blow all of it. Trust me, if you get lucky, get smart and find yourself a good accountant or some other professional who will guide you in your spending decisions.

I really hope that if you are young, you will take this seriously. If I had just saved ten percent of my income since I graduated from college I could retire right now. Ten percent is a lot for most of us but think of this way: if you work a few more hours each week, you will have the extra ten percent to save. I could have done that and most of us can. It's not like most of us are working all of the time. Most of the autistic and other disabled people I know have more free time than they need. You are a lot better off working, even if it's washing dishes, than you are sitting back at the group home, picking fights with room-mates or trashing your home every time you get upset.

It is amazing how much money you waste if you are not careful. My wife and I got lucky and had a large amount of money paid to us for rights to our life story. We wasted most of it. It is easy to do if you don't have a plan, especially if you have never seen so much money. But we learned from it and today we look forward to eventually owning our little home, adding a swimming pool and, we hope, an early retirement. It can be done if you have discipline and plan things. It can't be done if you just live for today. That is the way that I used to live, and it didn't work for me and won't work for you, either.

How to spend your money carefully is an important thing to know. The best way is to make a budget. List the cost of your

95

housing, food and other needs. Compare this to your income. Then list the cost of things you would like to do or have but can't afford. This makes it easier to see ways to reduce expenses and make money available for other spending.

Some expenses are hard to cut. You have to pay rent, and this usually doesn't change unless you add a roommate or move to a smaller place. Either alternative is not always a good one. You have to eat, but you don't have to eat all of your meals in restaurants. You can learn to cook for yourself. In fact, the best eating doesn't involve much cooking at all. Breakfast is easy: cereal, milk, fruit and that's all you need. Lunch and dinner are easy. The less lunchmeat you use and the more vegetables, lettuce, fruit and salad you use, the better off and leaner you will be. The amazing thing about food is that the best food, fresh food in the produce section of the market, is also the cheapest. It's the "fun" foods—chips, dips and other salty stuff that cost the most and do the most harm. And donuts? That's a no-brainer!

Here are some other ways to get the most of your money:

1. Movies: Matinees, early shows, are cheaper.

2. Free entertainment: Most areas have a weekly publication that lists poetry readings, nature hikes and other free fun activities.

3. Buses: Get a monthly saver pass for unlimited rides.

4. Gas: Car pool to work if you can. Walk to places that are not far and are safe to walk to. Use the car when you have to, not always.

5. Clothing: Second-hand stores and thrift shops have lots of stuff in decent condition.

6. Furniture: Buy unfinished wooden furniture, buy the finish and put it on the furniture. You will have beautiful bookcases, dressers and other stuff at a lower price.

7. Books and Tapes: Don't buy them; borrow them from your library.

8. Car repairs: Take an auto mechanics class. Don't look and sound like an idiot when you have to have work done on your car. Learn how to do your own oil changes and tune-ups. Keep everything in your car serviced on a regular schedule.

9. Coupons: Newspapers have coupons to save money on everything you need to buy. Use them.

10. Cooking: Take a cooking class at a local community college. Expand your appetite in a healthy way.

I can guarantee you that smart spending can increase the quality of your life without needing any more money. Not only that, but your wise and resourceful use of money will make you more attractive to other people. If you are too young to have a lot of money of your own, you can get ready for when you do. You can learn about how your family spends money and help in the process. If you behave, maybe you can help find items at the supermarket. Take note of the prices. Once you know what kinds of items your family buys, you can look for coupons in the newspaper, collect them and help your family save money. Even if you are a kid, you can have your own bank account. I did. The sooner you learn how to be really smart about money, the better off you will be!

There are a couple of other things we need to cover about money. One is taxes. You have to pay them. In most instances, they are taken out of your check, but not always. You need to know, with the help of an accountant, if you should save some money for taxes. The other is more complicated. If you work and are also getting income from public assistance, you need to report your income to those sources. They may reduce your assistance if your income is high enough, but the amount of reduction is never as much as the increase in your income. This is an important thing to keep track of.

Finally, you have to realize that you won't be able to work forever. If you can save anything for that time of your life, the sooner you start doing that, the better. It is never too late. Mary and I started a plan for our future last year and are glad of it. If you have any other income that will be available when you can't work, you should become aware of it.

There is another thing that you can do with money as long as you don't lose control. Gambling is fun and exciting; I enjoy the horse or dog races. There is a greyhound racetrack near my home. But I never take money to a racetrack or a casino that I need for other purposes. Gambling can be very addictive, and in most instances the odds are against you. Even in situations like blackjack or horse racing where some people actually try to make a living, it is very difficult to do. I hope that people who do that use money that they don't need for other purposes.

There is more to know about money, but this was a start. If you really like the idea of being smart with your money, there are lots of jobs for people in that area: accounting, financial planning, real estate etc. More than anything else, remember this: it's your money.

Getting Around Your Town, Safe and Sound

By now, you know that there is a life beyond your room, your home and school. You also know that walking is not the only way to get those places. You have ridden in a car or on a bicycle and probably a school bus. You may have traveled in a public transit bus, a commercial bus, a plane, train or a boat to distant places. This chapter is about how to safely visit places of interest in your local community.

The simplest form of transport available to most of us is walking. When I am fatter than I want to be and have the time, I walk to any place that is less than a mile away if the area is safe. I walk up stairs of buildings instead of using elevators if it is practical and I am not carrying too much to do it safely.

Even walking can be dangerous. You must only walk in safe places when crossing streets. These are called crosswalks. You will not usually find them unless you are at corners. Look to the right before you cross. Do it when you see no cars approaching that might hit you. Then look to the left. If there is a signal, begin walking in the crosswalk when the signal says "walk." After you start walking in the crosswalk, continue walking even if the signal says, "Don't walk." You don't want to wind up like poor Raymond Babbitt in the movie "Rain Man."

Walking at night requires more common sense. You should wear something light in color. Headlights of cars will show that you are walking and protect you from being hit. Avoid alleys and places that are not well lit. These places are dangerous at night. Avoid strangers. They will try to distract you, start a conversation to gain your trust and even offer you a ride home. You are better off walking, even if it is raining or you are tired.

There are other ways to travel in your community. You probably know how to take a school bus to school. There are other buses. They take people to work and to other activities. People get on them at bus stops. There are important differences between public buses and school buses. You probably always took the first school bus that you saw in the morning, since there would only be one going by the closest stop to your home. It is not that way with public buses.

Usually, public buses have more than one bus traveling through your neighborhood. They travel in fixed patterns, called routes. If you want to use a public bus, you need to find the bus with the route that gets you closest to where you want to go. To do this, you need to find the bus with the right route, its number and a schedule to let you know when it will stop near where you are. You need that schedule to find out how late the bus is running, so you can take it back to where you started your trip.

You also need to make sure that you are riding the bus from the right company. When I lived in Los Angeles, my local stop was served by buses from three different bus companies. Knowing the number of the bus was not enough. You need to know which bus system you are using. Each bus company usually has a distinct color pattern. The colors are usually the easiest way to spot the correct bus approaching your stop and get ready to board it.

If you use the bus regularly, you will soon know most of the times that your bus is in your area. You can get schedules for free and post them in your house. Look at the times and use your visual learning ability, which most of us autistic people have, to learn the schedules without trying that hard. You can get a map of the routes of all of the buses. The routes often appear on the map with different colors. If you hang that map up and just study it when you have free time, you will learn how you can use the buses to get anywhere, locally, that you wish, much faster than walking.

You should have the exact fare ready when you get on a bus. Bus drivers don't have time to give you change. If you need to take the bus to a stop and then use another bus, you need to ask the driver for a little piece of paper called a "transfer." If the next bus is from the same company, that transfer should be free. If it is to a bus from another company, there is usually a fixed fee to pay for that transfer. Either way, don't lose the transfer and be sure that you leave the bus at the appropriate stop to use it. You usually have two or three hours to use that transfer.

On the bus, you should walk towards the back if there are no seats available in front. If there is someone who really looks like they could use the seat more than you, like a really old person, offer the seat to them. You should not bring lots of packages on the bus or food that you are eating. It is no fun to have coffee spilled on you because the bus made a sudden stop. If you have to stand, there are handrails above you. Hold them when the bus moves.

Most buses have either a cord, or rubber strips, to press when you know you want to get off at the next stop. Pulling the cord or pushing the strip lets the driver know that you want to get off at the next stop. It is polite to pull or press once or twice. You don't have to stim on this. The driver is trained to hear that signal and stop when safe.

One last thing that I learned the hard way while riding in Los Angeles: you should sit near the bus driver if you can. Gang members and other troublemakers often occupy the back of the bus. They sit there so they can harass other passengers, drink and do other things that the driver can't see. There is no point in associating or trying to reason with these jerks. During crowded hours, they even enter the bus from the side exit to avoid paying.

I hate to say it, but it is not a good idea to try to help the passenger who is being taunted by these people. They never do this alone and they carry weapons. Just move as far away from them as you can. It is also not a good idea to stare at any passenger, especially someone engaged in an illegal activity. They can spot you, stab you and be off the bus before the bus stops. I am not making this up. You just can't trust everybody out there.

If you follow these suggestions, public buses will add a lot of freedom to your life. You can use them to shop, go to college, visit fun places and even go on a date. Buses are not the only local way to travel. There are ways that are "demand-responsive." In other words, there are travel options that you can use instantly, like driving a car or riding a bicycle.

You may not be old enough to drive a car so let's start with the bicycle. If you know how to keep your balance and ride one, then all you need to do is ride it safely. That means that you obey the rules of the road. You have to stop when the light tells you to. You ride on the side of the road in lanes for bikes and walkers. You should not ride on the sidewalk unless that is the only place to ride. If so, you must yield the right of way to walkers on the sidewalk.

Riding a bike also requires that your bike have reflectors and a light for riding at night. You should also have a lock and chain so you can lock your bike if you use it and have to leave it. Bikes are stolen and you don't want that to happen. Most shopping centers, schools and colleges have places to park your bikes and lock them. Those are the places to use.

The most important thing to remember when riding your bike is that you always pay attention to the road ahead. Look around you before changing your direction. You must not let your concentration wander and stim on some shiny object or other distraction. If that is going to be a problem for you, then don't ride a bike. It is only for people who can maintain their concentration. In addition, you should always wear a bicycle helmet, one that has a sticker inside saying it is approved by "ANSI Z-90."

I have another, important suggestion for you. You should always have identification. "ID" is any piece of paper or plastic that has your name, address, and picture if possible on it. If you are hurt and can't speak, that ID can help people help you. A good ID will also have your blood type and the phone number of a person to call if you wind up in an accident or other emergency.

In addition, many societies for people with different disabilities have cards which explain that condition to strangers. The Autism Society of America provides such a card, which you can carry with you. You may become so overwhelmed that you can't communicate. When that happens, you can show the card to someone and they will understand why you don't respond to them as they expect you to. This does not mean that you can act like a fool and use the card to excuse your behavior. It does mean that when you are in distress because of autism or your condition, you can use the card to alert someone and get help.

Beyond walking and bicycling, there is driving your own car. That is not something all of us can do. Certainly, you need vision, and it must be good enough to pass an eye exam given by the agency in your state that regulates autos, usually called the "Department of Motor Vehicles". The main thing you need though, is concentration.

Listen up because this is serious stuff.

Driving is not something that you can pay attention to when you want to, drift off, wake up and be okay. Good driving means that you <u>always</u> concentrate on the road ahead. This is not like a test where if you get 90%, it's an "A." The only acceptable grade in driving is 100% concentration on driving, 100% of the time.

I know people with autism who have Ph.D.s who don't drive. I also know people with autism who aren't nearly as well educated who are great drivers. Driving requires the self-discipline to keep your impulse to daydream, stim, or whatever completely under control while you drive.

I hope that you know yourself well enough, when you reach driving age, to know if you have this self-discipline. If you do, great. If not, you are better off if you don't drive now. Wait some more years and settle down before you drive, if ever.

I can't teach you to drive safely here. I can advise you to be patient about learning. Get to know the car that you will drive, inside and out. There is more to good driving than just twisting the steering wheel and hitting the brakes. You need to make sure that your car is in condition to be driven. My friends used to say, "If you take care of your car, it will take care of you."

That means that, at the very least, you should know how to check to see if your car has enough gasoline, oil, brake fluid and radiator fluid. When the car runs low on any of these, things get bad and expensive in a hurry. If your high school has an auto mechanics class, take it. You will learn a lot of practical stuff that will save you a ton of money in your lifetime. You will learn the common signals that cars give when they don't start. If you know those, you won't pay an outrageous bill to a mechanic when you need one. They just love it when people like us have the car towed in and look at them with a helpless expression. To them, we are sheep to be slaughtered!

Here are some other tips on driving safely and cheaply. And I have to admit, I drove for twenty years and had some accidents before I finally became a good driver. I haven't had a ticket or accident since 1985, but it took me way too long to find out.

1. Keep your car neat: Don't have stuff lying around that can suddenly move in front of you and interfere with your vision. Besides, a neat car makes a good impression on any police officer who stops you.

2. Minimize the distractions: You shouldn't smoke, so get rid of the ashtray and ask others not to smoke. Just because you have a radio doesn't mean you have to listen to it. Cell phones are dangerous. If you have one, there is a device that lets you answer it in your car without having to hold it. It's called a "hands-free unit." Get it.

3. Avoid tailgating: This is a huge cause of accidents, especially in rainy weather. If you find yourself coming to a stop, inches behind the car in front, or in the middle of crosswalks, it is time to be more patient and slow down.

4. Don't react to "road rage:" You might be too slow to suit somebody behind you. If you hear them honking, or see them pull alongside you, yelling, ignore them. They might be drunk or having a bad day. They also might have a weapon so there is no use in responding to them no matter how insulting they are.

5. Don't let passengers block your vision: Your friends may fool around and not realize that you can't see the side or rear because of their play. Tell them to allow you to see where you need to see.

6. Know what to do if you get "pulled over:" This is when you see a police car in your rear view mirror, with lights flashing. You might even hear a voice, telling you to pull over to the side of the road. Do that as soon as it is safe and then do the following:

Take your wallet out, put it on the dashboard, and put your hands in front of you. Be careful to show the officer that your hands are empty. Policemen carry guns and are always expecting confrontations. You do not want this.

Obey the police officer's commands. He may ask you to step out of the car.

Do not reach for your pockets. If he asks you for your ID and it is in your pocket, tell that to the officer get his permission to reach in your pocket or in your glove compartment for other papers. It will be easier for you if you always have your auto registration and proof of insurance in your glove compartment, in one envelope, on top of everything else. The less you make the officer wait, the more sympathy he will have for you.

The officer should tell you why you have been stopped. Even if you know you did something wrong, never admit it. If he writes you a ticket, don't argue with him. You can fight it in court. If your car is neat and you don't make him wait forever to see your documents, you may just get a warning which is not a ticket.

Never argue with a police officer. You argue in front of a judge. Arguing will only result in making the situation worse. You can be arrested for resisting the officer.

Last Detail: Get the badge number of the police officer if he does anything that you feel was improper.

7. Accidents: If you get in one, your first responsibility is your safety. Don't admit anything. If anyone needs medical assistance, call an ambulance or ask a passing driver to make that call. If there is an injury or more than minimal damage, a police report has to be made. To make sure that the report is accurate, police must be called right away. It is best not to move the cars involved, unless you are on a busy highway and it must happen. Moving the cars makes it harder for police to determine what happened.

The driver of the other car may not want to wait for a police report. Immediately get his license plate number. You can't stop him from leaving, but it's important to get his name, phone number and the name of his insurance company. You should let him have the same information from you. You both should also have the names and phone numbers of all passengers and any witnesses.

This may seem like a lot to think of at the time, so make a drill out of this: Have a list of things to do, stored in your glove compartment, in case you have an accident. You will have to make a report to your insurance company. They will determine who was at fault. If you feel you were not at fault, having all of your information organized will help you prove it.

Sometimes, the accident will result in only minor damage so slight that one person will offer to settle the matter for a small amount of money. If that is the case and you are the one paying, the other person should sign a form called a release of liability that should read like this:

> *I, driver of auto_____, hereby release (your name) of all liability for property damage and injury resulting from the accidental contact of his vehicle with mine at (time), (date), (address).*

Without a written release of liability, you can't just shake hands and drive away. The other driver can take your money and still have his insurance company go after you! And remember, if there is any injury or more than a small amount of damage (the amount depends on the state you live in), you have to make a police report.

I have dropped a ton of information on you about driving. This is not something to joke about. I hope you can make the wise decision to either drive safely or recognize that you shouldn't try. Driving is fun. You can even make a living, using cars or trucks to deliver things or people. It is a great privilege, but only for those who are focused and responsible enough to do it safely.

"It just has too many notes. Remove a few and it will sound fine..."
- Austrian Emperor Franz Joseph, to Mozart in "Amadeus"

Too Many Notes...
When the World is Too Much....

Overload is the name of the autism game. There are many things that some of us have in our act, but none of those are part of every autistic person's script. Overload is universal for us. Some of us hate to be hugged; some love it. Some of us won't look at people in the eye. Others stare. Some of us are nonverbal. Some never shut up. Some of us are picky eaters. Some of us, like me, will eat cement with the right fork. But if you had free tickets for a rerun of the Broadway Play, "Stop the World, I Want to Get Off!", you could fill any theater, anywhere, with overloaded autistic people faster than Raymond Babbitt melted down because of a smoke detector.

If I could think of two words to describe all autistic people, it would be: lousy jugglers. On a good day, I can juggle two oranges, but if you toss a third one at me, some poor orange is going to get dropped. Many of us have a few things that we can do very well if we don't have to do anything else at the same time. I can listen to music on a radio, walk over to a piano and play back the melody with one hand. No problem. I never had a piano lesson. But playing with two hands at once is still very hard for me. In fact, when I was a young boy it was that problem that led me to an event which inspires this chapter.

I was about eight or nine. I was in Pennsylvania, probably Lewisburg, where my Uncle Bill was a minister. Our family visited him and his wife, Aunt Jerry. (My first name Gerald comes from her "Geraldine") It was always fun to visit Pennsylvania in the summer. For one thing, it was less crowded than Islip. The river level varied each year and it was fun to guess how high or low the Susquehanna would be when we finally reached it. The gardens and parks were full of little toads to chase. And of course, there was Aunt Jerry, actually the craziest Jerry in the family, beyond even me.

She was nervous about everything, all of the time. But one of the things that calmed her, and that she shared with her younger sister, my mother, was playing the piano. We did not have a piano back home in Islip, so when Mom had a chance to play one, she took it. I watched her play with both hands. It was easy to play the melody in my head, but as I tried to read the music and play with the left hand, I never could stand by and keep up with her.

Finally, she took a break. I complimented her on the sound. She reminded me that my father also played. In fact, in college at Syracuse he was a piano player and bouncer at a local "speak-easy," a place where people went to drink when it was illegal to do so. His size, 6'2" and over 200 pounds, made him do double-duty when one of the customers was too full of suds.

"How do you do that? Play with both hands?" I asked.

Her response was orderly and logical as she always was. "Jerry, it was not easy for me when I learned, either. I teach the left hand how to play its part. Once that is done, I can play with my right hand and the left hand takes care of itself."

It was an inspiring statement, made by a woman whose apparent grace in life was probably an affected result of rehearsed spontaneity. After she died in 1988, I found a drawer, full of essays, poems and plays. Some were priceless anecdotes about my brothers and me, such as the time Jim broke the hearts of everyone at Sunday school by proclaiming that there is no Santa

Claus. My father found him on the steps of the church, grinning broadly.

My mother was obsessed with precision and measurement. She collected clocks and watches and wrote poems about units of time, money and different pronouns. I have to wonder if some of my Asperger's traits came from her. She refused an offer of a touch-tone telephone because "when you use a dial phone, you get to see all of the little circles go home."

But her mastery of the piano was the best. It really impressed me. What about her year's supply of lesson plans for school, which she delivered, year after year as if they were original scripts, written for only that eighth-grade math class? I already knew that stuff!

But the piano playing was something else.

Overload was hardest for me in early youth. It was too much noise in the cafeteria. Or it was the dreaded fly ball, headed my way. How to catch it and if that miracle happens, where to throw it? It was either not having the ball in basketball and wondering where to go or having it and being the immediate focus or target of nine other players and an audience waiting for me to mess up again.

Overload in the worst case made me shut down until it was over. I could feel it coming, a tightness in my gut was the most telling sign. I would just not say anything or do anything until I was calm enough to do so. At home, I did this most often when the conversation got too uncomfortable or there was too much action to pay attention to. I am happy that my father was wise enough to let me shut down and work my way out of it. I think he had moments like this, too.

The solution wasn't always peaceful. My worst moments were when I couldn't find something I needed, usually a car key. It was worse if time was running out. This was part of me even in 1988, the last year of my mother's life. I can remember a neighbor asking me to stop yelling when this happened, since my voice carried way beyond the little Santa Monica apartment that Mom and I shared. They knew it wasn't a domestic violence episode, but it wasn't fun to hear!

Sometimes, overload is cumulative. In 1986-88, I worked at an elementary school as a library clerk. Part-time, I was a cashier at the Santa Monica College student bookstore. Both jobs involved cumulative overload. At the college, I was very fast on the register. Because I was a part-timer, I had to work at different registers, sometimes switching in mid-shift. This distressed me, because I arranged items for sale, tapes and other frequent items below the counter so I could reach for them without looking if they were requested. When I had to change workstations, there was never enough time to duplicate my arrangement.

In the elementary school, most of my job was relaxing. When the library was empty—about half of the day—I shelved books and made arrangements, depending on the time of year. But when the students came in, that was another story. The worst were the third graders. They are in intellectual puberty! So many new interests at once: Scouts, Little League, instrumental music, chorus, reading books without pictures, an explosion of curiosity. In the library each of them wanted my immediate attention. Impossible for anyone, especially me.

Either work environment left me stressed out at the end of many days. The last thing I wanted to do for at least a couple of hours was talk to anyone. I wanted to go home, eat, watch TV and say nothing. My cockatiels would be enough company! My poor mom never understood this. By then, she never left the house unless she had to go to the doctor. Walking and moving at all was painful. Besides, she was a Newport. I could have taken her to church or given her a ride to Palisades Park just one block away where her friends played bridge and ate lunch with an ocean view. But not my mother! She could not stand looking vulnerable in public, so she wasted away the last five years or more of her life. I have to say that a person who won't let you buy her a touch-tone phone because of "the little circles going home" (each one at the same exact speed) is not totally normal.

But she had a great life, even though at the end, the high point of her day (and the low point of mine) was when I got home. The poor, lonely woman wanted to know everything I had done in school. I was in no mood to share it. I really feel sad about it now. Since I have learned to use her "teach the left hand how to play" principle, I would have handled that situation differently and both of us would have been better off. Too late, but she knew I loved her anyway.

There is another classic case of overload in my teen years. When I was in Boy Scout camp, I was between eighth and ninth grade. We were at Dan Beard campsite at Camp Baiting Hollow in Wading River on the north shore of Long Island. It was a two-week camp.

It was my third summer, and I actually had some success this time.

I made it to the swimmer's division in trials. I finally allowed my face to be in the water, jumped into the lake, swam the required 150 yards around a course, and got out on my own. That felt great.

But other stuff was not so great. I was tired of the teasing. It revolved around our outdoor showers. This was the summer of male puberty and many of them were quite interested in the relative size of our "trunks," to use an analogy. Some elephants have long trunks, long enough to skip rope with. Some elephants don't. My trunk was not rope-skipping length and the entire troop let me know it, every day.

That really hurt. I wish I could go back for a day and respond. Now I would say, "Why are you even looking down there? What kind of a goddamn queer are you?" or maybe," If I have to choose between a 'trunk' the size of mine and a brain as tiny as yours, I think I will live with my small 'trunk.'" or "The minute your girlfriend, with tits the size of town hall, realizes that you'll be working at MacDonald's forever, she will be putting out big-time for a small-trunk, future-rich guy like me, so enjoy your shower while it lasts, moron."

My "friends" knew something else about me. They knew that if I got stressed out, I cursed a blue streak. One evening, they decided to make a public show of me. An unsuspecting camp counselor, probably a high school junior or senior, suddenly found himself surrounded by a rabid sample of Troop 151. I was pushed to the front of this wild pack.

"Go ahead, Newport, cuss him out!" they said. I did. No reason why. I was just sick of the whole stinking camp experience and let him have it.

The counselor just listened. I finally stopped. He looked at me, just said, "Why?" and walked away.

So, in case you meet me at a conference and I look too normal to be your peer, a son or a sibling, it wasn't always that way and I have tons of witnesses.

It has taken some time to hit the heart of this chapter, but it is key to helping people live a full life who have to deal with autism.

Overload is a problem for many people, but much more for those with autism. I would feel like a real hypocrite if it wasn't part of my history. Having shown that, let's discuss how to handle overload. Master this and you are well on your way to a much happier, controllable life.

Overload, quite simply, is exactly what the word says: too much of a load on one's senses. Most people can hear, see, touch, smell, taste, etc. and they do combinations of those things at once, effortlessly. On the other hand, famous peers of mine like Donna Williams report that even as an adult, she can use one sense at a time, period. That may work if Donna is at home, writing, with no interference. But if she has to make a trip, deliver a presentation, answer questions all after a huge switch in time zones, she must use an elaborate series of strategies to keep herself together. She doesn't have a choice. Once you are a celebrity and a best-selling writer, it sticks, and it's a mixed blessing, I am sure.

Overload is when there is finally too much going on and your body is telling you that enough is enough. I have found, however, that most of my overload situations are not completely new. They are repeats of a previous overload situation. Here is a list of my all-time favorite overload situations:

1. I can't find my (keys, ID, shoes, whatever) and I need them, NOW!
2. Too many people are talking at the same time.
3. I am stuck in traffic. Some idiot is honking and tailgating me, but I can't get out of his way.
4. Someone talks to me while I am talking on the phone.
5. It's my turn to do something with the basketball, baseball, football etc.
6. My boss has just asked me to talk to him in his office...
7. I am at the airport and have lost my boarding pass.

8. I have lost my boarding pass, and the plane takes off in twenty minutes.
9. I am speaking in a room full of people, and some idiot just dropped twenty dishes, ten feet away from me.
10. The airline lost my bag.
11. I went to a baseball game and can't remember where I parked my car.
12. A police car is telling me to pull over.
13. Something that I am very used to having my way, has CHANGED!!!

There are many more situations for me and for you. Most, we probably share as a group, but some are uniquely part of your life. The first rule to remember, whenever you are in one of these situations or know that you are heading, that way is to remember,

YOU WILL SURVIVE IT.

Example: In 1993, my car was down for repairs. I had to take a bus from my home area to Brentwood to shop. It was not the usual route, but I just looked through the bus schedules that I had collected and found the closest stop and the next time the bus stopped there. That was no problem. But when I got on the bus, it was almost a disaster.

Perhaps the bus was running late. I was the last one to get on, and the bus began moving instantly, turning to the right. I quickly dropped my fare into the correct place but the coins got stuck. I was determined to fix that situation but I blocked the driver's vision.

It was a classic confrontation. I wanted to get the coins to drop where they belonged. The driver had to make his turn safely. Suddenly, in my mind, I saw the word, "temporary" appear. I have no idea where it came from, but I knew what it meant: "relax." The coins will not stay in the wrong place forever. The bus has to move. That is more important. Just find a seat and get out of the driver's way."

I did. As soon as he finished the turn and the bus was moving straight up Montana Avenue, the driver took a little screwdriver out of his shirt pocket and used it to jiggle my coins. They fell into the right place. I breathed a sigh of relief and was happy that had happened to me at the age of forty-four instead of four! But the lucky word in my head, "temporary" was never forgotten.

You have survived every situation so far, that seemed totally in control of your fate and hopeless at the time. You will survive many more, so this is a very useful fact to remember. This principle also works for parents and teachers when one of us drives you nuts. You, too, have survived every other line in our autistic script. You will survive this one, too.

Now that you have reminded yourself that there is a light at the end of every tunnel, here is the rest of the strategy:

Try to identify what kind of tunnel you are in. It may be one for which you already have a backup strategy in place. If it is, just use that strategy and happily head for daylight!

Example: I travel a lot. Sometimes, on the way to the boarding gate, I realize that I lost my boarding pass. No problem and no expense at all! I use E-tickets. When you make reservations with an e-ticket, and you lose the ticket or a boarding pass, you just go to any service counter for that airline, show a photo ID and get another one.

That could have been a disaster. I have been in situations where I had to come up with another seventy-five dollars to replace a lost ticket. Once, I had no money and a friend drove out at 6 a.m. on a Friday in the rain, to loan me the money! With e-tickets that will never happen to me again .

Another example is my ID. I now have a photocopy of my driver's license and passport sewn into my luggage and in my suit jacket or whatever I wear on board. So, if I go jogging on the morning of a trip, put my regular ID in my sneaker and forget it later, I still have a pair of backup IDs! If I wind up in a foreign nation with my baggage lost and no ID, there's another set of ID at home that someone can fax to me.

There are many situations that can easily be minimized with an appropriate backup system: spare house keys, car keys, etc. Lots of people do this.

Another problem situation is not being able to find what you need when you are leaving the house. I have solved this with this habit: if you are going somewhere and need certain things, put those items in a consistent place **before** it is time to go. When I worked at UCLA, things went best if my work clothes, car keys and briefcase were always waiting for me in the same space when I awoke each morning.

I added to that simplicity by pouring my coffee grounds into the coffee maker and loading the water each night before. I had all of the bird food ready to be fed and waiting in the refrigerator. This made getting up a lot easier and less confusing. I could do all of the routine stuff with no stress because everything was where it was supposed to be.

Backup systems are great and I find new ones all the time. I now have a local bus schedule handy in case my car doesn't start for me. I have phone numbers of pet doctors, plumbers and other professionals in case I need them. When I take a trip, I always give Mary the phone number of where I will stay, the flight number of the airline and any other number she might need in case of an emergency.

Not every overload situation is solved so quickly. But most of them are similar to something you have survived before, if not a replay. The first time I had to fix a flat tire was a pain, but it taught me something. I cursed a blue streak because it happened at night, I had no flashlight and all of the tools I needed were strewn all over the trunk. Today, if I have a flat tire, I do know how to change it and since the flashlight is in the glove compartment and the tools are neatly arranged in a box in the trunk, I won't have to curse a blue streak again.

You may wind up in a place where there are too many people talking at once. This is going to happen more than once, so it is not new every time it happens. It may happen in a new place with new people, but it is the same situation.

First rule: remember, no matter how uncomfortable you are, it will not last forever. Second rule: you may have options.

You can excuse yourself and look for a friendlier group. If there is a punch bowl or food around, you can walk over there and kill some time, even if you don't consume anything. If there is an outdoor area, a balcony or fresh air, you can go get some fresh air. If you have to stay in the group for some social reason, just wait until there is something said that you can easily react to and react. If it never happens, the situation is only temporary and will end. The light will come at the end of the tunnel and fussing and fretting and stimming won't make it come any faster.

I remember having to do a talk at a lunch event. These are tough for any speaker because you rarely have an attentive audience. There is usually at least one table full of barbarians who will eat and talk completely through your speech as if you don't exist, especially if it is an autism audience. It is a genetic condition. Add to that the sounds made by silverware and glasses.

I always walk into a place where I speak ahead of time, so I know what I can expect. Once something I never expected happened in the middle of my talk. Some poor waiter dropped twenty plates within ten yards of me!

If I had been ten years old, I would have jumped through the roof or at least ran out of the room crying. But I was almost fifty and had to finish a speech. After the sudden pain in my spine went away, I looked at the broken dishes, smiled and went back to talking. It was over. There was nothing to stim about. Life goes on.

Automobiles can trap us, especially in crowded cities where road rage seems the rule rather than the exception. You will never get completely away from tailgaters or other idiots. They may find you at different times on different streets, but you have to remember: They may have a reason to be out of control and acting like a highway bully. Just drive safely and don't do anything to make them more upset.

Two decades ago, I might have unrolled my window and flashed an appropriate signal to them with a middle finger. Today that is not wise. Some of these fools are on drugs or have guns. Just endure their insanity until they are out of your rearview mirror and have found another driver to irritate.

There is a logical, practical pattern for these overload situations:

First: remember that you will get past it. Second: identify the part that you have dealt with in the past.

It is another road idiot, another group of inconsiderate people at a social event, another flat tire, etc. That part you can handle with confidence. Just use the best strategy that you used in the past. There may not be a perfect strategy, but it will minimize the pain.

Those first two elements will free your mind to deal with any variations in the situation, based on what you have encountered before. It will give you more confidence in the overall situation. I can tell you that, as one on the giving end of much frustration, that a person who has confidence in dealing with whatever crazy situation I have foisted on him, has a much better chance of survival than someone with no confidence.

There are some situations that are rare, but you still need to prepare for them.

One is what to do if there is a fire or other emergency in your home. Have a strategy for dealing with either of these situations with a phone number to call and a safe exit plan.

We should all know how to handle some simple medical emergencies.

Once, a fellow had a seizure during my support group meeting. Fortunately, two of our members knew what to do. Another time, while eating at a fast food place, I ordered a bowl of rice and ate it way too quickly. I began choking and tried to drink some water. I kept choking and felt like passing out. A customer gave me a Heimlich maneuver and helped me dislodge the rice that went down the wrong way. His knowledge helped me live long enough to tell you about it!

The last situation, that of a sudden change in our routine, is a huge issue for us. When you are young, it may be that you are in the family car, expecting it to go one way and it goes another way! Or you go to school and your teacher, who knows your needs, is not there. She is sick and a total stranger is your teacher.

You don't have to be disabled to feel stress about change. All of us like to have order and consistency in our lives. None of us would want to wake up every day in a different bed, different house, with a different family, different name and new pets! We autistic people have a reputation for "unreasonable resistance to change." I think it's a bad rap. Nobody is always cool about change. Just watch how an elected official reacts when you try to replace him! Watch your favorite prima-donna athlete complain about being traded to another team.

Back to our gang. We like to know what in the heck is going on ahead of time. It is nice to know where your family car is going. It is nice to know who your teacher will be or what TV program is coming up next. This knowledge makes us feel secure and allows our overloaded little autistic bodies to chill out.

But it doesn't always work out that way. There may be some things you can do, as a drill, to make change less painful and terrifying when it happens. Here's a possible drill for when you go out in the car.

You: "Where are we going?"

Driver: "To church."

You: "Are we taking the usual way?"

Driver: "Yes, (No change!) or, no, we have to go to Bill's house and get him and his wife. Their car broke down. I am glad you asked me that because I need to warn you about this change. I will really appreciate it if you can stand sharing the back seat with a couple of people this morning."

You: "It's a big surprise but I guess I can live with it."

That is one example. Yes, you will have to live with a temporary change, but it would have been far worse if nobody warned you. By asking the leading questions, you found out that there was a change in the usual route. It gave your father or mother a chance to prepare you for that change and the temporary inconvenience of crowding in your back seat.

What about the substitute teacher?

This won't happen often, but it will happen. You need to ask yourself, "What does this new teacher need to know about me?" If you have an aide, that person should help you with this issue. It may be a good idea to carry with you, at all times, a little card that introduces you to any stranger who needs to understand why you suddenly act in a surprising manner.

Most disability advocacy groups, like Autism Society of America, as I mentioned earlier, have such a card available for children or adults. Hopefully, you will adjust to a day with a substitute teacher. But if you get uncomfortable, sharing that card will help the new teacher understand what you need.

Both of these change situations have one thing in common. They are not permanent situations. Your regular teacher will not be sick forever. Your family car will usually go where you expect it to go. With a structured strategy in place, you can reduce the pain that changes bring, have more confidence and flexibility and fewer meltdowns and embarrassments. I highly recommend that you, your parents and teachers try to think through as many possible changes as you can ahead of time and help you imagine how to react to them. It will make your life a lot easier!

Now you need to do some homework. This chapter can save you a lot of future anxiety. Make a list of the instances you can remember, as far back as you can, where you just "lost it" because there was too much to handle. Once you have a list, look at each situation. Wherever you have something that a backup system can either eliminate or minimize, put the backup system in place: get the extra sets of keys, etc., copies of ID to make life easier and use e-tickets when you fly!

There will be other situations. Look at what is predictable about each one. That part is consistent. Decide the best strategy to handle that part and visualize yourself doing it. Last, remember that all of these situations are survivable. You will reach that light, and it will come a lot sooner if you use any backup strategies available, handle the part you already know with confidence and move ahead through the new part.

Nobody gets through life without emergencies and feeling overwhelmed, and most of the time, it's not a totally new situation. You don't have to reinvent the wheel every time you have a flat tire. Just calm down, do what you know is best and you will live to laugh about it.

Time Out

This book isn't over. I wanted to give you all a break from the prison of earthly life. I have filled the first half of this book with a lot of well-intentioned practical advice. That is not the book I really want to write, but I had no choice what planet to live on, either. My words are intended to help you live in a world that is populated by people who aren't like you. Because they are the majority, they assume that the only way you can be happy is to be like them.

I am outnumbered, too. I accept it. I try to work with it. But I don't like it any more than you do. I have written every page up to this one in complete betrayal of my natural self. I have felt forced to keep focused, concentrate on relevancy and all of the stuff that normal people and publishers insist their books be filled with.

My brain is on strike. Just once, I want to stop the careening, drunken, road-raged auto that personifies the human majority and smear something on its windshield. This chapter is for me. It has no goal or purpose except to be fun and stim on whatever I think of when I write it.

I don't live to do the stupid, normal things that I do too much of the time. I compromise myself every day so I can do many of the things I used to do as a kid. But now I am an adult. I can do some of them even better. I love fans, especially six-blade fans. I hate five-blade fans. I will drive anywhere to sit, drink coffee and eat a slice of apple pie in the presence of a row of six-blade fans. I wouldn't walk across the street to be cooled off by a team of five-blade fans if it was 170 degrees.

Why? Because five-blade fans remind me of a Pentagon. I have never been a fan of the military. But six-blade fans are much higher functioning. For one thing, if you draw a straight line from the tip of each blade to the next tip and do that all around, a six-blade fan fits inside a hexagon. The side of a hexagon is equal to the radius of a circle in which a hexagon can be inscribed. Between each pair of blades in a hexagon, you will find an equilateral triangle, all sides equal. If you fold each triangle out from the center, you get six more equilateral triangles, twelve in all, within a star of David, my middle name. Twelve equilateral triangles, one for each tribe of Israel. Not bad insight for a WASP!

It doesn't mean squat, of course, but to me it's cool to know. To a young fellow, visually stimming on some geometrical relationship between his bent hand and his chin, or maybe moving his fingers close to each other and making hot dogs appear, it's just cool to know. Why is it so hard for the normals to understand that some things are just cool to know?! So cool to know that they can be known all day.

That part of me has never changed. Maybe that is why I love numbers. When I first met them, they weren't the flat numbers you make in arithmetic class, 1,2,3,4.... No, to me each number meant a set of points, like stars, to be manipulated visually as I pleased. So five meant a whole different set of possible mental constellations than four and six, seven and eight became more fun.

I still like to stim with numbers, bigger ones now because after almost fifty years, the smaller ones are road meat. I have never been to hell, but some conferences have put me in states where the license plates have only three numerical digits.

Nothing to factor! At least Hawaii had nice beaches. I was never a conventional math person, using induction and that stuff to prove relationships. My way was to just pour out a bunch of numerical Lincoln logs onto a mental table and push them around until a relationship appeared.

One of the first things I learned was this. Start with any simple fraction, like 3/2. Now, you create a new fraction using this rule: The denominator of the new fraction is the sum of the numerator and denominator of the old fraction. The numerator (top number) of the new fraction is the bottom number of the old fraction, times two plus the top number of the old fraction. So, 3/2 becomes 7/5 and that becomes 17/12 and that becomes 41/29 etc. The limit is the square root of two no matter what fraction you start with, as long as both numerator and denominator are positive.

If you decide to triple the top number instead of doubling it, the limit is the square root of three, etc. In the case I showed you, there is another cute thing that happens: Take the numerator times the denominator and square each result:

$$2 \times 3 = 6 \quad 6 \text{ squared} = 36$$

$$7 \times 5 = 35 \quad 35 \text{ squared} = 1225$$

$$17 \times 12 = 204 \quad 204 \text{ squared} = 41616$$

Each number on the right is obviously a perfect square but each is also a triangular number. It is the sum of a finite number of integers starting from one.

$$6 = 1 + 2 + 3$$

$$1225 = 1 + 2 + 3 + \ldots + 49$$

$$41616 = 1 + 2 + 3 + \ldots + 288$$

It works every time. I didn't know how to prove it back then. I didn't care. It worked whenever I tried it and that was enough.

I finally got old enough to prove some things I noticed. Like if you start cubing integers from one and add them up, you get the same result as if you just add up integers and square the sum. Example, sum of 1,2,3,4 is ten. Ten squared is 100. And 1 + 8 + 27 + 64 Is also 100. Just algebra.

But it didn't bother me whether I could prove it or not. If I could try out enough things in my head like visualizing an integral in three dimensions, it was enough.

It wasn't enough in college. I just wanted to write in my blue books, "I can see that it works. Can't you?" Unacceptable.

Today my favorite number is fourteen, as in my fourteen parrots. If each parrot occupies a different position, there will never be enough time to observe all of the parrot position permutations in our aviary. But it is fun to watch them change even if I lose track of them.

It was and always will be fun to know that our universe is blessed with an order and beauty that neurotypicals can never destroy, no matter how hard they try. And if you ask any orca mother who has just lost her calf to prenatal PCB poisoning as half of them do, you must admit that neurotypicals are still gaining in their fight to consume and sterilize our planet in their image.

It was and still is more fun to tune out and appreciate the order and sanity left than it is to tune in to a bunch of sadistic Boy Scouts who are waiting to ridicule me in a shower. Or another bunch of grade school brats, wanting me to strike out or drop a fly ball so they can feel better.

It makes you wonder, why are some "normals" so goddamn cruel? Why do they get so much pleasure out of making people feel bad?

Some stuff is just fun to know. Most people understand the expression, "as exciting as watching paint dry." I don't. I looked forward to every spring.

Middle brother Jim and I had a boat, covered up in our back yard. It got an annual sanding, varnishing and repainting. I have watched a lot of paint dry. It never dries the same way on wood. You can learn a lot about wood by watching paint dry on it. I think autistic people just like to watch paint dry. That's it.

My peers see beauty and order where others see nothing. My peers know that if they look hard enough, there is life in a desert. I know that because I live on desert property. Yet, every morning I water plants and watch tiny lizards, ants, bugs, flies and birds, and the desert is full of life.

Perhaps if you are one who is seen as a lifeless desert by others, you learn to give a real desert a long look before declaring it dead.

I know that this won't last forever. I have to go back to sharing what I know of life in a hostile, judgmental, arrogant planet. But I have no choice. I am stuck there just as you are. I wish I didn't have to live in a stupid body. It would be so great to be a free spirit and go anywhere with no worry of food, shelter, etc. I would spend months listening to music I remember, changing it subtly, replaying it, endlessly. But this world won't let us escape long enough for any of that.

It amazes me how normal people have screwed up the way I look at the world. I have spent over eight years, proud to be a member of various adult support groups. I am still proud but it finally dawned on me, why do we call them support groups? When I think of support groups, I think of stuff like AA, Twelve Steps and all that. What is it about autism or any disability that's such a sin that we have to get together and support each other?

We are making progress. Once in a while, people listen to us now. But I will know we have arrived when AGUA and my other groups are just what they should be, groups to hang out with and share being autistic, not support groups for people who want to learn to be normal. That hasn't been the case either, but why can't my groups just be autism clubs?

I am not yet ready to "write straight" again.

Life takes a daily toll on even marginally autistic people like me. I do a lot more compromising than I want to. It was over 100 today. Why wear clothes? I had to, and it wasn't comfortable. I spend countless hours answering email from people who just want me to somehow tell them how I fixed myself (I haven't. Ask Mary) so they can fix their kids. It doesn't matter how much I try to increase their understanding. They can't understand what they are too afraid to deal with. They only see one way out, an impossible way, becoming normal.

I sure hope there is an afterlife to make up for all of the time you and I are doomed to waste in this one. I hope there is enough time in the afterlife to see every possible constellation or all the stars.

I hope I can count all of the parrot position permutations and watch them all take happy rides on slow moving, six-blade fans. I want to spend at least a couple of hundred years, reading the solutions to every math puzzle I never solved, a century riding on merry-go-rounds and watching auto races, and another century surrounded by hamsters pushing liberty balls through deep pile rugs. I want to paint and sculpt by just telling the paint and material where to go, free from hopelessly self-conscious appendages. If I want to paint a dolphin in a sunflower, or have birds fly out of the wallpaper of a dreaming boy's bedroom and take his spirit out for a ride, it will happen.

I hope our spirits can all exact total revenge from the NT world that enslaves, medicates, "therapies," ridicules, abuses and tortures us. The ultimate revenge is to be happy in spite of them. Even if it is just a moment, seize that moment whenever you can.

This is my fantasy of collective, afterlife, autistic revenge: all of the autistic souls will converge near Palm Springs, where the rows of three-blade windmills live. (If you think of a three-blade fan as every other blade of a six-blade fan, it works.) We will gather there, all of us, millions. Included would be the great autistic person who once sat in a favorite place, imagined a neighborhood where everyone lived the same distance from him and invented a circle. Of course, we will have his autistic friend who turned the circle into a wheel.

Ancient people who measured the high and low tides and had the patience to record star movements will join us at the windmills, too. So will the makers of those little gargoyles on the Notre Dame cathedral and many other works of art and architecture. We will all spend a glorious day at the windmills, rising to do Tai Chi; a once and for all eternal autistic "AH" moment. It will be a long day. We will all meet each other. Everyone will mean what he says, and it will all work out.

We will all rejoice that most of history was ours. During most of it, people actually took the time to know each other. Recreation consisted of celebrating our relationship with the sun, moon, stars and nature. Nobody who enjoyed that was ostracized for enjoying it too long.

There was a time, our time, when one knew what one said had a universal meaning. Guile, treachery and deceit weren't yet desirable attributes. There was a time when people, values and principles weren't disposable. There was a time when people didn't just change partners, dwellings and alliances at the drop or rise of the next quarterly report or hot flash at Club Bozo. There was a time when nature and pure, uncorrupted humanity were respected. In that time, doctors would have treated people for acting normal, not for acting as we do.

It will be our party and nobody else's. Nobody but us will see us in our great team picture by the windmills. All of us who ever lived this way before and after today will come back to the windmills and share our common experience, rejoice and celebrate for a very long, high functioning day. And the rest of them will never know.

It is time to go back to work. I just wanted you to know that no matter how pragmatic and constipated a spirit seems when negotiating a peace in this world, I have not forgotten my roots nor do I deny the goodness and purity of them.

Some stuff is just cool to know and somebody needs to know that. Had a rough day? Do yourself a favor. After you finish the book, go out, find yourself some fresh paint, and watch it dry.

Jerry Newport and Mary Insight—As interviewed by Veronica Palmer for the Autism/Asperger's Digest Magazine on Social Relationships

One Size Does Not Fit All

A/AD: Mary and Jerry, thanks for inviting Future Horizons to help you compose this chapter on relationships. Because it's such a broad topic, in this chapter we'd like to concentrate on social relationships as you were growing up, talking just briefly about college and work. Then let's get down to the interesting and personal questions about romantic relationships, that I'm sure all our readers are interested in.

Jerry: No problem. A lot of people have fantasies about what it is like for two people with the same challenge to marry, and we'd be doing our readers a disservice if we didn't talk about it.

Mary: Jerry isn't saying that it doesn't work, but that it takes a lot more daily work than either of us new the first time around.

Jerry: We're a lot smarter now, (laughter) but we'll get back to that later.

A/AD: To start, why did you choose the title, "One Size Does Not Fit All"?

Jerry: Because males and females with AS, autism or any disability, don't develop socially in the same way.

A/AD: How do you think the sex difference plays out?

Mary: Society expects different things of men and women, socially. One sex is supposed to be the hunter and the other is the caretaker, the nurturer. That means that some traits will be more noticeable in boys than in girls: for instance, shyness in boys and aggressive behaviors in girls.

Jerry: A boy who doesn't make eye contact is going to be noticed more than a girl that doesn't have it. A boy who fusses about getting over-stimulated will stand out more than a girl who does the same thing. Certain Asperger's behaviors tend to fit a female stereotype more than they fit a male stereotype. That's probably why a lot of women who have the condition aren't being diagnosed. There's an interesting study about this by two Swedish researchers, Svenny Koop and Christophe Gilberg [European Child and Adolescent Psychiatry – 1992] They feel that if you remove gender bias, the male/female ratio for AS is much closer – maybe three to two, if not one to one. I bet that is also true across the autism spectrum.

A/AD: So you're saying that society reinforces more overt, group activities for boys, while reinforcing more docile, quiet and one-to-one behavior for girls?

Jerry: Passive behavior is much more acceptable for girls. Men are supposed to initiate socially. That's something you rarely find in AS. They usually show more initiative than high-functioning folks or regular autistic people. But in comparison to the rest of society, we are not really initiators. A passive woman will attract a lot of men. Too often, she attracts the wrong kind, domineering and abusive. That is not a scientific statement. It is based on what a lot of women have shared with me. However, a passive guy will not attract a lot of women.

Mary: When I sought a diagnosis, I was told that first, autism was not likely because I am female. The historically observed male to female ratio does affect the diagnosis process.

A/AD: *Do you think the gender differences play out in terms of any of the sensory problems or the types of repetitive stereotypic interests?*

Jerry: Sensory issues prevent most AS men from enjoying things like team sports, especially. That is an important bonding activity. You don't have to be any good at it but it's a group thing. You earn respect from peers just for taking part in the action. On the other hand, little girls aren't necessarily expected to enjoy those things. They have a lot less pressure to be in group activities. They have stuff like dollhouses to stim on.

Mary: I'm no statistics expert, but I do know that guys get busted for sensory sensitivity more than females because of gender bias. One thing that is overlooked on the sensory issue for females is anemia. Before my hysterectomy, I was crippled from photosensitivity and seizures. When my iron level rose to normal, those problems went into 100 percent remission.

A/AD: *How early do you remember trying to have any kind of social contact with another person?*

Jerry: My first clear memory was at Thanksgiving in 1952. I was four. We went to Uncle Bob's house and there were younger relatives present. I could see that in this large group the younger people entered the group interaction with ease that I lacked. That was my first experience with feeling out of sync and not liking it. Another experience came about a year and a half later. I walked home with a couple of people from kindergarten. It was a small town in upstate New York and we didn't have to worry about our safety. We came to a vacant lot and they played keep-away. When they threw the ball in my direction and I caught it, they rushed me like they knew I wouldn't know what to do. I walked home, looked in the mirror and asked myself, "What did they see? I look like my brothers; I look like everybody else. What is it about me that people see?" I was between five and six.

Mary: It was easier to form friendships up to the fourth grade. My early friends tell me, to this day, that they enjoyed my unusual play and were bored when my family moved away. My early friends enjoyed spinning with me. They enjoyed my unihibited weirdness. Autistic doesn't have to mean friendless.

A/AD: *So, at a very young age you were aware of being different?*

Jerry: I was aware of the difference but I didn't have a name for it. But it was such a subtle difference that I wasn't obsessed with it.

Mary: I became aware of my difference in the fourth grade. My earlier friends imitated me, but at a new school with new kids, they hated me for being so different.

A/AD: *Did you feel a need to "fit in" or to be like other people?*

Jerry: I don't know about wanting to be like other people. I just wanted to have friends. I was always kind of outspoken and actually I prided myself on being somewhat outspoken. I read history books at an early age and I knew that stuff like the revolution happened because some people said what nobody else was willing to. But I didn't want to be that way so much that I would be an outcast. As a kid, I felt like I was always five or ten minutes away from the next social blunder, where I would do or say something hopelessly awkward and everybody around me laugh. There was always that undercurrent. But I never felt like an outcast.

Mary: Not until the seventh grade. Between the fourth and fifth grade, I was just me. Starting with seventh grade, I tried really hard to fit in, using clothes, makeup and hairstyles. No matter how trendy and pretty I made myself, I still didn't fit in because my interests were so different.

A/AD: What helped you get ready to form your first friendships?

Jerry: Having to SHARE my parents with two old brothers was the main thing. I see too many families where the needs of the autistic person run the day. There has to be balance, between that very needy person and needs of parents and siblings. I don't care how needy he is, he has to learn that he is not the sun with the rest of the world as planets revolving around his every tantrum. I was very lucky to have two older brothers and two parents whose egos weren't totally tied up in what I thought of them or how I succeeded.

The real key in social learning is that you have to share time, attention, activity. Without sharing, there is no friendship or relationships.

Here's an example. One of our youngsters invited a classmate home. Then, he sat in front of his computer, doing all of the playing. The other kid just watched. The autistic kid was halfway there. He invited someone to come home and play. That is a huge step. But he still had an incomplete concept of friendship. His "friend" was a human piece of furniture to be around while he played just as he wanted, with his games and his rules.

The autistic kid thinks, "This is great, I have somebody here while I'm on my computer!" The other kid is bored.

Maybe you need to role play. Ask your autistic son if he would like to go to a restaurant and have to stand outside, look through the window and watch everyone eat.

Sharing is so hard because you have to give up control. You can't control what the other person will say or do. It was hard for me to allow even a hug because I had to trust that the other person, often bigger, wouldn't squeeze me too hard! The resistance to early sharing is very neurologically based.

So sharing involves giving up control and trust of someone else. That is an important bridge and the earlier it is crossed, the better! But to that, you have to help the child settle down and ABA and other intensive therapy only works on the brain and not the body. You have to develop both. I would say start with the body, first. School is dumb enough today that the brain has plenty of time.

When I had some years of exercise, sports, swimming, tumbling, etc. behind me, I relaxed. I didn't feel that I had to control the world around me. Finally, in fifth grade, I could walk into a school cafeteria, tune out enough noise and talk to other students. That is why small group activities are so important. You have to share the ball. You learn to be part of a group that works for a common goal. You can't be in chorus and sing what you want when you want. The same is true in band. But you sure feel good in a concert when it sounds right, after all.

I can't see how our kids will develop friendships until they learn to share like that. You don't learn that if everything is on a one-to-one basis with some help. One way or another, our children need inclusion in small, fun group activities.

Mary: Nothing prepared me for my first friendships. I was just wild and crazy and the young kids loved it. I was just me.

A/AD: So you had active friendships when you were young? Or how did those go?

Jerry: They were shallow friendships, most of them formed from Boy Scouts, swimming class or Little League. I didn't make friends just because they were people I knew at school. Some were classmates, but the connection surfaced from shared interests, rather than being in school together.

I don't remember opening up to anybody. I was always guarded in my conversation. I can't say that I had close friendships or relationships with anybody, even though there were a couple of people with whom I spent a lot of time. I think in comparison to the friendships that my schoolmates had, mine weren't nearly as deep. But in comparison to most people with Asperger's, I had more friends. I guess my last high school friend, Steve Lazzaro, was the only one who I ever halfway opened up to.

Mary: It was easier to have friendships at a younger age because younger children are less inhibited. As they mature, they try to be more sophisticated. They want social sameness. I think it's easier for an autistic to have earlier friendships because the nature of play is less sophisticated. That is the very reason pets such as dogs are so good. They just want to romp and play and love unconditionally.

A/AD: Did you choose to participate in these activities yourself, or did your parents prod you to be more involved socially?

Jerry: I had the good fortune of having two older brothers whose behavior I could model. My brothers were in Cub Scouts, I went to Cub Scouts. My older brother was in Little League, I went to Little League. My brothers played musical instruments so I played an instrument, too. Literally, everything I did through elementary school was simply copying what John and Jim did before me. That made it a lot easier.

Mary: My parents were totally aloof to my social life. We lived in a neighborhood with a number of children who were my age. We approached each other out of curiosity. I was always outside playing, doing things like spinning, rolling, tumbling on the front lawn or climbing trees. I was totally unsupervised (which I don't recommend), but it gave me exposure to other children.

A/AD: While you were in elementary school, do you remember anything special about getting along with your peers or your teachers?

Jerry: I got along better with teachers than peers. Sometimes I said or did things that squarely showed a lack of empathy toward my peers. I think what finally got me included in elementary school was people making a big fuss about me being a math brain. They showed me off to new students. It was a unique identity.

My father helped me share my skill by teaching me all of the sports numbers. Soon I was the one who kept everybody informed on all of the sports statistics and stuff. But the lack of empathy was a barrier.

Mary: I, too, got along with teachers better than children. Teachers liked my early talents in music and art. They tried to help me become more socially acceptable.

After the sixth grade, I no longer had one teacher all day. I had seven! That was a disaster because I became a face in the crowd and the one-on-one relationships disappeared. I went from an A student to a D student with one friend who did everything to corrupt me.

A/AD: How involved were you in sports?

Mary: I loved kickball and played as well as the boys, so I played with the boys a lot. They couldn't allow themselves to like me openly. Social stigma. But they always wanted me on their teams.

Jerry: I loved to play them but I wasn't very good. My favorite sport was baseball. I became a decent hitter but my fielding stank. I loved to ride my bicycle. It was fun in the fall when hurricanes came. I sailed home on them, letting the wind fill up an empty paper-route bag.

A couple of guys tried to teach me to play tennis but that was hopeless. Even though I wasn't very good at sports, I'm glad that I was given a chance to fail. I ran track and cross country for four years and never won a race. But it got me in good shape and helped me focus. My grades improved every year that I ran.

A/AD: What did the failure teach you?

Jerry: That it was okay to fail—a very important lesson to learn. You need to be able to fail.

Mary: In my family, failure was a cause for ostracization. Any failure devastated me.

A/AD: *How did you relate to your math abilities? Did it contribute to your sense of self-esteem?*

Jerry: I think people who have special skills, real savant-level skills like Mary's and mine, are misunderstood.

I remember in third grade somebody was showing me off to somebody else. I multiplied some numbers for them and I saw, out of the corner of my eye, that somebody was looking at me and doing some nonverbal signal to indicate that while I was very good in this one area I was really kind of "off" otherwise.

From that day on, my attitude towards numbers and math in general was, "If I don't have to work at it, it's okay." But I wasn't really interested in it. I go into this in detail in another chapter so that's it for now.

A/AD: *Getting back to that gender difference, did the girls accept you more than the boys did?*

Jerry: In elementary school, I had little contact with girls, other than if a girl sat next to me in a class, we'd occasionally say, 'Hello.' My contact was exclusively with either teachers or the boys. I noticed the pretty ones but was too in awe of them to do more than look.

A/AD: *Mary, did you find that girls accepted you more easily than did boys?*

Mary: Boys accepted me more than girls. I shared their interests and was very rough and tumble.

A/AD: Did you have to be taught some of the social skills that neurotypical kids have? Did your parents spend time with you practicing?

Jerry: My parents saw that I was a wallflower but they weren't comfortable discussing it with me. The best attempt they made was hinting that I should ask out the daughter of some people they played bridge with. Her steady dates were guys who could have crushed me like a beer can! They hoped that maybe my middle brother would teach me but he was in college too soon to do that. They probably regarded themselves as late bloomers too and weren't too worried about me. I remember them talking about how other students came back from a couple of years of college, "all grown up."

When I was a senior in high school, my friend Steve, said, "Jerry, you have to make a conscious effort to do what the rest of us do naturally."

And he was absolutely right. I still know that guy; he's in Manhattan. He was very opposite of me in many ways. He was always well groomed and socially appropriate. But we had great memories in common. I had to deliberately think about how to behave and how to react in certain situations where other people could just do those things without thinking.

The first really embarrassing moment for me was in sixth grade. We were in a structured dance class, ballroom dancing. It was easy to pick up the dance patterns. That was kind of fun. By then, I could tolerate holding a girl's hand and putting my arm around her waist. So the night arrived when it was time to show us off to our parents.

143

Everyone is crowded into our combination auditorium/ gymnasium, and we're dancing. The next dance was a ladies' choice. However, I didn't realize that. So the ladies are on one side and the boys on the other. I went over to the girl's side trying to pick my next partner. They're all looking at me really confused. Suddenly the whole place was just a sea of laughter, and I realized what I had done.

It took me a good two years to work up the courage to ask anybody to dance after that, because I was just so humiliated. The dance that broke the streak was Chubby Checker's "Twist." If you have any autism at all, you have to twist!

Mary: My parents themselves lacked any social skills. They taught me nothing. My neighbors (in the 6th-9th grades) taught me etiquette and grooming. They didn't let me be an autistic slob. They helped me learn manners and beauty. To this day, I thank them.

A/AD: Did these embarrassing moments happen a lot in school?

Jerry: Well, not a lot, but the problem I had (which I share with my peers) was that my recovery time was very long. Most kids, if they had done something like that, would laugh it off. Maybe they'd feel funny for a couple of days, but that would be it. It wouldn't take them two years to recover.

The problem I had then, and the problem I see today in my adult peers, is that they don't engage in social experiences often enough to wade through the learning curve. It takes them so long to recover from one disappointment and then try again that there is no learning curve.

A/AD: Why do you think the recovery process is so long?

Jerry: We try so hard to find sanity in our world. When we screw up like that publicly, it hurts more than it would for a kid who's not spending most of his time waging war with the world.

That's the thing. I was spending a lot of time just at war with the world rather than feeling a peaceful existence within it in comparison to normal kids.

Mary: The recovery process is so long because of the ridicule factor. No one praised me for my skills. I just got ridiculed.

A/AD: Did you feel angry towards the kids? Did it make you feel depressed?

Mary: I wasn't so angry as depressed. That's not to say I wasn't angry. It is just that the depression was overwhelming. I wanted to die.

Jerry: I don't remember feeling angry at that age; maybe envious at times. From the minute I saw that kid sending out that signal to the other kids, "Well, I don't care how fast he can multiply, he's still a nut.", I've got to say for the next 35 to 40 years I spent most of my time wanting to be anybody but me. I looked at my math talent as a curse rather than a blessing. I remember thinking, "I guess I have to live with this and make the most of it, but it doesn't mean I like it."

I wanted to be anybody but Jerry Newport. I was angrier with me than with the people around me.

A/AD: Mary, was your experience the same, or is it different for girls?

Mary: By the seventh grade, I was keenly aware that I was a nerd. Embarrassment happened daily when I was ridiculed. I just came apart and couldn't function. This is where etiquette, beauty and becoming sexy helped out. It helped me dig myself out of the nerddom and enter a social circle.

Did I say, "sexy?" Yes. Face it.

Sexual interest begins in the seventh and eighth grades because of puberty. Becoming sexy and beautiful can especially help a girl find social interest. Face it. You need to have that sex talk. Sudden beauty attracts sudden interest and girls, especially, need sex education.

A/AD: Was jealousy part of your peer experience?

Jerry: I felt very misunderstood because most of my peers were jealous of me for having this skill – jealous to the point that times when I was about to make a fool of myself again, they rejoiced. I felt jealous of them. They were part of the flock in a way that I didn't feel like I was.

Mary: If it was jealousy, it was expressed as pure hatred.

A/AD: Did you keep all of this to yourself or were there people you talked to about it?

Jerry: I never talked to anybody about it – not my brothers or even my parents. I just kept it all in.

A/AD: How about you, Mary?

Mary: No one talked with me. I kept it all to myself.

A/AD: Jerry, did you keep all of these feelings to yourself because you didn't want to talk about them, or because you didn't know how to put them into words?

Jerry: That's the way my family handled things. I can remember in my house whenever my parents reached a point in any discussion where there was emotional content, it felt like the whole place was about ready to crash. Neither one of my parents wanted to deal with anything like that openly.

Mary: Ditto.

A/AD: Tell us a little bit more about your family relationships.

Jerry: I was always afraid of my dad because he was so big. Yet he was not an abusive guy at all.

My oldest brother was seven years ahead of me and it seemed like by the time I was old enough to have even a halfway intelligent conversation with him, he was off to college. So it was Jim that I knew better. Jim was a little less than three years older than me. He was, by far, the more advanced person socially of any of us. Some of my friends would see Jim, who was dating girls even in sixth and seventh grade, and say, 'Well, why is your brother so cool and you're not?'

The three of us were not close; we tolerated each other. My older brothers are like oil and water. They were rivals for parental attention. I was like a neutral little country in comparison. I never got any attention in the way I wanted. I got way too much of the attention that I didn't want. Nobody ever told me I was popular, coordinated or cool. They always told me how smart I was until I was sick of hearing it.

Back to my older brothers. It seemed as if we had an unspoken treaty where we agreed not to kill each other because we would all eventually grow up and escape. It seemed like all of us felt like prisoners in that family.

My mom and dad got married for whatever reason, but by the time the three of us were born, they were sleeping in separate beds. I remember watching my dad in his car. He was always happy when he drove away and scared when he came back. It seemed that if there was any activity to do to keep away from home, he did it. A lot of fathers do that in our community.

They were very responsible, and totally involved in the community, volunteering. After my older brother got married, at one point he asked my parents to talk to his therapist. They refused. My dad had a classic response, "Your mother and I have co-existed peacefully for almost forty years and you have to learn to do the same." There is a huge difference between that and marriage. I mean, can you imagine Khrushchev married to Kennedy?

Mary: I was ostracized by everyone in my family. It was pure hell to have almost everyone hate me. My parents did nothing to mediate family relationships. There was a lot of sibling violence among seven children. And my only friend was violent toward me. All of this made me take a vow in the fifth grade that none of this would ever happen if I had a family. I lived up to it.

A/AD: It must have been a difficult environment for your social and emotional development.

Mary: It wasn't just difficult. It was devastating. My daily schedule was to go to school, get ridiculed, and beat up. After school, to my "friend's" house and get beat up. Dinnertime, go home, get ridiculed and beat up. I was suicidal.

Jerry: Mom and Dad stayed married for us boys. It had to be very unsatisfying for both. It does a lot to explain Dad's smoking and their obesity. Trying to work with me on social stuff would have opened up all of the wounds.

A/AD: *Puberty is a highly emotional time for most kids. How did that affect your relationships?*

Jerry: Once I discovered my natural erector set, I became obsessed with it and that really bothered my parents. They finally took me to see the school psychologist to see if he could straighten me out on that point. [laughter] The problem was that I was too straight!!

This was when I started thinking about dating. Some of my friends dated already. By the end of the eighth grade at least half a dozen of my classmates were regularly dating. And by the end of ninth grade, a whole lot more were dating. In tenth grade there were still enough other people not dating that we could show up at a party solo and that would be OK.

At the beginning of my sophomore year somebody threw a party and my best friend told me that I couldn't go because they knew I wouldn't have a date. Looking back, I wish I had said to him, 'How did you get your date?' That might have led in some positive direction. But I just saw a wall.

It was two more years before I had a date. The frustration I experienced is probably what most kids today are experiencing in sixth, seventh, and eighth grade. It's happening earlier. Middle school today is just the absolute pits. I didn't get picked on because my parents were teachers and it was a small high school, but I was lucky.

Mary: Puberty helped in some respects because I became sexy. I did everything to cultivate my looks. My peer's reactions began to change in the ninth grade. I was not ridiculed so much. Puberty was hard because adults were having sex with me and offering me marijuana, alcohol and LSD.

I totally came apart at the seams and became incommunicado. My parents put me in a cult. Out of sight, out of mind.

A/AD: What advice would you give someone with AS in seventh or eighth grade about helping himself socially?

Jerry: I would tell him to be realistic and say, "Look around your class. I'll bet you'll find some girls out there who feel just as left out as you do."

Heck, most of them have this self-destructive fantasy that dating some normal girl will be the best thing for their image. Heck, why not date a young girl with some other kind of challenge, not necessarily autism? There might be more empathy to share.

What kids really need at that age is practice. They need to acquire comfort and experience in simple, shared experiences. That's the first step. Instead of fixating on some class queen, be realistic and you'll have much better success.

I'd also suggest they seek out girls or guys who have common interests. It could be they like to read the same kind of books, or have the same favorite subjects you have. Common interests are a good way to start building relationships.. Also, do things on weekends with other people who don't have dates, either. Isolation just leads to social stagnancy.

Mary: Do everything to look and act like everyone else. That's the rule in adult life, too.

A/AD: *Do you think part of the social developmental process for you was just getting a little bit older? Did things ease up as you got into high school and you just understood things more?*

Jerry: Socializing got easier the last couple of years of high school. When I got a driver's license, I was somebody that could give other people rides to places. [laughter] I finally worked up the courage to go out a few times, my senior year.

Mary: My social life improved in high school as far as peers go. It was the adults in my life who made me crack.

A/AD: *What other strategies worked for you in social situations as a teenager?*

Mary: I only had relationships with adults. None of my friends were my age. My parents got rid of me because of this. I got no help.

Jerry: Well, I don't know. I went out with girls a few years younger than I was and from neighboring towns. I figured they didn't know I was a hopeless nerd or they didn't know enough to reject me.

You know, when you're a senior and they're a freshman, they are so impressed by the fact that you're a senior, you don't have to work hard at the rest of it. I didn't have good social coping skills. I just had the advantage of age. [laughter]

A/AD: *It sounds like you had a healthy dose of self-esteem. So many kids with AS don't have any.*

Jerry: I had more than the average peer, but my self-esteem was really skewed. If you charted my self-esteem there would be a high point if you asked me, "Well, how do you feel about your professional potential? Do you think you will grow up, go to college, graduate and make a lot of money?"

But if you asked me questions like, "Do you think people really like you? Do you think you'll ever be somebody that people really want to be around or will they just tolerate you because you're so smart?" then you would have seen real doubt.

Even though I wasn't crazy about math, it was there. Whether or not I wanted to spend a lot of time on it, it was part of my act. I think my self-esteem in general was maybe higher than most of my Asperger's peers. The big difference was that I would take a social risk. But in comparison to society in general, my self-esteem was lower. It was in college that I became more aware of that. However high my self-esteem was in comparison to peers, it still caused problems.

A/AD: *Jerry, how did your lack of self-esteem, compared to most people, cause problems?*

Jerry: The main problem was my lack of social discretion. I did dangerous things to win social approval. It started in high school.

At a couple of parties, the other guys wanted to see how much I could drink, so I obliged. The first time, I was only fourteen, and when I got sick to the vomiting stage, they called my father to pick me up.

The other time, I was a senior and got really smashed. They let me drive home. It was a win-win situation for them.

They got to see me "drive funny" and if I had crashed on the way home, they could have said, "Look at what crazy Newport did!"

It got worse in college. As a senior turning twenty-one, tradition was that you went down to a local bar and had twenty-one beers. I had a phony ID and went along. I decided to drink twenty-one myself, just to show I could do it. I managed to do it but was quite out of it.

Fortunately, I did not drive that night. Later, I began smoking pot and using drugs to fit in with the bell-bottom crowd.

The irony was that others took these drugs to feel messed up. They made me feel normal! The common denominator in a room full of high people is like group autism. Nobody really communicates. People stare off into space, perseverate on ice cream and pizza crusts and say, "Groovy" or "Far out."

I fit in more in that social arena, actually an antisocial arena, than normal. My great visual memory enabled me to replay these "trips" so I actually didn't use drugs as often as some others. But street drugs are dangerous because you have no guarantee of what you have consumed.

To sum it up, the real danger of relatively low self-esteem is that a person can be so desperate to make friends that he shows poor judgment. He does dangerous things to win social approval. I was very lucky to survive the drinking and drugs.

A/AD: Mary, how about you? What was your self-esteem like?

Mary: I had no self-esteem.

A/AD: Mary, you became a parent at a young age. How did your AS influence your relationship with the fathers of your children, and your children themselves?

Mary: I got married at age sixteen. It was an arranged marriage. That was a cult practice. My marriage was terrible because there was no love, just sex. When I became pregnant, it was a joyous occasion. I was bringing someone into the world who would love me. I knew my baby wouldn't despise me for being different like my husband did.

There was a lot of love between my sons and me. I did everything to protect them from bad school situations. I home schooled them in their middle school years. If there were problems, we talked about them. AS was a strong point in raising my children because of my savant talents. I helped my children with their gifts.

Jerry: If I can interject something here... Mary did a remarkable job as a mom, with little support. Her sons were better off being home-schooled overall. They are grown, responsible adults now. They are much better adjusted than we were at their ages.

A/AD: Jerry, did you find it easier or more difficult to make friends once you went off to college?

Jerry: I found it easier. One of the reasons I went to Michigan was to be anonymous. I was seven hundred miles away from my hometown, and out of 35,000 people, only one senior knew who I was. I moved into the dormitory and fell in with the rest of the dorm. We did lots of things together.

Freshmen there were at a real disadvantage socially because there were almost three men to every woman on the undergraduate level. So, to not have a date on a weekend was not a big deal. Most of my freshmen peers didn't. During my first year there were a couple incidents where people tried to send me signals.

I went out with a girl from my math class and I thought we had a good time, so I asked her out about 13 or 14 times. I asked her out so many times that she quit the math class to get away from me. A guy in my dorm came up to me one day and said, "Jerry can we talk? You know this girl named Becky? You realize you've asked her out 14 times? Don't you get it? She's not interested in you."

After that, I went by the three-strike rule. I felt badly that apparently she dropped out of a class to avoid me. It was pretty humiliating to feel I'd done that to somebody.

Other people commented on strange things I did to get attention.

Occasionally in high school I tried to be the class clown, which didn't work. The teachers told my parents, who were teachers, and that ended it. In college I tried to do things to gain attention and impress my friends that were inappropriate. My dorm mates let me know about it. I joined a fraternity right away, because I thought frats were cool and I wanted to be cool. It was that simple [laughter]. I must have rushed a dozen houses and one asked me to be a member and I pledged. I would have pledged any house that asked me. I just wanted to be in a fraternity.

Mary: I was twenty-three and a single mother when I went to college. It was music school. It was easier to make friends because we were all a little kooky. There was mutual respect for our gifts. I liked college because people were mature and it was much easier to find a social circle.

A/AD: What about dating during these years?

Jerry: I developed some practical ways for me to find dates in college. I looked for girls who did something that interested me. Maybe they had read a book that I had read, or maybe a common book we had for a subject. The school was so big that it wasn't surprising at all to see somebody else carrying the same textbook you were carrying. Or I would notice that they were members of a certain sorority – I'm a Greek, she's a Greek. It was a connection, some excuse to talk to them.

And the funny thing I remember is that it really didn't matter who the girl was or whether we had anything in common or not. I would go out with anybody who would keep going out with me. Until they decided not to go out with...they always had the upper hand. Each girl was THE one, until she decided she wasn't the one.

It was funny, because I wound up with some very, very attractive freshmen. I remember one girl in particular, somebody I met during orientation. She grew up in Ann Arbor, so she already knew the college, very intimately.

She immediately pledged the most popular sorority on campus and she was not only very attractive, but a very mature, well-dressed girl, just an absolute doll. Here I am an absolute turkey taking her to my pledge formal. The guys in my house were quite mystified about how I managed to do that. I guess that at first, a lot of girls would find my genuine curiosity about them to be attractive. Being a math major was no longer seen as something to shy away from, and they're sitting there thinking, "I probably wouldn't have anything to do with this guy in high school, but five to ten years from now he might be a good bet." [laughter].

College students are more open socially.   But, I remember a story that fits in here.

It was the middle of my sophomore year.   I lived in a fraternity house.   One day, I heard a bunch of my fellow sophomores sitting in a room discussing me. I walked right by the room and they just kept on talking. I guess they figured I was so out of it that I didn't hear them. And they were saying things like, "Yeah he can get a date with anybody." And somebody else would say, "Yes, once." Then somebody said, "You don't suppose old Newport is one of those idiot savants, do you?"

This was 1968.   I went to the library and looked up the term *savant* and I found a picture of this guy in an institution in France who could multiply and do calendar dates. I thought, "Well, there's just not enough here to relate to.   I've never been in an institution, and I'm never going to be. I can't possibly be like one of these people."

That was my first exposure to anything ever remotely connected with autism. It was almost 20 years later that I had any further exposure to it.

Mary: Dating was much easier because music was a common interest. I also dated non-musicians.   My identity was musician-artist. I did everything to be attractive and it worked, socially.

A/AD: What dating tips would you pass along if someone is going to college?

Jerry: Tips...well, as if I'm an expert.   I'd say number one is to accept who you are. My biggest problem was always trying to be someone else. When I went out with girls I either said nothing or talked all night in an effort to try to impress them. Neither approach worked. They don't want to do all the talking and they don't want to do all the listening. I never found a middle gear.

First, be yourself. If you are really yourself and comfortable with yourself, than you should be comfortable sharing the conversation.

Second, be realistic. Go out with women you've got something in common with, that you can share.

Third, be patient. A big problem with me was I had this fantasy that all my friends went to bed with girls on their first or second date. It didn't work that way. I knew guys who had girlfriends from their freshman year. They were seniors and pinned,* and they were still virgins.

Just be patient, for God's sake. On the first three or four dates you shouldn't be worrying about whether to kiss them or anything else. The main thing is, "Are you comfortable around this person or are you constantly feeling like you're stepping on eggs and you're doing or saying something that upsets them?"

Sometimes you might end up as friends, but romance is not meant to be. When things are working, it's effortless. In a certain sense, a hand fits a glove. But you still have to work at it.

Another rule, a good one: three strikes. If you ask someone out three times and it's always "no," forget it. There's three billion other fish out there. Too many of my peers get really stuck on one person, usually for the wrong reason, and just keep trying and failing.

received a fraternity pin.

Oh, one more. If you don't have a date and it's a weekend, go out anyway. Find some dateless gender peers and share an activity. See a movie or a game. Go to a poetry reading. Show some independence and you'll feel a lot better than being alone. You will also learn some things, and it is amazing how many single people you will see, of the opposite gender, doing this to. It makes you look more attractive, not less.

But the main thing—and parents reading this, listen up—is that the earlier in life that you start, the better.

Mary: Do everything to be like others. That's the rule at work, too. "But I'm autistic" doesn't cut it. Finding a person's interest helps. It's good conversation and it helps you grow. People are flattered if you want to hear about their interests. Jerry and I both used autism to help us make sense of our lives and negotiate with a non-autistic world.

Too many of our peers see a new diagnosis as an excuse to go off at anyone, any time. That's social suicide. If it wasn't for Jerry's involvement in the autism community , the word would never come up. Autism just isn't a big deal now.

A/AD: Was sex on your mind a lot when you were in college?

Jerry: Oh, all the time. ALLLL the time. I was on a crusade to find a perfect girl to convince everybody who had ever known me that I really wasn't a crazy person after all. I'd think, "Look at this beautiful girl. If she loves me, then you should, too."

It was a much, much bigger deal than it should have been. And that girl would have been a pretty piece of furniture to make me look good.

Mary: Sex was of great interest. I had several lovers. I was devastated that none of them wanted to get married. I was looking for a husband. They were looking for casual relationships.

A/AD: Was sex part of your college experience?

Jerry: Well, my left hand was sure interested in it. I tell you, if I'd put lipstick on my left hand I probably would have gotten engaged to it. I think I had an unusual amount of interest in it and frustration with not actually experiencing it. My first experience was pretty hilarious. It was about the end of my sophomore year when I visited San Francisco with a hooker. I was probably the most passive trick she'd ever had in her career. But it's funny. If I mention that I had any sex in college, it impresses most AS male peers.

Mary: Yes.

A/AD: One of the things I've read is that some men with AS feel they have to have a woman. It becomes almost an obsession.

Jerry: Boy, you've got that right. I spent more time in the last two and a half years of college trying to line up my next date than I spent studying. I wasted so much time. Several girlfriends lasted anywhere from three to six months, but the reason none of those relationships ever went anywhere was because I didn't have any sense of direction about my future, and I didn't have any real self-confidence. So, once people started to get to know me they could see that my interest in them was really superficial.

Mary: Men with AS have it harder than women, socially. Women can just get hair and wardrobe to be sexy. Women aren't held to macho standards like men. We're just kooky girls with great hair, wardrobes and bodies.

A/AD: Where do you think it comes from?

Jerry: It comes from the frustration of our youth. Most of the people I know who have really gone overboard in that direction are twenty-five or older and never had a date.

A/AD: Is it a longing to connect with another person?

Jerry: Absolutely. It's a total fantasy. They want this thing so badly, yet they're clueless about getting anywhere close to it. The saddest thing is that the older they are, the harder it is for them to ever get in that ballpark.

Check this out: The number one reason that my male peers lose jobs and have legal trouble is from inappropriate behavior, often seen as "stalking." They don't know what they are doing, at work or other places.

In elementary school, most of my friends experienced a gradual escalation of contact with girls. For me, I was just oblivious to them. I did miss out on some of that contact, but in comparison with most of my peers, I didn't miss out on nearly as much. It wasn't like I had the automatic stigma of being in special class or walking around with an adult albatross, an "aide," attached to me. Aides are a mixed blessing and the sooner your child can shed them, the better. Socially, they are the kiss of death.

I see too many parents harp on the academic side. That's because it's simple and predictable, compared to social growth.

Let's face it: you only need a two-word vocabulary to get a college degree now: "Point" and "Click." This is a generation that uses little calculators to do arithmetic. Critical thinking has all but disappeared from the curriculum. Give me a break.

Our kids don't become miserable adults because of brain shortages. It's the social stuff. The longer they wait to start learning social skills, the harder it is. The older they get, the more it means to them, and the more anxious they are. If they even get half a chance to do something, they are so full of self-consciousness and anxiety they almost invariably drive the other person away. You have to start them young. Let them kick and scream all they want. Better earlier than later.

Most women don't find my peers attractive socially because they lack confidence. They're so self-conscious. Nobody wants to spend an evening with somebody who's constantly fumbling, stuttering, tripping and insecure.

Men are supposed to be the captain of the ship, right? It's not fun for a girl to be out on this boat for the evening, constantly picking the captain up off the deck, reminding him where the ship's supposed to go, reassuring him that it's not sinking.

Women don't want to be put in that position. They want at least some illusion that the guy knows what he's doing. Even though most men don't know what they're doing anyway! I don't have to tell you that. [laughter]

A/AD: That's right; it has nothing to do with Asperger's. [laughter]

Jerry: But most men at least know how to fake it. We don't

know how to fake it because with guys with AS, what you see is what you get. By the same token, my brothers and my father expected me to be a good card player like them, especially with my memory. But I wasn't because I couldn't run a bluff. I was too busy, arranging all of the cards by number and suit. I remember one day, another player said, "Jerry, play your jack." I said, "How do you know I have a jack." He said, "The whole town knows you have a jack, play it!"

A/AD: What helps prepare people with AS for these types of social encounters?

Jerry: They need special coaching at a much earlier age. Some of that can come from professionals. If they can have a support group of peers with different challenges, they can trade what they know and maybe even make an initial friend in that group. It gets a lot harder when you deal with adults who were in segregated, abusive settings.

I can't stress enough how important it is to get our people started early in the social area.

Mary: I've already said it. It's hair, makeup, clothes and learning about other people's interests. You can do all of that in your way but if you wear your condition on your sleeve, it won't help at all. Besides, a lot more women have traits like me than you think, without a label. Most of me is as normal as most people. It's the other 5% you stim on.

A/AD: Do you believe there is an autism culture that has its own set of rules?

Jerry: Yes, but I think it's overdone. My peer support group has a unique comfort zone and social rules of its own but that's .5 percent of the time, three hours a month. It is too bad it isn't longer and sometimes, I wonder what an autie commune, trading and co-mingling with its surroundings as necessary, would be like.

There's much to be said for having a few hours a month where you walk into a room and you don't have to apologize for being who you are because everybody else there shares your AS.

So, yes, there's definitely an autism culture--people who know exactly what they want to know and when they want to know it.   And they don't settle for less.   You should have been there when Margaret Bauman spoke to an AGUA meeting.   Some of us had questions to fire away like arrows in a quiver.   Did we ever wear her out!

Mary: I'm very detached from the autistic culture.   I focus on being like normal people so I can make it in the world.   I consider it to be personal growth.   I find happiness and achievement in it.   I follow normal people's rules.   When in Rome, do as the Romans.   It means daily compromise but I am still autistic when I really need to be.   In that sense, I put on a "work-face" like the normals do, too.

I am happy, have a job and go to school to get a better job. Autism is never an excuse that others must accept.   I only mention autism when I have done something praise-worthy.

A/AD: *Do you think that people with AS use their lack of social skills as a crutch in a relationship, so they don't have to work as hard as may be needed?*

Jerry: Way too often.

Many peers say, "This is the way I am, I can't change it

because of my condition." They seem to believe because they have AS or autism, everything about them is cast in stone. It's very self-defeating to have that attitude. The autism community track record, in marriages, is even worse than the norm and rigidity is a big reason for that.

There are certainly limits to how much accommodation you can make. But in my AS community, I see too much rigidity, too much insistence on, "Oh, why doesn't the rest of the world just lighten up?" Well, guess what? We're in the minority. 99.8 percent of the world is not going to totally change to suit .2 percent that is afraid to. Compromise is needed.

There are a lot of things about me that I would change, but I know that there are parts about having this condition that I really like and that really helped me. Just like everybody else, I make a lot of compromises. Maybe I don't want to get up four or five times a week, go out and make a living, but I do it. There are lots of things I don't really feel like doing but I do. On the other hand when I have free time to stare at the birds for hours, watch our sunflowers grow and record it, or do any of the other things that really are still classic AS behaviors, I still do those things. But I don't insist on being that person all the time, everywhere.

Temple Grandin can't just flip out every time something bothers her at a conference. I'm sure there are things that go on at any conference that drive her up the wall in a sensory way. She doesn't do it. I don't care who you are, you have to have self-discipline. I think you have to see the big picture.

If you really want your life to be something, you've got to make some kind of peace with the rest of this world so that you can live enough of life the way you really want to live it.

I'll tell you, some people I know in my community are not going to like my book because I'm urging people to take responsibility for their lives and stop using their condition as an excuse. It may be harder but it is not impossible, and this is the only life I get.

Mary: You can't focus on deficits. It's like being an athlete. Refuse limitations. Meet or exceed every goal. Always say, "Yes, I can!" Social skills can be learned. Observe normal people. Incorporate behavior. Still be yourself but also like them. Consider it growth.

A/AD: *And do you think that's part of what prevents them from forming relationships?*

Jerry: Sure it is. It's that rigidity, that absolute insistence on the world following their rules all the time. I've "known" some people through the Internet and I've met some of them at conferences. Most of them are educated, talented adults who are full of anger. They feel absolutely no obligation to control it. It makes them totally unemployable. They have no control over their lives, but they insist that's the way it has to be and they're perfectly justified in their reasoning. That is a sad waste of a lot of lives.

A/AD: *Do people with AS understand how their behaviors affect other people?*

Jerry: I think they do some of the time; I know I do. But I still say things and don't realize the social impact on the audience. We may not get it when we say something but might, after we think about it. Or maybe somebody points it out to us, that what we said ruffled his feathers. I think a lot of us have reached that point. I don't think that Theory of Mind is beyond our reach. I don't think it's a high priority for us.

We're born in a world in which we are constantly fighting to stay afloat and survive. There's not a lot of peace. I think when you're in that kind of world, certain things that normally might be a part of your thinking, like other peoples' perceptions, don't get onto the screen very often. Too many other things crowd it out. It's like you're an air traffic controller and there's just too many planes on the screen. The Theory of Mind plane won't fly until you have those other planes landed.

A/AD: *In your relationships with people, have you learned how to say you're sorry?*

Jerry: Sometimes people tell me, "Stop saying you're sorry. Just don't do it anymore."

I don't think the problem is learning to say you're sorry. The problem is the social learning curve, not being fast or steep enough to suit most people. It was that way in the workplace. It took me a long time to understand that my supervisors didn't have nearly as much time to spend with me as I wanted them to have.

A/AD: *As we close this chapter, what advice would you offer to other people with AS to maximize their success in relationships?*

Jerry: You've got to accept the fact that in certain ways you're always going to be fundamentally different than a lot of other people. Just accept it. Stop fighting it. It's just that way. But on the other hand, you have to keep yourself open to finding ways to negotiate through this world and arrive at a compromise between the way you'd like to be and the way that your workplace or your friends or whatever relationship you want, requires of you.

You have to have some flexibility. You have to forgive yourself for not being normal. There are a lot of well-meaning people around you who think that the only way you could possibly be happy is to become normal. You're never going to be that. You have to take stock of your strengths and your weaknesses and make the most of them. You don't have to be normal. You have to be the best available version of you.

Mary: Love your differences. You are unique. Always be interested in their interests. Tell yourself you can grow. Become a loveable person. There are some people who like people with differences. Once you find someone, try to grow to include him in your world.

A/AD: Do you feel your AS has removed choices from your life?

Jerry: I have different choices. AS people are not usually good managers. On the other hand, we are people who do one part of a big project very, very well and very reliably. There might be a Michelangelo in back of us, deciding how this mural is going to be painted and he tells me that I'm going to paint the whale. Whales are my passion and I would probably produce a great whale. But I won't coordinate that whole mural. That's not me. There's a lot more room in the world for good worker ants than queens.

Many of my peers and most people with disabilities feel differently than I do. I have never felt that AS was a disability, even when I lacked a name for it. I just think I am able and incompetent in a skewed, very different way. But I am not disabled. Nobody ever told me I was. I know too many people with more severe levels of autism and with tougher, obvious disabilities, to think of myself in that light.

Mary: I've certainly had a hard time, but I keep going. Right now, AS doesn't impede me. I'm popular at work and in school. My identity is as someone who works hard and has a sense of humor. At cosmetology school, I am nice to everyone and do well, learning hair, nails and facials. I have lots of options and a bright future.

Married with Stepchildren

Jerry and Mary Newport were one of the first AS couples to gain public attention. In this part of our interview, they talk candidly about what attracted them to each other, and what eventually broke them apart.

A/AD: How did you both meet?

Jerry: Well, this is funny. It was the summer of 1993. I got a call from this lady living up in Hollywood. It was a frustrating call. The clip on her phone kept pulling in and out of the wall. It was driving me crazy and she kept talking and talking nonstop, louder and louder. She had heard about AGUA, the support group I started for people with AS, from ASA activist Kitty Rivet and wanted to know about the next meeting. I couldn't get her to shut up.

In September, the AGUA group was going to a conference in Long Beach. I didn't think it would be a very good idea for her to meet us in a room with 500 people. So I said, "Why don't you wait until October. We're having a Halloween Party. I have to say goodbye because I'm going to go work on my whale costume." That was it. I didn't think anything of it. The next thing I knew I'm at the Halloween party and she came out of the bathroom, dressed as Mozart. I was dressed as a whale and I licked her with my tongue and that's how we met.

There was another factor: Mary had just gotten over a difficult relationship. It was a relationship that didn't go anywhere and she felt like she'd been used. She was living up in Hollywood with her sons. She was very stressed out when she came to our group. She talked so loudly that literally everybody in the meeting ended up in another room. So, I talked to her briefly. I went to the meeting with another guy, and I remember at the end of the meeting I was trying to talk him into asking her out. I didn't have any interest in her.

She showed up again at the next meeting; this time she was calmer. I noticed that with most of the other women in the room, you had to go up to them and talk. A lot of AS women come across as self-centered and egotistical. I think that's a cover for insecurity. Mary was different. She walked around the room, introduced herself to different people, and talked to people who normally didn't have anybody to talk to. I thought that was nice. The next day she called me up and just said, "I'm sorry I didn't have more time to talk to you yesterday." So we agreed to go to the zoo the following Sunday.

A/AD: Mary, is that the way you remember it happening?

Mary: Yes.

A/AD: What attracted you to each other?

Jerry: I liked what I already mentioned. She showed genuine interest in others. She was smart and liked the same animals that I did. She was more social than most of our women. A lot of them come across really generic with no social affinity. Mary had feminity and sensuality that many of autistic women lack. She was an extra in some

172

TV shows and she had a style—unconventional, but it was there.

Mary: Jerry came across as a genuine activist/caregiver. He also was walking the room, talking to those too shy to talk. I loved that he was also a savant. I wanted more than anything else to have another savant to share the gift phenomenon. Then when he said he had cockatiels flying around the house, I knew then, the day we met, that I had to have him!

A/AD: How did the early part of your relationship go?

Jerry: The best thing about it was that I didn't feel uncomfortable. Probably from the first date, I felt like there was so much we had in common. More than anything else, I didn't feel self-consciousness. That was a very new experience, and she felt that way too. So, we started seeing each other on weekends. In January we started thinking about finding a place to live together. She was over at my place the night of the Northridge earthquake, and as it turned out, the earthquake ended up ruining her apartment. So, she wound up moving in with me right after that, which was a little fast.

Mary: We were honeymooning and exploring each other. We loved seeing each other and talked a lot on the phone. Things did happen quickly but that was ok. We were like two parts of the same sponge, just soaking each other up.

A/AD: Mary, how did you feel about Jerry at that point?

Mary: I felt he was a gift from God, and I still feel that way about him.

A/AD: How did you two work out some of the early issues that people in relationships had to deal with? Things like housework, spending time together or alone, money, etc.

Jerry: I worked full-time. She started working part-time over at UCLA and had the part-time extra work in Hollywood. I don't think there was a problem in the beginning with how much time we spent together. My place was such a mess that I know it had to be difficult for her to move in. There wasn't enough room in that place for all of her stuff and all of my stuff and all of her animals and all my animals. So, you know there were a lot of animals and furniture. The other thing was that we were both desperate to have somebody else in our life. There was a lot of smoke in the room that didn't get breathed right away.

Mary: The practical difficulties seemed to be overcome with new-found love.

A/AD: Were you able to talk about things openly at that point in your relationship? Did you just accept the fact that you were together, or was it something that you talked about?

Jerry: I think we quickly had a mutual sense of being a couple. I noticed that I missed her more during the week, and when we were to meet at a bus stop, there was an anxiety of anticipation that was new. It was so totally unexpected for me that I didn't look at it closely. It was more like, "I have nothing to lose, so let it happen."

Mary: We have always talked about our difficulties. We have always been very open, expressing the full spectrum of our relationship.

A/AD: How did you both relate on a physical level? Did any sensory issues impact that part of your relationship?

Mary: We made up our own sex games. Jerry was very self-conscious about his attributes but I saw a mature, long-lasting relationship as being more important and fulfilling.

Jerry: That was a big gulf. I had very limited intimacy experience in comparison to her, married twice and a mom. My idea of sex and intimacy was much shallower. She must have noticed it, but probably thought it would improve and it was not the most important thing to her. I think the companionship and feeling of commitment I offered was something that her lovers had not offered before.

A/AD: All couples, as they get to know each other, start noticing little things that get to be an annoyance. Was that part of your relationship?

Mary: Yes! Jerry became very touchy and tactile defensive. He was like hugging a cactus for the last part of our marriage. When we separated, I planted about thirty cacti around my property. I love them. I found that getting rid of the environmental, big-city irritants made Jerry into my loveable teddy bear again.

Jerry: It wasn't a problem in the beginning, but it became a problem. Both of us had a lot of unresolved anger. It didn't start to become a major impact on the relationship until the second year.

A/AD: How did it manifest itself?

Jerry: When I look back and see the early signals, I know something happened in the fall of 1994. Mary was cleaning something in our apartment; there was some kind of ungodly odor that was bothering her. She inhaled something and all of a sudden she could hardly breath at all. She had to be hospitalized a couple of times. I felt really guilty about the place being so dirty that something like that could happen. But what I remembered was the fact that even though she was in the hospital and not doing very well, she didn't seem to care. I didn't realize that until a long time later, after we'd been married about nine months. So, I reverted to my old touchy self. If she touched me accidentally, I just yelled out. Mary called it "barking." I was thinking, "Wow, I'm married to somebody like me, so therefore I can do anything I want at any time I want." And, of course, that doesn't work.

Mary: I have experienced violent tendencies over my unresolved anger. I slapped my ex-lawyer and bit a police officer during an "autistic tantrum." I am on probation and in therapy. I know that I must control myself and work out my anger in positive ways. "Autistic tantrum" is no excuse. Nobody in court said, "But she's autistic and can't help herself. Look at the little card she carries."

Jerry: It was a very stressful situation. She had been married twice before, and had a great need for intimacy that I was not satisfying, at all. Not a bit. And between the lack of intimacy and the lack of feeling loved, coupled with my negative reactions to her, it was difficult. One time I yelled at her in our car with her sons there for a stupid reason, and they never forgot that. If I said something to her and she didn't respond right away, I would ask the question again right away. I think she felt like she never had enough space in which to react.

I didn't see it then, but I see now that relationships are a lot like a dance. If you're dancing with somebody whose toes are constantly too close to yours and who is constantly stepping on yours, no matter how you try to compensate, it's no longer fun. This was November of 1994; she'd already figured out that this wasn't any fun anymore. And, it was so ironic that we hung in there for another two and a half years before she finally threw in the towel. It was right after Valentine's Day of 1997. We had this initial romantic upsurge after moving in together and getting married, but the last two and a half years we lived together were downhill.

A/AD: That's an interesting comment about the initial romantic surge. It happens all too frequently between people. They base their decisions on romantic feelings, instead of finding out how compatible they are as partners. How were you defining love and the idea of committing yourself to somebody else before you got married?

Mary: At first I was looking for the romantic ideal. Now, eight years later, I am much more practical. My primary concern is that I have a friend to negotiate life with.

Jerry: We came from very different families. I had two parents who lived and slept in separate beds as long as I knew them. Their relationship was more a co-existence and an intellectual sharing. I guess for me, at 46, that was enough. Mary's parents were more intimate with each other. They had seven kids. Obviously they spent a lot time in the same bed. [laughter] So she grew up with a different relationship model than I did. I mean, they were clearly different models, and what would have satisfied me at that point was clearly unsatisfactory to her.

FHI: What was your vision of your marriage together?

Jerry: More than anything else, I just wanted somebody to come home to. I wanted somebody that I could do things with. That disappeared after the first year; she didn't want to go places anymore. She didn't want to drive with me because I was too irritable. She couldn't touch me while I was driving. Or I got impatient if we were lost. So a lot of the things that I wanted from the relationship just weren't there.

Mary: The things that weren't there are there now. Jerry is no longer irritable in the car, for one example. Most of what got lost or screwed up the first time has been fixed. We are very happy now that we have both put work back into our partnership.

A/AD: *The situations you're describing could be part of anyone's relationship. How did your AS traits help or hinder this?*

Jerry: I think part of it was that both of us had sensory issues, and living in a place like Los Angeles probably made them worse. Especially for Mary, LA was a very difficult place to live in. She was having a lot of seizures. Living in Tucson, where we are now, is a lot easier on our senses.

Mary: Our AS traits both hindered and helped. We had games like reading and speaking street signs backwards and the other person had to know what was said backward. Or one of us would walk outside and say, "The rule for today is that all buildings wear sunglasses" and we would have to imagine that all of the buildings wore sunglasses." Once, we drove under the LA airport runway and Jerry said, "All planes have crests." That is quite a sight, to imagine those huge airplanes take off and land like giant cockatiels, with crests.

But sensory issues tore us apart. We were both hypersensitive. Neither of us was willing to work on it. That made life together very difficult. Being apart gave us time to think about the trade-off of working on issues or not. I am much happier now that I have my sensory issues under control. I get rewards from life now.

A/AD: *Were you able to pick up nonverbal signals from each other during your relationship? Or did the AS interfere with that too?*

Jerry: I didn't pick them up enough. It was often a matter of not giving her mental space to respond to me. Mary is sometimes more of a one-track person than me. Thinking back, I can remember the distress in her eyes and body language when I pressed her, but I rarely got it when it counted.

Mary: Reading body language is not an issue for me like it was years ago. I took a class in Yoga and body language in 1980. These things can be learned.

A/AD: *You mentioned "unresolved anger" before as being a major conflict between you.*

Mary: We came to a point on Christmas in 2000 that we said we would fully and unconditionally forgive each other. We both decided we can have everything we want in life if we just throw away all of our anger issues. It is working. Hanging onto anger is very painful. Complete forgiveness is the door to pleasure. Along with forgiveness is the commitment to not doing things that require forgiveness!

Jerry: Both of us expressed this anger too often towards each other. It didn't have anything to do with us; it was just anger from our past. No matter where we lived, that would have still been there. Without counseling at a real early stage to help each of us understand and express our anger... well, we still would have split up...

We express it differently. I usually let it loose as soon as I feel it. But sometimes, I was like the rest of my family. I repressed talking about something until I couldn't control my feelings when I finally did.

Mary had a cycle: She got frustrated because she didn't think people listened to her. Actually, the ASLA board and parents are uniquely rude in that way. It built up to where she didn't even try to communicate. Then, she blew up and found fault with people for not understanding what she never told them in the first place. It was like living with a volcano. You don't know the meaning of the word, "bitch" until you are in the presence of an AS woman who has completely lost it.

A/AD: Did you do any marital counseling before you split up?

Mary: I had the attitude that everything was Jerry's fault. So I refused therapy. Boy, I was wrong! Being apart and alone with my problems gave me the challenge to fix them after getting into a great deal of autistic brat trouble.

Jerry: Yes, but it was way too late, in the later part of '96, after the *60 Minutes* story came out about us. We went to one session together, but she'd already thrown in the towel at that point. It was dead in the water. I was dead in the water when we went on TV. The only reason that interview happened was that we wanted our people to have some hope. I was desperately hoping the relationship would go on and survive. But I know Mary knew it wouldn't. But there was a mutual feeling between us. We wanted people in our community to see something that, even if it wasn't good then, used to be. We wanted them to know that relationships were possible between two people with AS.

*A/AD: You wound up getting a lot of publicity—the front-page article in the **LA Times**, "60 Minutes" and a movie contract. Did all that publicity affect your marriage at all?*

Jerry: I don't think it affected it negatively. I think it probably kept it alive a little longer. It was a positive feeling that what we were trying to do would, in some way, be beneficial to people around us. Through all the publicity and the contact with people like Spielberg and Ron Bass, was the fact they were saying, "What you people are doing or trying to do has some value." We had lost sight of that. That part was good. I have to say that it was probably more positive than anything else. The best thing for me was watching how hard those people work. It raised my own standards quite a bit.

Mary: Ditto.

A/AD: *How did you communicate with each other? Can you describe your communication or lack of it?*

Jerry: The first time around, both of us wouldn't communicate about things until it got to a point where we couldn't avoid communicating. Usually by then it wasn't in a normal tone of voice; we were yelling. Mary would just plain shut down. She would say, "I need to be alone." And I — this is a very, very common thing with the males — I had an immediate urge to fix the situation. I wouldn't give her space. A couple of people whose marriages are in distress have come to me for advice. In both instances it is the guy who crowds the woman like crazy. They just don't get it because they want to fix a bad situation right away like I tried to do. It makes it worse. You have to give people space. I didn't get it, either. That's the difference this time. Now, if there is even the slightest signal, I back off immediately and Mary does too. In many instances it might just be a matter of giving each other an extra second or two to think or relax. But for people like us, that's a very critical extra couple of seconds. It's the difference between feeling like you're sleeping with the enemy or sleeping with a friend.

Mary: Ditto.

A/AD: Were any other factors involved? In-laws, step-sons, infidelity?

Jerry: Nothing that really mattered. I wasted time complaining about her sons, and she wasted time complaining about my family. Today, those issues are where they belong: way, way on the back burner. Sure there was friction with other people, and at the end, some infidelity, but you have to be really clueless, beyond autism, to think that isn't going to happen. The bottom line is this: Other people don't break up a good relationship. Our marriage was dead anyway. Nothing on the periphery really mattered.

Mary: I had my sons, and they didn't accept Jerry. It was like a living Molotov cocktail. Now with my sons out of the nest, it's just Jerry and me. I had a brief relationship after we split up but it wasn't a factor before separating. It was a factor in realizing I wanted nobody for a few years.

A/AD: So, you split up and got divorced. And now, four years after Mary moved to Tucson when you were hardly even talking to each other, you're back together. What makes you think it will work this time?

Mary: We have an equal commitment to not offending each other. Also, he is number one, not my grown sons. They both have a number one in their lives now. Jerry and I have pleasure things to do and personal regimens to reduce the tactile issues. Our cockatoo Shayna is a great shared stim. We also love to watch greyhound races at a track just two miles away. Jerry has learned more about sizing up the dogs visually and I have learned about the stuff in the racing form.

Jerry: There is a mutual awareness that we can't assume that the other person's going to automatically accept everything we do or say; that's a part of our condition. In issues like anger or when we feel irritable, we can't just let it go. I think we both realize that we have to show each other a lot more consideration in certain ways than we used to do in the past. I think there's also a greater acceptance of certain things that may never get resolved.

Here are a couple of examples: When I wake up, my brain is in full gear right away. Mary needs a lot longer to warm up. I have to accept that and not just motor mouth her into a coma! Lots of my old friends are very professional and wouldn't think of me as an organization man, but in our house, I am the one who does that stuff. I accept it and it's worth it. I am going to live a lot longer, happier and fuller. I am very concrete in some ways. I make lists, schedules and outlines. Mary doesn't.

I think we both understand that it's really important to work hard on the relationship and to have constant communication, trust and patience with each other. Also, Tucson is a much better place for people like us because there are less of the daily stresses: traffic, pollution, and general social coldness. Big cities are horrible places to grow up with a disability. If you stay there because the early services are better, the ideal thing would be to move to a more rural, relaxed area once you have outgrown those initial services. Most of our peers would be much happier in a place like Tucson than in any big, ugly city.

A/AD: Do you think the fact that both of you have AS gave you a better chance for success, or did it you cause more problems?

Jerry: Overall, more unusual shared interests that neither of us had with other partners. Those helped, along with tolerance for some of our "isms": my stimming on visual stuff or her spacing out on pretty patterns. It was far more of a help. The problem for us, first time, was the shared illusion that we could each be ourselves with no restraint and not worry about making the other uncomfortable.

Mary: I think both are true. AS has its toys and its problems. We share the toys to play with and the problems we work out. One big difference now is that we both share our savant turf with the other instead of gaurding it jealously. Jerry has taught me some things about numbers and I am showing him new things about art.

A/AD: Do you think that the two of you are an exception, or that your apparent happiness can be shared by other people with AS?

Mary: I think AS couples are much more common than anyone knows because they are not commonly public or officially diagnosed. We are a savant couple which must be more unusual. But there may be more couples like that in places like Silicon Valley.

Jerry: I think more of our peers can have what we have but not necessarily with an AS partner. It is better for them to seek partners who have a challenge but not the same kind. The main thing is for our people to accept themselves and be open to people who have common interests and natural mutual comfort. Relationships work best when there is common experience and complimentarily. That's important. If you are totally like someone else, just marry yourself and save the effort.

A/AD: In closing, what advice would you pass along to people with AS involved in romantic relationships?

Mary: Get a treasure chest. Write down all of the AS things you love to do together and make sure that chest is opened and used often. Get a wastebasket. Write down your negative traits. I mean write what you don't like in yourself and not necessarily what you are told not to like. Throw those away. Keep throwing them away until they are at least under control. Which would you rather do, dig through the trash or dig through the treasure?

Do all of that and notice how much better life keeps getting!

Jerry: It's simple and it isn't. You have to love yourself first. Be yourself. Be realistic and patient. Make peace with the world around you and relax. Always remind yourself that you have value and are an important addition to life around you. Make the most of what you can do and accept and avoid the things you can't do. If you do that, you will live long enough to meet someone who appreciates you.

"Just tell me, what do you want?"
                    Kevin Spacey in "Swimming with Sharks"

If You Can't Speak up for Yourself, Don't Expect Anyone Else To

You can't assume that society will be fair to you. The history of human rights for people with disabilities is not a pleasant one. We have been burned at the stake in medieval times and many "deformed, different" people were victims of Hitler's holocaust along with millions of Jews, gypsies and Russians. The rationale was that "for the sake of purifying the human gene pool, it is necessary to eliminate those who can never carry their own weight and will always be a burden to mankind."

I guess words like "deformed" and "different" apply to many readers as well as Helen Keller, Franklin D. Roosevelt and scientist Stephen Hawking. Fortunately, at least in the United States, there are legal safeguards that outline the rights of people with disabilities. You take social studies in high school. It is required for you to know American history to be a good citizen. This chapter is about the social studies that people with disabilities need to know. It is not a complete course but enough to let you know that our history is not totally like that of normal people, and we need to understand that for our own good.

For those of you who are members of the autistic community, this is an especially important chapter. I don't know of many other groups that have been abused as much as we.

In the name of therapy, we have even been shocked. That is rare today, but there are still places that use pepper spray, excessive restraints and other barbaric measures. This will not stop until enough of us know that we have basic rights and get involved enough to change people's opinions as well as government and agency policies.

There are two major pieces of legislation, both within the last quarter of a century, that advanced our rights in broad, significant ways. The parents and professionals who work for people with autism had much to do with the passage of these laws. People with disabilities also marched, wrote letters and peacefully demonstrated. I am sorry to note that persons with autism were not a large part of those efforts. That can and must change in the future. The last part of this chapter is designed to help you see that we have a voice in the future.

The first law to understand is about your education.

Public Law 94-142 says that anyone with a disability "is entitled to a free and appropriate public education in the least restrictive environment." There are three main points to that. The education, as it is for everyone else in a public school, does not require you or your family to pay for it. Taxes pay for it and all of us pay taxes.

Your education must be appropriate. That means that, as you get older, your education must be aimed at teaching you the most important skills that you can learn, depending on how far you progress. The vehicle for insuring this is usually known as an IEP, an individualized education plan. You are the individual. The plan is for you. There are lots of rules governing IEP's. The IEP is supposed to define what efforts are made to educate you specifically and even to redirect your behavior when you are not behaving at your best.

The last part of the aim of Public Law 94-142 is about "the least restrictive environment." This is very much an individual matter. Being stuck in a separate room on the same campus, with no contact with the other children, is a violation of this rule. On the other hand, being in a regular classroom with no assistance is also a violation if that is too much for you to handle.

You can help your school and parents help you. You can tell them when you want to be with a class of people with disabilities, when you want to be in a regular class, and when you want to learn with a teacher or an aide, by yourself. All of this will depend on the subject and/or activity.

You need to communicate. Tantrumming is not the best way to do that. It is better to talk or write and tell people what you want. You won't always get what you want, but you will get a lot more respect if you communicate in a way that does not disrupt.

Respect is what people feel when they think that someone is worth listening to. Respect is not easy to gain, and if you lose control, it is a lot easier to lose respect and even harder to get it back.

You can win respect in school or at home by sharing with your parents and your teachers your view of what is working for you and what needs to be changed. If you can learn to do this for yourself, you are making a big step towards becoming an advocate. An "advocate" is a person who speaks for his rights or the rights of others. An advocate is a good person to be and a good person to know.

Advocates had a key role in passing the ADA, Americans with Disabilities Act. This is considered to be the most important civil rights legislation in the last quarter of a century. It is said to do for people with disabilities, what the Civil Rights Act of 1964 did for blacks and other ethnic minorities. The ADA recognized great discrimination in employment, transportation, access to public buildings and businesses, access to communication and other areas.

This is what causes new buildings to include ways for people with wheelchairs to enter them. It mandates availability of TDD devices for people who can't speak on a telephone or who are deaf. These devices use typewriter keyboards attached to a public telephone. For most of us, the most important part about ADA is that it prohibits any employer from denying you a job or firing you simply because you have autism or another disability. If you can do the job, that is all that matters.

The access issue is more important on places like college campuses. Most colleges and universities have an office for students and workers with disabilities. One of the people in that office should be an ADA Compliance Officer. That person can help you correct any situation in which you feel that your rights to generally participate in your community have been reduced because of your disability.

The best way to make sure your rights are protected is to know them, use them and become an advocate yourself.

Once you are old enough to vote, you should register to vote. The 2000 presidential election shows that votes do count. If the disability community had been better organized, our voters could have been the deciding factor for either candidate. The presidential race only happens every four years, but there are thousands of other elections held every year for local officials. These people may vote on a matter that directly affects you. They may appoint people to various boards and policymaking bodies. They need to know that people with disabilities vote, too.

If you happen to really like a certain candidate, there is usually a campaign office with lots of volunteer work to do. Even with the tremendous amount of money spent in campaigns today, volunteers do much of the work. There is always a lot of work to do in a campaign and never enough people to do it. Some of the jobs, like stuffing envelopes for mass mailings, or examining voter registration forms to make sure all of the information is filled out, are the kind of monotonous work that many people hate. But some us, especially autistic people, like to do these jobs.

I found many different ways to help. Most of the time, it was for my fellow Democrats, but not all of the time. What got me started was a union meeting in 1974. The guest speaker was Jim Bates, a San Diego City Councilman, seeking election to the County Board of Supervisors. He was very impressive and energetic, but the biggest impression came after the meeting. I learned that Jim had once driven a Yellow Taxi, like me, after he left the military. The fellow who told me that, Bob Rennie, also mentioned that he knew Jim while both were on the party central committee. It was very encouraging to feel that my taxi driving peers could have such an impact!

Soon after that I met a young fellow running an uphill race against a long-term incumbent Congressman. His campaign office was near where I lived. I helped King Golden out a little, walked some precincts and was hooked.

By 1976, I volunteered for Jimmy Carter and other candidates. The next ten years saw me do about everything but run for office. I actually threw my hat in the ring for City Council in 1979, but withdrew once I saw too many candidates splitting up the same vote.

The part that was hardest for me was walking precincts. You just never know what you will encounter when you enter a person's yard.

Once I was walking in Chula Vista, near the Mexican Border, when the biggest Republican german shepherd I ever saw bounded out of the rear of a yard and headed straight for me. I bolted out the gate and slammed it on the defiant dog, but not before I dropped my remaining Democratic Party literature in his path. I walked away in one piece while the growling GOP calendar doggie triumphantly shredded his catch.

Another problem with precinct walking was my grooming. One friend, running for City Council, gave me a choice: either shower or give up helping his campaign. I wisely decided to shower. It was a warm August, and I just didn't realize what I looked like in the afternoon, after walking for six hours. I am not sure I would want to go back and find out!!

The most successful effort was closer to home. In 1976, my taxi company went on a long strike. After a month, some of the drivers decided to see if they could go into business as taxi owner/drivers. That was not possible unless the city council allowed it. By the end of the second month, I added my name to a growing number of aspiring independent taxi owners and joined the lobbying activity. My contribution was a statistical attempt to show that the city had room for more taxi competition.

Eventually, we won, and by 1979, hundreds of new taxi drivers and owners had their own companies. A friend of mine, Vic Burnett is still president of CO-OP Cabs, a loose confederation of individuals who share one phone number and the same color (silver) so people know which taxi to wait for after they call. It is the second largest taxi fleet in San Diego, with more than one hundred taxis, and I am proud that by my advocacy I helped that become a reality .

In 1978, my photo appeared with that of forty-nine local newsmakers in the annual review of the weekly, <u>San Diego Reader</u>. It showed me behind an independent taxi, wearing a custom-made T-shirt that said, "One Man, One Cab." Later, in 1982, I found my true niche.

Jim Bates ran for Congress, in a new district. A friend Ken Erhardt and I went to the county registrar of voters and copied all of the important election results for Jim's new district.

That became our pet project—a productive one. We spent two warm weeks analyzing and rating over six hundred precincts for voting patterns that either meshed with Jim or needed special attention. It was all for free. It helped Jim's campaign decide where to concentrate volunteers and direct mailings. The payoff came on election night when our man won with over 70 percent of the vote.

The rewards of working on a campaign are many. For one thing, it helps kill time. During the campaign period, if you are bored, the office is probably open and politicians are glad to have you helping out. I have also made friends while volunteering on campaigns.

Another reward is possible if the candidate wins. In that case, he is willing to listen to the people who helped him. He is supposed to be accessible to all of the people in his district, but usually a winning candidate is more willing to give time to people who helped him win his election.

Campaigns attract all kinds of people. I have even found jobs through people who I met during a campaign. I was also exposed to some events as a volunteer that I never could have afforded to attend on my own. By helping to register other people who paid up to $100/ plate for some fundraising dinners, I was able to hear people like Jerry Brown speak and get a free meal without paying $100 for the experience!

The best part though is knowing that you have helped make something good happen. There is always the excitement and suspense of election night when you go to the local Election Central and watch the vote results come in. It's like the Cinderella Ball: until the winner is known, everyone is in the dance. But the minute there's a winner, some celebrate and the rest are history. I have been on both sides of that result and learned that in a loss, there is victory in enabling one's values to be shared in public forums.

The winner, if he isn't your candidate, has to respect the views of a loser who wages a good campaign. In a way you win either way. Being a participant is the main victory. Not enough of us are participants.

The potential for political action is not just in campaigns. Most state parties have conventions either annually or at least every other year. Delegates to these are picked at local meetings, usually state senate or assembly districts, called caucuses. Anyone who is a registered voter and member of a party can attend that party's caucus in the district where he lives.

If a person is really serious about becoming a delegate, it helps to bring some friends to vote for you. I didn't know any better when I attended a caucus in 1978 and won enough support, with a little speech, to be an alternate. The State Convention was in Sacramento and gave me a look at the party structure on a much bigger scale. There were at least a couple of thousand people there: elected officials, delegates and all kinds of VIPs.

The most important lesson, though, was to see that the elected officials of major parties pay attention to the leaders of their party, especially those who run the state caucuses. These have the same name as the meetings that elect the delegates, but a state party caucus is a committee of party members that focuses on a certain issue. Typically, you will see a labor, education, disability, gay, lesbian or other interest group represented by a caucus. That is an ideal place for a grass roots person like you or me to have an impact on the laws of your state that govern services for us and other issues of importance to people with autism and other disabilities. But you don't have to limit yourself to that. I was also interested in the Labor caucus as a union member and in the environmental caucus as someone concerned with ocean pollution and its threat to whales.

There are more places to be an advocate than anyone has time for. It is best to get an overview of the types of opportunities available and explore from there. You will be wanted and needed wherever you involve yourself. I think it is wise to go where your interest is the strongest. It may be in disability activism. It may not. I believe that we need our people involved in all important issues of society so we will be accepted as part of the new wave of leadership.

Rather than bog down in the nuts and bolts of how to rise in any particular advocacy network, I will look at disability activism in general and list what appear to be the skills needed to be an effective advocate:

Individual:

- Basic understanding of the ADA and Public Law 94-142.
- How to help out at IEP and other education-related hearings.
- How to make an ADA compliance complaint and participate at a hearing.
- How to educate your local community on its responsibilities to us.
- How to deal with support staff: negotiating skills and basic rights.
- How to chair/participate in a support circle meeting.
- How to file a claim in small claims court.
- How to file a traffic accident report.
- How to appeal a decision by an agency.

Collective:

- Knowing the names of one's elected officials and members of policymaking bodies.
- DDC councils, Regional Area Boards, Boards of P&A Inc. etc.
- How to apply for, or encourage peers to apply for, these positions.
- How to start/maintain a peer-run support group.
- How to participate in your party's district caucus.
- How to join your party's disability caucus and/or impact it.
- How to run for your party's local central committee.
- How to write a letter in support of a position to newspaper and/or elected official.
- How to testify at a public hearing.
- How to register your peers to vote.
- How to raise money to support an issue, like a class action lawsuit.
- When to endorse an issue by another group and when not to.
- How to run for office or run a campaign for an initiative.
- The need for time-out, avoiding burnout.

That is a lot of skill. Some activists have been at it for decades. Some are far more effective than others. The most effective are the ones who master how to listen to their peers, how to lead and how to motivate. They also have patience and focus on their side. I have found that much of what I learned as an advocate helped me professionally and socially. It also gave me a feeling of pride, of being part of the way that our democratic world continually evolves.

Before closing this chapter, I want to dispel one myth: that of a common advocacy agenda.

In the disability arena, there are four main players: government, professionals, parents and consumers. We all live in the same world, but our basic goals are not completely the same.

Bluntly stated—
The government agenda is to spend as little money and maintain as high an illusion of tranquility as possible: That is the only way they keep a job, by minimizing bad publicity and embarrassing incidents that reflect negatively on their department, bosses, and the elected officials who appoint their bosses or otherwise control their funding.

The professional agenda is to stay employed: Professionals can be super advocates but their number one agenda is self-preservation. They have a lot to offer, but in one way they are more autistic than we are. They will resist change in any way that threatens their income. That may mean keeping an outmoded program like a mental health institution open, rather than opting for humane, community-based living. Change is threatening to the professional status quo.

The parental agenda is to keep the consumers out of their way: Parents love their kids, but kids like us usually exhaust them. Peace of mind for them may not necessarily agree with our real needs. I doubt if I could survive a week if I had to be a parent.

The consumer agenda is to have a life: Self-explanatory. Much of the time, all players may have a common goal, but not always. It is better to be realistic and hope that, if all players practice enlightened self-interest, general good will be served.

Most advocacy skills will help you no matter what cause is your passion. Depending on the subject of interest, the only major changes would be what major regulations you would understand. If you are going to be an activist for the environment, then you need to know more about the EPA than the ADA! But any advocate for any cause needs most of the rest of what I list.

Most advocacy organizations have workshops to help people learn new skills. They also have plenty of different committees. Not only will you help make something better in your world, but you will meet new people and maybe new friends. Most advocacy organizations have a lot more work to do than people willing to do it, so you should be appreciated. Just be patient. You may walk in with a ton of ideas of your own, but don't expect everyone to just drop everything and listen to it all. Usually, the people who do the most work are the ones who end up having their ideas accepted the most, and that seems fair to me.

I would like to see more autistic people become advocates. Compared to our peers with other disabilities, we don't have the same impact on our autism organizations, disability councils, advisory boards, caucuses, programs and legislation that affect every part of our lives. Most of the groups that I just mentioned, hundreds of them in our nation, have NO autistic people on them.

That must change. More of us must become advocates. You can start at a local ASA chapter or join a local People First organization. That organization believes that people with disabilities should be thought of first as people. If you are patient and sincere, there will be a place for you to help advance our community.

Nationally, there must be training in advocacy for people with autism. Also, there should someday be a peer-run advocacy organization, one that is run, owned by and made up of people with autism spectrum disorders. There is no group like that now and there should be.

We have lots of issues. We need more public awareness of our attributes and needs. We need better job, social and housing options. We need to live in a world that maintains interest in us for our entire life span and doesn't forget us once it is obvious that we won't be cured. We must be accepted as we are.

The best way to find out if you want to be an advocate of any kind is to look for advocacy organizations in your community that might interest you. Attend their meetings, read their publications, even check out their websites. Take your time and once you decide to join up, be patient, listen and learn. Rome was not built in a day, but it will easier with you helping than it was before.

YOUR LIFE IS NOT A LABEL

"Jerry, you can't ever act as if you are too smart to take your job seriously. If you do that, you will never get the job that you really want."

Bill Perry, McDonald's Co-Worker, 1966

Any Job Worth Doing ... is Worth Doing Well

I will never forget Bill Perry. I met him in 1965 while working part-time at a McDonald's near my home. I was finishing my junior year at Islip High. Bill was a student at a local community college and a night manager. He worked hard at everything he did including the stuff that was way too hot for me to do, cooking burgers on the grill.

Bill noticed me right away, just standing when I didn't think there was anything to do. I was a cashier because they knew that I could handle that. Other duties included making an occasional milk shake. My main task was to take orders and inform the cooks when different items ran out or when if there were special orders, like a fish filet with extra tartar sauce.

Often the other cashier was Peter Toeg, the only fellow in my class with a higher rank than me. The similarity ended there. Peter was always immaculate, and I rarely saw him standing around. His car was never messy, and he was just that way: a consistent class act. If Bill had his way, I am sure that he would have hired two Peters instead of Peter and me!

I can't remember exactly when Bill told me the quote at the top of this chapter. I know I frustrated him. I could do the job, but I never put my heart into it. I guess a manager doesn't like to see people standing around. McDonald's had a way of evaluating its stores by looking at the ratio of sales to payroll, so when I idled instead of keeping busy, I didn't help the image of my store.

When Bill made his point, it didn't register at the time. But he was right. For one thing, there is never enough work around for everyone who needs a job. If you have a job and think you deserve a better one someday, then you have to do your best at the job you have. It's about developing good work habits. Without them, you can wind up in trouble. Once you start losing jobs, it is hard enough to get hired anywhere, let alone move ahead.

Most of us, when we start working, begin at "entry level" jobs. For example, a busboy at Denny's is an entry-level job. His manager is not. His manager might have been a busboy once, then maybe a waiter, a cook, and finally a manager once the store's owner saw him perform well enough to be trusted with that responsibility.

I think the common thing about all entry-level jobs is that there is only one direction to move: up. If you can't do an entry-level job, there usually is no alternative but to fire you because there isn't any job at that company that requires less skill or work. Most people don't expect to do an entry-level job for the rest of their working career. They do the job to prove they work well and can eventually be promoted to a job with higher pay and more responsibility.

However, most of us, unless a relative owns the company, will start our work life in an entry-level job. No matter what kind of job it is, such jobs are important in this way: they are opportunities for new workers to learn basic skills that they must master before they move up the job ladder.

These are the most important skills that most entry-level jobs teach:

1. How to be on time, every day.

2. How to listen to or read instructions.

3. How to accept criticism gracefully from co-workers, management and customers.

4. How to dress appropriately.

5. Personal hygiene.

6. Honesty.

7. How to work independently.

8. Flexibility: how to work in a team and accept changes in your official duties when needed.

9. Focus: how to look busy when there seems to be no work to do. How to not get distracted or distract other employees.

10. Diplomacy: how to be patient when other people have lost control, without letting them abuse you.

Some of these skills are easy for most of us people with autism. Number one is probably the easiest. I have rarely heard bosses complain about my peers being late for work. We also are known for not being absent too often. One way to insure that you will be on time is always leave your home or apartment with more than enough time to get to work, and to call your employer if it appears that you will be more than a few minutes late.

Number two is much harder. I still don't like to try to understand something that is said to me. I would much rather have it shown to me in writing. If there is any visual way to learn duties, that is by far my preferred way to learn. However, that is not always possible. I think that this is something that can be disclosed to a supervisor before you are hired because it is an important—but not impossible—feature of many of us as employees.

My last boss had a relative with autism. That was a mixed blessing but it did make her aware, ahead of time, of my sensitivity about interruptions. I was lucky that much of my work involved working with a computer. Whenever she had time, she e-mailed me instructions and I was usually able to open a file and see what had to be done. That made it much easier. But there wasn't always time to do that and I tried to deal with listening, very carefully, to instructions that were often said by a person with a lot else on her mind. That's life.

Numbers three and four are two skills that will get you fired in a hurry if you lack them. Part of this is because most of us really try to do a good job. We are really hurt when somebody points out that we made a mistake or could have done something better. It happens to everyone. Nobody does a job perfectly. This is important to managers. How you handle criticism will have a big impact on your future and your chances of promotion.

Now, imagine yourself as the boss. Which employee would you rather have: one who always takes criticism personally, insists that he is right and acts resentful or an employee who listens, asks how he can avoid the same mistake again and thanks you for helping him do a better job? When managers have to correct their employees, it is not fun for them. They just want to get it over with and get back to more important matters. They don't want to argue with people who think they were right and they certainly won't want to give those people any more responsibility as well as more opportunity to be a pain in their butt.

So, when you are corrected, even if you are 100 percent sure that you are right, listen first. Don't overreact. Listen and make sure that you completely understand what the person thinks you did. If you still think you were right and can show it in a minute or less, offer to do so. Most of the time, you should just ask how to avoid the situation again, hear the response, and go back to work.

My defensive behavior cost me several good jobs. One was paying me ten dollars an hour, back in 1989. I worked in a library and just kept arguing with my supervisor over really trivial stuff, like whether I misfiled a record. The job paid well and was easy. My refusal to cooperate and let people guide me through my training period cost me that job. It was five years until I found a job that was as good as that one, five years of going back to delivery jobs and other jobs that didn't pay nearly as well. That is a high price to pay for having too much pride and being stubborn.

One rule to remember: the customer is always right, even if you know he is wrong. Some customers get impatient and accuse you of things that you didn't do. You don't have to raise your voice in response. You will never look good if you do. You need to politely tell the customer that if there is a dispute, the manager will have to help settle it. If the customer curses or threatens you, then politely tell him that you don't have to listen to that. If it gets that bad, definitely get a manager or other higher-ranking worker to look at the situation. Some customers have a bad day and take it out on you, but unless you want to be fired, you can't respond to them in the same way. That may not seem fair, but keeping your cool is part of what you are paid to do. It is part of being a professional at anything.

Numbers four and five are often areas where we slip up. Most workplaces have a dress code. You have to obey it. If they say no beard, shave yours. If they don't allow Levis, don't wear them. They have the legal right to set those rules, so you have no defense if you are fired because of your appearance. Some places will provide you with a work uniform to wear. That should make it easier to stay within the dress code as long as you keep the uniform clean. But you have to always brush your teeth, shave, wash your hair, and clean your nails before going to work. Clean socks, underwear, and clothes are always the rule, and you should always make sure your fly is zipped after you use the restroom. If that much attention to grooming is not a habit, it has to become one. Just do it.

Point six, honesty, is not usually hard for us. If anything, we are too honest for our own good. It is best to let our co-workers know when we have erred, right away, so it can be corrected with minimal effort. On the other hand, if some co-worker or customer is being rude to you and asks you what you are thinking, it is not a good idea to tell them what you probably are thinking! Trust me on that one.

It is also not a good idea to admit that you have done something that will get you fired if it has not done any harm and your word is the only thing that can put you in that position. If someone else knows what you did and is going to make that known, then your goose is cooked and you might as well cook it yourself and admit what you did.

Here's my most infamous example: I drove for Yellow Cab in 1975. I was sent to a house where two young men wanted a ride to downtown but had no money. They offered me an ounce of pot. I figured the pot was worth more than the fare and had enough tip money to make up the meter, so I accepted the offer. On the way, we were on the freeway and one of the passengers offered to light up some of my newly acquired stash. He leaned over to the front seat to pass the joint to me.

All of this happened on the freeway while a vice squad unmarked police car was right behind me. They had no idea that we were smoking pot. I think my passengers were known to them as downtown hustlers, and they thought that I was being robbed when the man in back of me leaned forward to offer me the joint! As soon as I was off the freeway, the undercover police told me to pull over. I did and they rushed out. One opened the rear door and immediately began handcuffing my passengers. The other cop came to the front of my car, looking past me at my passengers shouting, "You're busted!"

I was totally in the clear and didn't know it. By now, the police were frisking my passengers and paying no attention to me at all. But all I could remember was the cop shouting to me about being "busted." I thought he meant that we had been seen smoking pot and that I had to get rid of the pot in my trunk.

I walked back to the trunk, found the pot and swallowed it. One cop saw me and ran over saying, "What in the hell are you doing? "

Like a good, undiagnosed twenty-six year old, I told him, "I'm swallowing my pot. That's what I'm doing!!"

So, I wound up in handcuffs, too. But I swallowed all of the pot, and there was no evidence for arresting me. I was released. I was still free after amazing stupidity, but I had to go back to Yellow Cab and explain what happened. The night supervisor handed me a report form and a pen and told me to make a full report. I did...and in complete detail.

Guess what? They fired me!!!

I wound up driving another taxi. I became the laughing stock of the local taxi industry: a guy with brains and absolutely no common sense. I guess I did the right thing, but the price was too high. So, I have to tell you, honesty is not always the best policy. I ended up hurting myself by being too honest.

Point seven is not always a part of your first job. It will be at some point in your work life. Once you have been trained to do the job, you are expected to do as much of it as you can, alone. You don't want to go to your supervisor ten times a day because you want to be absolutely sure that you did something right. The person who manages you doesn't have the time for that.

It is a good idea, if you do need to ask for some advice and it is not something that must be known right away, to ask your manager for some time to discuss it at his convenience, not yours. That is much preferred to your interrupting him from other work and asking for time. Sometimes, you may have to do that but the less you do it, the better.

In an entry-level job, some of you may have the services of a job coach available. This is someone who is paid to help you learn to do your job well enough to keep it. I think that if you feel a need for constant reassurance, then you are better off with a job coach, at the start, than bothering other employees constantly. However, if you do have a job coach, you have to understand that his goal is to help you become independent of him or at least reach the point where you won't need him at the worksite but can call him up if there is a problem. If you can't reach that point, then you can forget about ever being promoted.

Job coaches deserve a little more attention. They are a mixed blessing. They can help, but not in the long run. Just being seen with one at work is a signal to the rest of the workforce that you don't have your act together. I have met some very dedicated job coaches, but the sad truth is that they are not paid enough. One of the sickest jokes about them is that most of them wouldn't have jobs if they weren't job coaches!

So, if you start a new job with a job coach, your goal from

day one must be to gain enough skill in your job to do it without the job coach. If you and your coach focus on that, it can be a good situation for both of you. You grow out of your need for him, and the job coach will find someone else to coach and be proud of how he helped you. Everybody wins!

Point eight is a huge one: Flexibility or the lack of it is a big reason why many of us with autism keep getting fired or never ever do anything beyond an entry level job. It is, ironically, a result of our wanting to follow all of the rules and be a great worker.

However, some of us are overzealous about the schedule thing. The good part is that we get to work on time. But some of us think that our breaks will happen precisely the same time every day or that we will always be able to go home at the same time. That depends on the company you work for. It is not always possible for you to take a break at the same time every day. Let's go back to my first job at MacDonald's.

I would have liked to take my break at the same time every shift, but it rarely happened that way. That is just the way that fast food and service businesses work. You can't just look at your watch, in the middle of taking an order and say, "I'm on break!" and leave the customer. Maybe the person who is supposed to relieve you has to help unload a truckload of food that arrived late. Stuff just doesn't happen on schedule and you have to get used to it or prepare for a short career.

This is not easy for us. Most of us are very dependent on schedules and structures in our early lives, more than most people. Those devices help us learn and settle down and make some sense out of the world. But the working world requires us all to be more flexible than we are used to being. I remember that, in my earlier years, it was difficult for me to accept that things wouldn't always happen on schedule. I got mad and acted that way. I felt cheated and misled. It wasn't that way at all. Once I got older, I noticed that even my manager didn't get to take breaks when he wanted. In fact, he often had to stay in the office overtime, without pay, because some stuff had to be done whether it was done in the normal work period or not, and he was responsible.

Point number nine, focus, can get you in trouble. You may reach a point in your workday when there seems to be nothing to do. That is when you can get in trouble if you don't find something to do. You can't just wander off and start a conversation with a coworker who is busy and distract him. You can't sit there and start daydreaming until there is something to do, and then your boss walks by and notices the glazed look in your eye and wonders what planet you are working on today.

It will help to have a list of things to do when there doesn't seem to be anything to do. If you work at a desk, you can always make sure that your desk is completely organized. Make sure that you have supplies of everything you need. For example, at a restaurant, you can check to see that every table has napkins and everything else that should be there. You can wipe the tables clean even if they already look clean! There is never going to be a table that is too clean. After all, that is where someone will sit down to eat. Who wants to sit at a dirty table?

Let's suppose you do everything on your list of "things to do to look busy." Don't give up. Make sure that you can't see anything to do. If that really looks like the case, tell your manager that you think you are caught up and would like to help somewhere else. Tell him you are willing to learn something new if that will help the company. Trust me, managers like to hear this. What you are doing is saying that you are dedicated, doing your job and are flexible, willing to learn more skills. There will never be enough employees like that!

Some potential distractions are a real turnoff to other employees and your boss. You don't want to use "free" time to call your friends on the phone. Other people will hear you while they are working, and they will not like it. You don't want to surf the internet on a computer while at work. I got in trouble for both of these actions, and I just didn't get it for a long time. I thought other people were doing it, so why not me? Well, the answer is this: when your boss objects to you doing things on the job that are not part of your job, you need to listen and forget about what anyone else at work is doing. Your boss is not talking about them. He is talking about you. Trust me, this almost got me fired from one job and did get me fired from another.

I can't overstress focus. It is essential. You are at your job to meet the needs of your employer and his customers. You are not there to do personal business, flirt with other employees or do other things that have nothing to do with the job. You men have to really watch yourselves around the women coworkers. It is okay to notice a pretty woman. It is sure death to stare at them or keep trying to get their attention. And never, ever share with them any silly joke that has any sexual material in it. It may seem funny to you, but work is not a gym class locker room.

If you say or do something that threatens women coworkers, a sexual harassment complaint can end your career in a hurry. It just shouldn't come up, but my male adult peers cite this kind of indiscretion as a leading cause of termination. It's simple: you are at work. DO YOUR JOB. PERIOD. If you focus exclusively on your job, you will be more appreciated and more respected by your coworkers. If you don't, they will not miss you when you are fired.

The last point is difficult for people in general. I don't like it when people speak to me using profanity or insult me. My natural tendency is to tell them to get out of my face, and being larger than most people, relocate them if they don't hear me. But what if your boss is under pressure and loses his composure? Punching him is not the answer. It is better to listen when others are angry and out of control. The longer you listen, the better your chance that they will finally get a grip and appreciate that you kept calm.

If you work in a store and have lots of contact with customers or answer the phone a lot, you will encounter this more often. The easiest way to encourage patience on your part, is to remember the last time you called some company, got put on hold, got hung up on or transferred forever. How did you feel when you finally heard an innocent voice ask, "May I help you?" Patience is a big part of what you are paid to do. The customer has a right to expect instant service and a right to be frustrated when it doesn't happen.

Of course, there are limits and you should usually learn about those in training. I have always been told that if language is excessively abusive, that I can tell someone that I don't have to listen to that. You certainly don't have to accept any physical abuse. But that is rare. However, if you are at a place where a theft or robbery could occur, you should be trained in how to handle that, so as to minimize the danger.

Guess what? I forgot something and this does happen. Your first job may not offer you any room to move up. This is often the case when you get a job through an agency. They are more interested in numbers of placements than quality. You may discover, after a couple of months of cleaning toilets and sweeping, that your boss has no intention of finding more challenging work for you. He may be one of those fools who "knows how much you can do since you have a disability." If that is the case, you have company. Some of my bosses have been idiots like that, too.

So, now that you know that you need to find something else, the first rule is, do the job you have as well as you can, until you have a better one. If you lose interest and get fired because you couldn't care less about your "stupid job," a better job will be a lot harder to find. The next thing to do is to talk to people who know you, about jobs that you can reasonably think of doing. If they actually know people who hire for those jobs, ask them, not the system, to recommend you.

The best jobs I ever had, including my last job at UCLA, came because people who knew me spoke up for me to people who could hire me. That is much more effective than relying on some underpaid, overworked bureaucrat to find you a job. My father helped me get several jobs because he would see some work in the community, someone stocking shelves at a store, and he would talk to the manager and say, "I have a son who can do that work. Could you try him out part-time?" It worked and it worked a lot better than any other system ever will.

Face it. The system exists to serve itself, to generate reports about us, to keep all of the files neat. People who work for the system (government) don't have the time to know us like our parents, teachers and friends do. They also don't know usually much about autism, and what they know is probably wrong. So, you are better off in your job hunts if you rely on personal contacts to open doors to interviews that aren't even advertised in the paper.

Now about interviews: there are good books on this, as well

as on how to find a job. They are listed in the appendix. The best news is that some of my peers are actually writing these books for people like you. In an interview you should always know something about the business that would hire you, what they do to make money. You should act interested and pay attention to the interviewer. Dress neatly and sit on the edge of the seat to look really interested, as long as you don't lose your balance! And stay alert. You may think you already understand what is being explained about the job but don't lose attention and wander off in a daydream. Ask intelligent questions. Don't tell stupid jokes.

If you can get someone to pretend to be an interviewer, practice before the real thing. You should have a few good questions to ask if given the opportunity. Make sure you understand their questions before you answer. Don't be long-winded. It is a big turnoff to have someone incorrectly answer the question or go on and on. When the interview is over, thank the person for his time; then ask him what the next step in the process is and when you can expect to know if you have been hired.

One important thing to consider is whether to tell a possible employer that you have a disability. That word sends the wrong message to many people. If an agency has arranged the interview, the employer probably knows. If a job coach will be involved, it is obvious. In other interviews the decision about this, called disclosure of your disability, may be up to you. I have never felt the need for disclosure myself but that is only my opinion. I honestly believe that where people have thought of me as someone with a disability, it has automatically resulted in a lower opinion of me as a fellow employee as well as a limit on my professional potential that didn't need to be there.

Too many people concentrate on the "dis" in "disability."

Once they hear the word, they believe that you will not be promotable, that the best strategy is to find the job that you are least likely to screw up and hope that you stay there forever, never complain and never embarrass them. That is just not a fair estimate of me or you.

Money doesn't buy everything, not even in Los Angeles, the land of two-digit IQ scores and eight-digit appetites. I decided that I had better things to do than be anyone's token Asperger's employee. Pride is not something to lose. Money can't replace a basic lack of dignity and respect. Only people who value you as a coworker can do that. But my "superiors" (in their dreams) "knew better."

That is my experience with disclosure. If you have a choice on this, you should ask yourself what part of the job is most difficult for you to do because of your disability. If it really is something that can't be avoided and must be adjusted for, then disclosure is better now than later. If it is just something that is a little harder for you to do but not impossible, what's to disclose? What is your real motive? Are you looking for special treatment? Or is this really something that will help your employer and coworkers get the most out of having you as an employee? I can't answer this for you. You can tell it is not a favorite topic for me. It is something to decide on before you have an interview. If you have an employment counselor, you want to agree on the best strategy to present yourself. Disclosure is an important consideration.

There are three other common work options. One is self-employment or the independent contractor. This is a popular option for people who want to work from their home with a computer, have a flexible schedule and enjoy other advantages of being your own boss. One of my AS friends is self-employed.

He does medical transcription. He is paid by the job, by a company that pays him and other independent contractors to do the work.

The main advantage is that he decides when to work. The disadvantage is that there isn't always work available. He also has to pay self-employment tax on his earnings, which is a higher percentage of his earnings than social security would require. In his job there are no fringe benefits, vacation, health insurance, etc. However, he often makes ten dollars an hour and sometimes more. It all depends on how fast and accurately he can work.

Self-employment is great for people who want to also attend college, or pursue acting or another profession whose demand is very unpredictable.

For example, Mary was an extra on several television shows. One never knows when that work is available. It is like the motto of the Army: "Hurry Up and Wait!" But when the casting company calls, you are told where to be, what to wear. It could start at two in the morning and last up to sixteen hours. They don't care what you are doing. They want you when they need you and not one minute more. If it sounds like Hollywood is a self-centered, demanding business, it is.

That is the extreme case, but lots of us might find self-employment to be a much better alternative than a regular job. It takes extra discipline to be self-employed. Depending on what you do, the income is often greater for the effort but not always as consistent. To a degree, this book is an example of self-employment. So far, I have not made a dime off it. If enough people buy it, I will be rewarded for my time spent. But there is no guarantee that will happen.

Here are some of the self-employment options that I know are being done or have been successfully done by a person with autism, AS or another disability:

- Newspaper route (morning or afternoon)
- Delivery (pizzas, packages, etc.)
- Seasonal delivery of phone directories and other periodicals
- Hot dog or other concession stand
- Freelance photography
- Freelance writing, reporting
- Gardening
- Furniture moving
- Truck driving
- Hairstyling, cosmetology
- Elderly, convalescent home care
- Respite care, aide to persons with disabilities
- Petition circulation, signature gathering for political candidates or initiative campaigns
- Temporary job agencies
- Income tax preparation
- Pet sitting and grooming
- House sitter
- Boat sitter
- Computer repair
- Website design and website managing
- Certified financial planner
- Movie or TV extra
- Auto repair and body work
- Painting and construction work by contract
- Real estate
- Notary public
- Bicycle repair
- Appliance repair in general

- Swap meets (sale of items bought from surplus outlets)
- Airline reservations using a computer
- Tutoring in all subjects
- Reading to people who can't
- Medical transcription
- Delivering cars cross-country
- Inventory of supermarkets
- Book sales at conferences
- Freelance computer programming, research
- Stock broker
- Piece work – assembly
- Airline courier

I am sure there are more than that. I think that many of you should consider self-employment. You may want a partner, at least someone in the beginning, to help you with the public relations aspects. You have to make sure that you are "legal." Many of these activities require licenses or registration of various types. You need a special driving license, for example, to drive a big rig truck.

Don't get the wrong idea about these options. Many of them are more rewarding and offer more independence than being an employee, but it takes more self-discipline to be self-employed or an independent contractor than it does to punch a time clock.

There are two more job options and they can be good ones. One is where you have a future job goal and work for the company while you are in college. This is called a co-operative arrangement. Usually, it means that you go to school one semester and work for the company every other semester, until you graduate. it takes a little longer but the advantage is that when you finish college, you have a working relationship with a company that is already four or five years old. I had a chance to do this in the actuarial field. Actuaries are people who help insurance companies manage their investments and decide what each kind of insurance policy should cost. I wish I had done that, but it's too late now. But not for you. If you think you will go to college, you should ask your guidance counselor about co-op programs. There may be one available for a job that would interest you.

A variation of the co-op idea is an apprenticeship.

Years ago, Mary learned how to tune and refinish pianos as a apprentice. She worked for a man who did that for a living until she could do it on her own. She was self-employed for years and tuned pianos in Carnegie Hall, Radio City Music Hall and other neat places. Unfortunately, it also meant tuning pianos in apartments where children had a TV or video games on, full blast. That makes tuning a piano a real nightmare, especially when you have the sensory problems that Mary has.

Many trades, such as carpentry, electrician, etc., have apprenticeship programs available. These are very good options because you are being specifically trained to do a job and there is usually a very good chance of being employed once you have passed the apprenticeship period.

A variation of this is a trade or technical school. You have to be careful about these. Some are great and some not. If the school really trains people to do the jobs it lists, it should have a high percentage of its graduates working in those jobs. If not, the school is not a good place to go because you will owe the school money for your training whether you get a job or not.

My stepson went to DeVry Technical school and is a lead computer programmer after less than a year of work following college. He had almost straight "A's" and the school had the right courses and a good job placement record. Mary is now in a nine-month cosmetology course at a local school where students can pass the professional exam and work in cosmetology at a very high rate.

These are cases where technical, focused training for a specific job is a better bet than college, where you are supposed to decide what classes to take, what major to get a degree in and then hope that some company thinks you are worth hiring. That for us, is a very abstract way to bet on our future.

The ultimate apprenticeship, if you are in college, is to join ROTC. This is a training program for people who become officers in the military: Navy, Army, Air Force or Marines. I am not saying that the military is a picnic. It is a necessary evil. It is like taking martial arts class. You don't want to use the power, but it is nice to know that you have it. Not all of the nations in the world are trustworthy, and we have to be able to protect our borders as well as live up to our friendships with our allies.

The ROTC usually helps a college student pay for his school expenses, and in return the student, upon graduation, has an obligation to be an officer in his chosen branch of the military for up to six years.

I went to college when this was not a popular activity but that is different today. Several of my high school friends chose this option and all have done very well since. None of them made a career out of the military, but two are commercial pilots for UPS and American Airlines and make very good salaries. Considering how much I love birds, it is amusing how many of my friends fly for a living.

We have explored some basic steps to finding and keeping a job and moving ahead in a career. If you master these, you should succeed at any job within your ability.

Nobody reads through this chapter and just gets it. Learning this comes only from doing. Once good work habits are established, they will help you for your life. Remember, work will occupy more of your adult life than any other activity.

I apologize for not having the space to visually show you, for your particular job, how to put all of this into practice. I encourage you to exhaust all of the resources available to help you become a good, reliable worker. Who knows? Maybe for example, if you really get the art of delivering pizzas down to an exact science, you will be the one to write a "how to deliver pizzas" manual or videotape for your peers! The more of us who share what we learn, the better off we will be.

The bottom line is this: if you ever want the kind of job that buys you a house, a limo, and anything close to that, you will have to do every job before that one as if it was the greatest job in the world. Just make believe, if you wind up cooking hamburgers, that every burger will have a photo of you on the wrapper, saying "cooked by...." Do every job to the best of your ability because you are proud of who you are and always do your best. If you do that, you will get the most out of your working days.

YOUR LIFE IS NOT A LABEL

"Once a man found out that over ninety percent of auto accidents happen within five miles of home. So he moved."

Dumb joke

Where You Will Live, Depends on You

This is not an easy subject, but it is important. Many of us are so caught up in what is right in front of us that we don't look way down the road. You might be only fifteen years old today, but you will be twenty-five, thirty-five and a lot older than that. It is not unlikely that some of you may live over a century. Most of that time will be spent as an adult. Once your become an adult, usually at age of twenty-one at the most, nobody is obligated to take care of you anymore. After that, where you live and how you live, more than anything else, depends on you and what you make of your abilities.

It will be easier for you if you prepare to accept an eventual change in where you live before the failing health or death of your parents forces this reality on you. I am grateful to my parents for what they did but I have to say that I live more independently and fully now that they are gone. I had no choice. My father died when I was in college in 1969. My mother died when I was almost forty. For most of my adult life, I lived on my own, but I moved back in with Mom, just after my thirty-seventh birthday. It was a mutual benefit. She wanted someone to do things she could no longer do. I had run out of luck in San Diego and needed a fresh start.

When Mom died, I took over the apartment. The logistics were simple. I went to the apartment manager and had the lease put in my name. My mother had the foresight to have a will with everything very organized and left in the charge of her hairdresser, a wonderful man named Maurice Mize. He walked me and my brothers through the steps needed to settle the distribution of Mom's estate according to her wishes. There were no disputes, and it was done in a matter of months. The most surprising thing for me was helping Maurice to file a tax return for Mom! Even though she was gone, it had to be done for 1988, her last year alive.

So for me, that part was not hard. It was hard to live in a place that we shared before. It was like living in a ghost town. The interior of the apartment was a reflection of her personality, and I have great difficulty making changes. I would have been wise to redecorate the place with my personality in mind, but in 1988 I was so rigid that if a piece of paper fell to the floor, it could stay there for months because it was too emotionally wrenching for me to pick it up and change its predictable position. When Mary saw my apartment for the first time in the fall of 1993, she said it was if my mom had died and nothing ever changed from her last day.

If I had looked ahead, it would not have been that way, but I just assumed that Mom would live forever. I hope you can avoid falling into the same situation. So, here's step one: Accept the future. Someday, you will not have parents. You will live in a place without them and it probably will be a different one from your home. Step two: Educate yourself about the options available to you for living, before the inevitable happens.

The most common options are as follows. (After I list them, I will tell you what I know about them. Where you end up will depend a lot on how you anticipate the future and whether you make the most of what you can do for yourself.)

There are several possible living situations. I personally rate them by several factors: how much control you have over your life; how much you can include yourself in the community; and how much potential each allows you to grow as a person. I will list the most common options, starting with the most desirable and ending with the least desirable.

Adult Options for Living Arrangements

1. Living in a home or apartment, independently.

2. Supported living in your own home or apartment.

3. Group home.

4. Institution.

Number one describes me, for most of my adult life. At times, I have had either a roommate or a wife. I found that having either was better for me than living alone. The advantages were having someone to do things with, splitting the cost of rent and other bills, and having moral support when I needed it.

The downside of any live-in companion is that you have to be considerate of that person. You can't just watch TV or do other things whenever you want and expect to keep a self-respecting companion very long. I think that the social growth required for having a roommate or wife is well worth the inconvenience.

Another advantage I enjoy is that nobody else, so far, makes any of my decisions. I discuss important issues with my wife Mary but that should happen with all couples. We make many joint decisions on things: how to spend the money we have left over, once all of the bills are paid; what to do when we have a day off from work and school. My point is, nobody makes those decisions but me and the person I chose to live with. It is all a matter of personal choice.

The last advantage I have is social freedom. I can be as much a part of my surrounding community or as little a part of it as I wish. I can walk to a local park and watch the daily neighborhood baseball game or walk a mile further and watch the dogs race at the greyhound track.

It means Mary and I go to movies, poetry readings, or other events when we want to and can afford it. It also means we stay at home with our animals if that is our wish. Any way it happens, we make the decision.

I know peers who live in such a manner, and they generally see it as I do. They like the amount of independence and control that living in your own place, with or without a roommate/ spouse gives you. However, as we look through all of these options, you will learn that the more control and independence you have over your living situation, the more responsible you have to be.

Mary and I have to remember to pay bills, taxes, feed our pets, water the plants, clean house, keep the cars in working order, do laundry, shop for food, cook and do everything else. That is the kind of self-discipline you need to live on your own or as close to it as possible. You don't just wake up being able to do this. It is the result of a childhood and young adulthood spent in getting an education, learning to socialize, and learning how to be a good employee and responsible person. If you haven't seen the value of school so far, maybe this will make it clearer.

Mary and I are actually one step further up on the independence ladder. We own our home now. That means that instead of paying rent to a landlord, we pay a monthly payment, called a mortgage payment, to a finance company. This is not as impossible as it may seem. There are several programs that help people with disabilities own their homes. Interest rates are usually low, and often little money is required to start the purchase.

Once again, there is a tradeoff between freedom and responsibility. If we want to change the color of our walls or add an outdoor aviary for our parrots as we did, we just do it.

However, if we don't make the monthly mortgage payments, we can lose our house. We also are responsible for the annual property taxes. But from a money standpoint, just look at this situation: in Los Angeles, I paid $900 a month to rent a one-bedroom apartment. It was a very nice place but after almost four years and paying almost forty thousand dollars in rent, I owned nothing. What's more, because of the mess my birds made, I lived in constant fear of being kicked out of my apartment!

Today, in Tucson, Mary and I own a home, three bedrooms, space for us, our pets, computers and other toys. We have almost a third of an acre with a garden and enough room, someday, for an outdoor swimming pool—all of this for less than five hundred dollars a month. We will own the home in twenty-five years. After that, we will not have to make any monthly payment to anyone. Chances are good that we will pay the home off way before then. So, given the choice of paying $900/month for nothing or $500/month for something, it was not a hard decision. You don't have to be Raymond Babbitt to understand those numbers.

Recently, I started a nonprofit corporation to help my peers get current information on home financing and hopefully, raise money to do projects similar to Habitat for Humanity. The name of this group is "Homes for Independence."

As I write, HFI is getting started. It has a board of directors, all adults with AS or autism, an advisory board and several honorary board members. Board members include Steve Shore, Liane Holliday Willey and Jean-Paul Bovee. Advisors include Margaret Bauman, Ron Bass and Carol Gray. Honorary members include Wayne Gilpin and Dr. Bernard Rimland. There is more information about HFI in the appendix, including its website address, which should be up by the time you buy this book!

I don't think my life could be better now. But I have to accept the fact that I will get older. So will Mary. One of us may reach a point where we can't make all of our own decisions. That is scary to consider, but I am still thinking about what I want done if that happens to me. It might be wisest, if one of us reaches a point of mental incompetency, to have our income in a trust to make sure it is not wasted and we have the food and other things we need.

Eventually, I will decide what is to be done with me once I am gone. I think right now that I want my ashes scattered in the ocean so I can become part of a whale who swallows the water. That is all part of life. But as hard as some decisions are to make, I like having and using the power to decide things myself. As long as you are able, you should, too.

The second housing variation is life in a home or apartment with some support in the areas where you need them. For most of our population, this is probably the most possible and practical living situation to transfer to, outside of your home. Supported living is the most common name for this.

Ideally, you have as much decision-making ability as you desire. The emphasis is on community inclusion and lifetime growth. One of my friends, Ilene Arenberg, used to live in a group home. She was the first person, supported by her agency to go into supported living and is much happier.

Ilene has a career-level job at a local university. She does most of her own shopping and house tasks and takes a bus to work. The most important part of each month is her circle meeting. This is a voluntary evening where staff, family members and friends help Ilene address the current issues in her life. Ilene sets the agenda and chairs her own meetings. I have been part of her life for ten years and am proud of her continued growth and absolutely positive attitude.

That is not to say that Ilene lives completely without support and is always a happy camper. No, she has ups and downs like everyone else. The beauty is that her family and friends give her the chance to keep growing, keep going to college, working at more challenging jobs and enjoying victories and defeats, earned or suffered by her own efforts and decisions. She has a maximum of independence with the right assistance available when it is needed. Most importantly Ilene is developing a natural circle of friends that will be there after her parents are gone. I am confident that Ilene will keep growing as long as she lives. Her life is as good as it could possibly be. I see no reason why thousands of other peers can't do the same thing and I think Ilene would agree with me.

There are two living options left. They are similar to what I just described in one respect. There is a wide variance in quality among the agencies that support any of these options. Much of the quality depends on the people who provide support. The more dependent you are on others for support, the more you are at the mercy of a society that still does not value your needs enough to pay these people enough to keep the best qualified people around.

I have never lived, thank God, in either a group home or an institution. I have visited both and am glad it was just a visit. The negatives far outweigh any positives. Given the choice, I would live in a group home. My problem with them is, as I mentioned already, the low wages paid to staff which results in high employee turnover, minimal training for staff in general and the "hothouse" atmosphere. The "hothouse" is the result of up to half a dozen disabled people, usually with the same condition, sitting around with little to live for besides menial jobs if any, endless hours riding in vans to different silly activities, and boredom.

Few of these people ever show up at support group meetings where groups are available. "Thanks" to their group home experience, many of them have learned to dislike others who have disabilities. They sometimes learn to dislike themselves, too. The people who need peer support the most are the least likely to seek it. It is an all-around sad situation. In addition, most of one's day is not decided by or for him. It is all determined by the staff. The schedules, van rides, etc. are to make it easier for staff, not the residents. You rarely see any pets. Staff doesn't want to clean after them. In general, you rarely see much life or happiness in a group home. You see a lot of walking, prematurely dead spirits.

Well, I hope that convinces you that you need to become independent enough to try a less restrictive living situation with more potential for growth. But there actually is one alternative even worse: an institution.

I remember my first exposure to such a place. It was a mental hospital in Central Islip, New York. The residence buildings were along a public street. When I was a kid, I remember my family driving through. I watched the inmates sitting on benches with blank stares. Not a pretty sight.

I heard older kids, with new driving licenses, brag about a local rite of passage: "mooning the nuts." But two adult experiences convinced me forever that such a place could never be for me. I was a taxi driver and my company had a contract to provide rides to mental health patients. One day I gave a ride to a fellow allowed out to visit some relatives. I was feeling low and about ready to just give up on living on my own and check into County Mental Health myself.

I asked him what it was like, and he quickly understood why I asked.

"Don't even think about it!" he said. "It may seem like your life is hard but it's a lot harder in here. They can do anything they want to you. You have no rights because nobody respects you or listens to you. Stay where you are and tough it out. I would be glad to trade places with you."

So I asked him, "Why are you in there, if it's so bad?" He just turned away and said, "I'm just too afraid to try living on my own."

That was all I needed to hear. But years later I met some truly miserable people, homeless mental patients in Santa Monica.

I was working but sometimes ran out of food money between paydays. I met them at a free food line in a park. One of them was a sad case. The government paid him a lump sum of several thousand dollars in assistance. He wasted it all on drugs.

Another little guy, a schizophrenic, used to stand in line and count his money in front of everyone. These people were obvious, vulnerable targets. I have to wonder where they slept and how often they got robbed or worse. Yet all of them said they would rather sleep under a park bench than have the "security and safety" of an institution.

I think the homeless situation is immoral and disgusting. But it does exist, and I met some people, before I even knew of autism, who were homeless and probably my autistic peers. There has to be a better way to protect some people from themselves without the oppressive nature of an institution or even a group home.

You know what option I chose for myself. My advice to you is this: appreciate your family as long as you have them. Maybe you have a sibling who will let you live with him someday but you can't count on that. The best thing you can do, while you still live at home, is to make the most of every opportunity to become more responsible, educated and employable. It is not easy to make friends, but there is a huge difference between just one good friend and none.

By far, the best situation is for you to eventually get a job and your own place like me. But many of you may not reach that point as fast as I did, if ever. One thing is true for all of us. It is far better to face the future and prepare for it than to have it dumped in your lap!

The sad truth is, sooner or later, you will have to leave the nest. If you can't see the day when you can fly out on your own, then you need to let your family know that you eventually want to have the best living situation possible and prepare for it while there is still time and they are around to help you find the best situation.

You can visit potential places to live and explore what is available. You can find out which places really believe in supported living and which places go through the motions. The best way is to meet some of the other consumers who those places serve. See how life is for them. This may not be fun to consider, but if you do it right, you can have as hopeful and fulfilling a life as possible like my friend Ilene Arenberg. You will be an adult for most of your life. You will outlive your parents. Preparing now will make it a lot easier for them and you.

YOUR LIFE IS NOT A LABEL

"You know, buddy, you'd be a great guy if you could just stop being so autistic."

Anonymous AGUA member

Self-Service Support

AGUA, "Adult Gathering, United and Autistic", was a regular part of my life for so long, eight years, that it is hard to believe that such groups are only a recent development in my community. AGUA is based in Los Angeles. It has monthly meetings at the office of ASLA and various homes in the county. Attendance is usually between fifteen and thirty people. Most of these people have been diagnosed with either autism or Asperger's Syndrome, but not all of them. Some people just feel more comfortable there than anywhere else.

There are similar groups around the nation. Mary and I started another group, after moving to Tucson. We plan to start another one in Phoenix. There are adult support groups that I know of in New Jersey, Boston, Atlanta, Chicago, San Francisco and Vancouver. As recently as ten years ago, I knew of none. We need a lot more of them, but it is easier to have more of a good thing when you have a few that work already.

Huge barriers remain to these groups. The biggest barrier is the mindset of many adults with autism. By now, they are so frustrated that the last thing they want to do is go to a meeting of people like them. Professionals have done us a huge disservice. Some of the earlier efforts in "behavior modification" were done by people who convinced parents that even the word, "autism" should be driven from the family vocabulary as soon as possible. Now, that's a fine lesson: the one word that describes you is a bad word. That must do wonders for your self-esteem!

Too many of my peers don't like themselves for being autistic. They hate living in places full of autistic people and the ones who need peer group support are the least willing to seek it. Most, if not all, of the active AGUA members and similar groups are adults who live on their own and have not been brainwashed and burned out by the group home experience.

Peer support groups are easier to start in urban areas but are possible everywhere. There is a big difference between something that is difficult to do and something that is impossible. The main obstacle in starting anything new in autism is inertia. Parents and others who dominate local ASA chapters and advocacy organizations have had a lot of frustration. They tend to at find reasons why things can't be done, rather than figure out a way to do them.

So it was, when I joined the Board of Directors of the Los Angeles Chapter of Autism Society of America (ASLA), the largest individual autism society chapter in the world. It has over twelve hundred members. ASLA is larger than most national organizations of other nations. My main goal was to help improve the quality of services for adults. That was 1992 and it was still a new area. Our community knows much more about the first twenty years of an autistic person's life than it does about the rest of that life.

Truth is, we are adults for most of our lives. Some of us from the new generation may live to be ninety or even one hundred. But the majority of attention, when I joined ASLA, was on the needs of newly diagnosed children and, of course, whatever the most popular cure happened to be. There is always a new cure. We have gone through more cures than there are people who need to be cured.

The board was nice enough, but burned out. Most of them were from families with adults who were in group homes and had very little to look forward to. They really didn't think that adults could make a meaningful contribution. Nobody else wanted to chair a new committee for adult services so I volunteered.

I called a meeting at my apartment. Two board members showed up and spent the evening talking to each other. I may as well have been in the next county. But that was the prevailing attitude: adults with autism are to be seen and not heard.

The funny thing was, at the grass roots level in support groups dominated by parents of children, I was quite welcome. They hadn't been around long enough, I guess, to "know better," like their board did. Eventually, I suggested forming a support group for adults. The reaction was underwhelming. I don't think anyone thought it could be done. After all, everybody "knew" that adults with autism weren't social, so why would they want a group?

My support group idea got passed from one committee to another. I knew it was dead. But I got lucky. A couple of other local ASA chapters decided to have a spring conference.

It was unusual. The focus would be on adult issues, which was rare in 1993. They asked me if I would like to try forming an adult support group at the meeting. The plan was simple: part of the conference would be a panel of adults. The last part of the day would be reserved for anyone wanting to be part of a support group. Notices were sent out to as many adults as we knew. I had no idea what to expect, but it was worth a try. At least someone didn't write off my idea without trying! In autism, that is most unusual.

I guess part of that was from knowing the two organizers, Kitty Rivet from ASA San Gabriel Valley, and Mary Preble, the godmother of ASA Long Beach. I met them both at the ASA State Conference in 1992, where I also met an inspiration, Temple Grandin. It was a point in my life where I was trying to figure out where I fit in the autism community.

Kitty and Mary knew some other adults, and later that summer we had a picnic at Mary's house. It was unusual and fun to see as many of us in one spot, and that is where the idea for an adult support group really started.

Finally, the day came, Saturday, April 24th, 1993, in the public library of Glendorra, California, an eastern suburb of Los Angeles. I knew some people would show up since I wound up in a carpool with one parent of an adult with autism and two other adults. The panel was all people whom I knew: Ilene Arenberg, daughter of an ASLA board member; Geneva Wulf from Anaheim; Alan Myerson from Thousand Oaks; and John Newell from Palos Verdes. It was very informative, well received, and set a good tone for our organizing meeting that followed.

The time finally came and there were fourteen of us there, at least ten more than any of us expected.

It included one grandmother and several men who still had not had a date. Ages ranged from seventeen to fifty two. Work experience ranged from none to three decades or more. Some people had even been to Africa and Europe. Others had never left their state or ever lived in more than one city.

The only thing we had in common was autism. That was enough. We also had the help of Patrick Breen, a part-time comedian, and a brother of one of our adults, Terry, who moderated the adult panel. Patrick chaired our first organizing meeting.

We had one corner of the meeting area. In the opposite corner, simultaneously, was an organizing meeting for a county-wide support group for parents of adults with autism.

The meeting was amazingly efficient. There was a quick round of introductions. We grabbed a blackboard. We listed what we would like to see come out of such a support group. Friends, information about jobs and/or housing, information about autism and research, support during crises, and fun things to do together were the more significant things we listed. It turned out to be almost identical to the list generated by the parents on the opposite corner of the room!

Most of the fourteen had a chance to share a little about why they had come, where they lived, and some of their background. There were four women and ten men. Most of the people lived in their own places or shared houses with friends or family. Only one was from a group home, an unfortunate trend that has not changed to this day. That was the beginning, and I have already shared the first few meetings in another chapter.

AGUA is bigger today than ever. It has much to offer, as do similar groups. It has strengths and shortcomings. Its greatest strength is its monthly consistency. Eight years of regular meetings is a good track record. Other strengths are variety of people, degrees of autism, age, gender, race, religion, jobs, social experience, and political persuasion.

In all of those measures, AGUA members defy a stereotype. Another strength is that people don't usually get put on the defensive for what they share at meetings. It is a supportive atmosphere for anyone wanting a three-hour break from the normal world.

There are still some weaknesses. One is the lack of initiative. The burden of running meetings, scheduling them, planning events, and talking to new members has always been in the lap of one person with some help from others but not much. That was me for seven years. It is not that the members are selfish or lazy. It is that even the smartest are reluctant to take the risk of involvement. It means taking the risk of doing something wrong.

However, AGUA as it is, is far better than no AGUA. In another eight years, it may reach its potential. Maybe it will offer more information and more speakers on issues of adult interest. Maybe more AGUA members will become advocates as Ken Brewer, Heidi Lissauer and Arthur Ringwalt have.

In the meantime, there probably is not a group like this where you live and there should be. In the appendix, I have some outlines for how to start an adult support group. It is based on what was done to start AGUA and several other groups. There is also a list of groups that I knew about at the time this book was finished. I see no reason why the method for starting an autistic adult support group won't work for other disability populations.

With that in mind, you should see if your local regional center or DDD office has a support group already. That can be an additional alternative for members of your population. It can also help you find people for your group as well as a place to meet. Once your group is going, there are some elements that should always be in place.

1. Confidentiality: What is shared at a meeting should not be shared elsewhere, without the permission of the people who took part in the discussion.

2. Members first: The group's mission should be to enable its target membership (i.e. adults with autism spectrum conditions) to run the meeting, decide what is discussed, share experiences, and feel comfortable doing so. Other people, parents, professionals, etc. may be allowed to come but should not be allowed to take over the meeting. Unfortunately, some of them will try to do that.

3. Regularity: Meetings should occur at regular monthly times in places that are easy to reach for most of members.

4. Safety: No alcohol should be permitted. If meetings are at homes, all members should know enough to ask for help if they need aspirin, etc. rather than just opening the medicine cabinet. People with epilepsy or other potential medical emergency needs should inform the group in advance. It is a good idea to have a first-aid expert appointed and available. A first-aid speaker is an excellent idea.

5. Participation: New members should always be introduced and given extra time to share their background as they wish. Nametags are helpful whenever there are new people present. Every person at a meeting should be invited to comment at least once.

6. Continuity: Signup sheets can record new people, other visitors, addresses, e-mail addresses, etc. A regular reporting of meeting proceedings and attendance will encourage continued support from any sponsoring organization.

7. Accessibility: Identify drivers and people needing rides. Having a car or a ride is a strong predictor of regular attendance.

8. Security: New people should first contact someone from the group before attending a meeting. If there is a sponsoring organization, a website can post information about the group, its purpose, membership, and meeting times and places.

9. Threatening behaviors: Some people will bring issues to a meeting that may be beyond the ability of peer-support to help. The first aim should be to make sure that any controversial or threatening remark or action is understood before any action is taken. Violent behavior is intolerable. It is a difficult fact, but no one person's agenda can be allowed to dominate meetings to the point of driving other people away.

These are good principles that belong in any peer-support group. Let me finish this chapter by talking about, without specifics, some of the more common issues that concern my adult peers. I can't be specific because meetings are private.

In general, there is a lot of interest in social development. The sexes differ on this. Some males come to meetings, hoping to meet a female to date. The females are fewer. Rarely has any of them attended a meeting looking for a date.

In general, autistic females have had more social experience. They are far more likely to have had boyfriends. Many of them have been married once and some even are mothers. The male/female ratio is smaller than the observed 4:1, but not equal either. In any event, some women go to one meeting and never return because too many men pay attention to them at once.

Other concerns are work, or the lack of it. Isolation is a key issue. Most people seek new friends and activities to share. One interesting issue on which we differ is the one of "disclosure." In other words, at a job, who should know that you have autism or any disability? That is a personal choice. Most of the jobs I have had were before I had a diagnosis. In my own case, I wish that my diagnosis had remained a private matter. It gave my last employer a mistaken view that I had limited potential. No thought was ever given to help me train myself for any move upward. But others don't feel this way.

It is impossible to stereotype AGUA member's opinions. Some of us want to be cured of autism and many just want some things about them cured. Some of us voted for Bush and the rest for Gore and Nader. What was good was that many of us voted at all.

There is one thing that we all agree on. We are better off with a group that brings us together. If you find some help and give this support group idea a try, you will know why we feel that way.

Footnote on Electronic Support:

You may not have a peer support group in your area. In the meantime, there are some electronic support groups for all of us. You can share experiences with peers and network whenever you want. The appendix has a list of groups that serve the autism community. If you search, you can find lists for just about any disability community or other interest that suits you.

I am not an expert on how to get along on these lists, I must tell you. I don't suffer fools well and you will find all kinds of people on these lists. If you follow some simple rules, this can be a good addition to your life.

1. Before you join any list, examine who the intended participants are. If you want the company of peers, then don't expect everyone on an open list to be one. A general autism discussion list will include people with autism, parents and professionals, for example.

2. Read the user agreement: These vary in detail. They usually prohibit threatening behavior and use of the list for commercial promotion. They may or may not, specifically prohibit profanity. They usually prohibit excessively aggressive, insulting personal attacks, bad language, etc. both on the general list or in private mail to list members. Make sure you understand it and live up to it.

3. Avoid "instant reacting." A new list is like a new toy. If you respond to every topic from everyone, you will be old news in a hurry. Be selective in responding. Ironically, I still make this error every time I am on a new list!

4. Indent and punctuate. Keep your messages legible and concise. Paragraphs of 500 words are death to read.

5. Privacy: Don't share your phone number, address or other personal information on any general list. Share it discreetly only when you need to, in private e-mail.

6. "Internet Road Rage": If you think someone flamed you, do nothing for a day. Reread THAT post. If possible, send the person a private message. Ask for clarification of what was said that offends you. See if you can state what you think he meant. This can go a long way to avoid feuds. Avoid online protraction of the dispute. Your fellow list-members will appreciate this.

If this does not resolve things and if the other person continues, then forward all future messages from him, to your list owner and ask for help in stopping the situation. That may result in someone being warned and in extreme cases, get someone suspended from the list. I've been on both ends of this process, so I am not without sin nor do I pretend to be.

7. The Human Factor: You will read some stuff that really seems stupid to you. Just remember that some other human wrote it, and it may make perfect sense to him. The screen is not your private video game to find people to hurt.

8. Priorities: It is easy to let new "net hobbies" take over your life. That is not healthy. Limit your time on lists and use them for specific needs: networking, information, new friends, etc. If you find yourself spending most of your free time on the "net," take a day off and rethink that situation. Make sure your life is in balance.

9. It isn't democratic: Every list has people in charge, called List Owners. They vary in how much you see them on line. The most effective do their best work in e-mail, mediating disputes. The worst make den-mothers look aloof. Bottom line: it's their list, and you are a guest. They make the rules and you have to follow them.

With the internet available, you need not feel alone anymore. One way or another, even if you have to use a computer at the local library, you have others who walk in your shoes, waiting to meet you!

"Jerry, you gotta travel. It'll change your life."

Jim Newport (1970)

It's a small world, so why not see some of it?

I remember the time my brother told me that. He was right, but it was almost three decades before I knew it. The first time my middle brother Jim went to Europe was 1966. I was graduating from high school in Islip, New York. Jim had one more year to go as an advertising design major at Pratt Institute in Brooklyn. He had worked part time during his junior year and saved enough for a summer trip to Europe.

He was the first Newport to go anywhere that you couldn't drive to, but as my father said, "He's an artist, and he needs to go over there and see the great stuff." Within a couple of weeks, postcards began to arrive with beautiful comments on them, surprising my parents who knew Jim was artistic but didn't know he could write so well. There was also a clever photo of Jim, sitting in London's Trafalgar Square in vintage hippy garb surrounded by pigeons, reading Europe On Five Dollars a Day.

But there were other benefits to that first trip overseas. He met a woman from California and traveled with her much of the summer. They wound up married five years later. I can't guarantee that a trip to a new place will net you a spouse, but having traveled a lot now, myself, I agree with my brother that traveling is not only fun, but will have a very positive impact on your life.

I didn't always feel that way. Up until 1996, with the exception of a trip to California, my traveling was limited to carpools, weekend trips to football games, and endless trips between San Diego and Los Angeles for family gatherings. The idea of going to places completely unknown to me, changing time zones too, did not appeal to me at all.

It changed for me in a hurry in the fall of 1996. The phone rang. It was Wayne Gilpin from Future Horizons. I knew who he was, sort of. A friend, Tom McKean, wrote an autobiography that Future Horizons published. I was hoping that he was not going to ask me to write a book. Since my marriage was heading down the toilet, I was in no mood to do that! He didn't.

He had seen Mary and me on "Sixty Minutes" and wanted to know if I would come to Hawaii and speak at a conference. So far, so good, but the catch was: I was going to replace Temple Grandin. In autism, that is about as attractive a proposition as pinch-hitting for home run king Mark McGwire! However, I had always wanted to see Hawaii. I had written a report about it in fifth grade. Not only that, but Sea Life Park in Oahu had my favorite animal, a Wholphin, a hybrid of a whale and a dolphin.

So, I accepted the offer. I would at least see some of Hawaii and the Wholphin, even if Temple's disappointed audience threw pineapples at me. They didn't, but that wasn't necessarily a good thing.

It was good that I wound up getting more chances to travel. The downside was that the audience was automatically more sympathetic to me, a person with a disability, than a parent or professional. They had a lower standard of performance, one that I met. Heck, anyone able to stand up and mumble anything, without walking into a wall or scratching his crotch in public, would have gotten a standing ovation from that crowd! It made me a bit more impressed with myself than I deserved. I needed another three years to learn how to give a presentation that would meet any audience's standard.

But the main benefit was the experience. I actually flew over an ocean, sitting in row thirteen of all places, and liked looking down at the water. The time change worked in my favor. I woke up while it was still dark and took a barefoot, moonlight walk along a beautiful beach. The local license plates were low functioning, though. Only three digits. I don't need any effort to factor such small numbers.

But the rest made up for it. I also got to see an old roommate, David Morgan, who had moved to Hawaii in 1993 and knew it well. Having a friend who could show me the real island helped a lot. He showed me the University of Hawaii where he goes to use the Internet in the library. David also knew the local bus system so well that my plan to rent a car was scrapped. We saw Pearl Harbor and I was moved, just as millions of visitors have been, by the documentary of the attack and the boat ride visit to the memorial on the sunken U.S. Arizona.

The best part was finally seeing the wholphin. This creature's name is "Kekeimailu", Hawaiian for "the peaceful sea." She was born on Wednesday, May 15, 1985, at Sea Life Park. Her mother was an Atlantic bottle-nosed dolphin like Flipper. Her father was the surprise, a false killer whale, a smaller relative of the orcas made famous in the "Free Willy" movies. It was great to see her in the lagoon with dolphins and false killer whales. She has the body of a large, dark, tubby dolphin, with a shorter rostrum (beak) and bigger fluke. She jumped higher than her playmates.

That was my first time off the continent. It was far more fun than I expected. Since then, I have been to London and Toronto and taken over seventy trips in all. The travel has helped me learn a lot more about how the world runs in general, and has increased my knowledge of an expanded variety of approaches to autism. It has given me confidence in everyday life and probably made me a more interesting person. Certainly, I don't feel so left out of the world. However, despite the great luck I had on my first trip, there have been some bumps on the road.

Murphy's law says, "Whatever can go wrong, will." I have had about every kind of misfortune happen during my trips. They don't happen as much now, since I am better prepared. I have lost my airline tickets and boarding passes. I have gone jogging on the morning of a trip, left my driver's license in my sneakers, and arrived at the terminal without a picture ID. I have landed in new cities, expecting to have a free shuttle to a hotel, only to learn that the hotel was fifty miles away, and at the late hour, it was either take a taxi or wait until morning to take a bus. I have forgotten to bring everything from socks and toothbrushes to my speech outlines. But I learned from all of this that if you are reasonably prepared, most of this can be eliminated and you can have a lot more fun than frustration.

Traveling has a way of throwing people off balance. The term "jet-lag" means how a person feels after traveling from one time zone to a place, several time zones away. Suddenly, your body is out of step with everything. You wake up too early or too late. Or when it's time to eat, you aren't hungry yet. The more out of balance one feels, the more likely he will forget something or just get disoriented instead of enjoying his trip.

With that in mind, it helps to have checklists to follow, so you don't lose things. When you stop to get your ticket, have your bags checked at security, or take a bus or a cab after arriving at your destination, you can forget something because you are tired. My rule is that I don't move anywhere unless I know that everything I am supposed to have is still with me.

For some of you, this may seem impossible. Travel, to me, means going to a place that at least means driving if not flying.

Maybe you don't drive. I have many very capable friends in the adult community who don't drive because there are too many distractions and they wouldn't feel safe driving. No problem. There are other ways to get around, and if more people used them, our air would be cleaner.

You can start expanding your travel horizons in your hometown by exploring the points of interest where you live.

I used to collect maps. It was fun to put a map up on my wall, of any place that I was going to visit. If I did this far enough ahead of time, I often had a very good idea of the streets of the city I would visit, before I got there. You can get a map of where you live and start by hanging that up. If you want to visit a local museum or zoo, you can probably get a floor plan or map of it to put on your wall. In a few days you will feel a lot more comfortable about visiting that strange place.

I recommend the map and floor plan strategy because many of us in the autism community are very good visual learners. If given the choice between hearing verbal instructions or seeing a picture of what someone wants us to do, we would much rather look at the picture. The maps let us make autism work for us.

Another great kind of map is one of your local bus routes. If you get to know this map and learn how to ride a bus safely, it will really expand the scope of the world within your immediate reach.

Although I have usually owned a car since 1965, I have used a bus to commute to work because of the cost of parking at work and the early morning rush hour traffic. That's how I learned the safety tips on riding a bus in chapter ten.

If you learn to ride a bus on your own, it will open up a lot of possibilities. It will make it possible for you to go to a school or to a job that would be too far away to walk to. Even if you need someone to ride along with you, that is okay. By growing enough to ride a bus with some assistance, you are enabling yourself to do new things. I think there is a lot to this statement: "The journey of a thousand miles begins with one step." So it is, with learning how to travel safely. You start with learning how to ride a bus. In some cities, there are also subways. Some of you will also learn how to drive safely. After that, you can learn how to ride trains and planes. These can take you anywhere in the world.

I want to say something about subways before talking about the kinds of transportation that take you to distant places. Subways usually run often enough that you don't need a schedule. You can usually find a subway map, near the waiting area, that shows the different routes using different colors for each route.

You need to make sure that the subway you take is going in the direction that you want to go. If you are not sure, you can ask someone. The most important thing to remember is this: Do not stand close to the track. You can get seriously hurt, especially since some subway trains don't stop at every station. I have seen them go by at over sixty miles an hour and you don't want to be standing at the edge of the waiting area when that happens!

Once you have learned how to use your local transportation system, you may want to visit another city and see something that you read about or saw on television and always wanted to see, like a museum or maybe a team playing a baseball game. To do this, unless you drive or know someone who would drive for you, you will need to take a bus, a train or a plane.

These all have some things in common. They have schedules of where they go and when they go there. All of them usually allow you to take a limited amount of baggage to your seat. If you have more than that, the rest is carried in another area and you are given a "claim ticket." You must carry that in a safe place, so you get your belongings back when your ride is over.

There are some differences. You usually don't have to reserve a seat on a bus or train. Airplanes are different. The earlier that you make a reservation, the cheaper the cost of flying. Making an airline reservation can be done from a home computer or by phone. The first time around, it is best to have someone help you. I also think that on your first trip out of town, you should have a friend or a staff person travel with you.

You may want to travel to meet someone who you met on the Internet, or as a pen pal. That can be neat because having a friend who knows the local streets and places to go in a new place can make a trip a lot less confusing and a lot more fun. But for your own security, if the person is not a relative, a friend of someone you know personally, or someone you have already met, it is important to make sure you can trust this person enough to visit him. If the person is trustworthy, he won't object to your meeting him in a public place. He also won't object to you bringing one of your friends along with you. If he does object, I would not visit him. The sad truth is that we autistics have a reputation for being easy to take advantage of and there are some people willing to do that.

Traveling to another country involves more planning. For one thing, you need to get a passport. A passport is the best form of identification in the world. It has your photo in it, your address and is issued by your government. In the United States, you can apply for a passport at most post offices. You need to have a copy of your birth certificate and a driver's license or some other photographic ID. If you don't drive, you can get an ID card from the Motor Vehicle Department office.

A passport is not something that you can get in a day. It usually takes at least six weeks. So, if you plan to fly to another country other than Mexico or Canada, you will need to apply for your passport at least six weeks before you fly. Once you have bought your airline ticket, the airline will help speed up the passport process, but it is best to apply as soon as you plan to travel. The passport is good for ten years and may be renewed. It is a very valuable item. Once you have it, you should make a copy of it to keep at home and also put another copy of it in your luggage, in case you lose the original one. In a foreign country especially, you must make sure that you don't wind up without identification.

However, accidents do happen. But we can survive them. If you have a copy of your passport at home and the worst happens that you lose your passport and the airline loses your luggage, you can call home and have someone fax your copy of your passport to whatever country you are in. The same is true for your driver's license. This is why I always have "backup" copies of every form of identification I need, at a safe place at home, where a roommate or trusted friend can get them and have copies of them faxed to me if I need them.

I have not told you everything that you need to know about travel. You will find more references about traveling in the appendix. I have told you enough to show that it is fun and can give you a lot more to live for. I hope what I have shared is enough to convince you to prepare yourself to take some calculated risks and expand your ability to move and explore throughout this world. Travel, if poorly planned, can be a nightmare. But when you learn and know what you are doing, it is fun and exciting.

"To be or not to be, that is the question...."

William Shakespeare

The Glass is Never Full, but It's Never Empty Either

I am happy to report that there are some things at which I was not able to succeed, despite repeated attempts. I am a complete incompetent at suicide. In the great game of suicide, I am now a pathetic zero for three. Even considering the horrible pain, albeit momentary, of those who actually do blow off their heads, dive off bridges or swallow cyanide, I can't say that I am alive because of more courage but because I had less.

This is the chapter that I hope most people never have to read. But as one whose past close calls surprise those who know me, I know that many people who seem fine on the surface are mere blocks away from throwing themselves in front of a UPS truck. Suicide, along with self-destructive thoughts that lead to it, is happening far too often today, even among people in grade school.

If that is not where you are, good. This chapter will help you, if you ever reach that point, to find more hopeful, safer ground. If you are there, then I hope that you will read this chapter before going any further with your recent thoughts. I don't write this as some goody two-shoes fool or whatever, whose peak of anxiety was the day that her poodle didn't match her new drapes. I write as one who is lucky to have survived, three times, having made the attempt you should never make.

There are common paths to this bad place. One of the most common is the trap of "all or nothing" thinking. People who take their own lives have reasons, but they are usually built upon premises that represent totally unrealistic viewpoints. The

255

reasons are a tragic failure to accept that life is never all that we want it to be.

Take my three attempts, for example. All were inspired by failures in relationships. In the first case, I couldn't accept the lack of interest or even friendship of a girl who outgrew her former boyfriend, me. I was willing, at age twenty-two, to toss my life away because one girl, out of two billion on the planet, had decided that the party was over. Oh, I was obsessed and all that, but looking back at what I would have missed in the last thirty years, it does seem foolish.

Yet I went to a pharmacy, bought some sleeping pills and swallowed them. They apparently took slow effect. Waiting to die, I shared what I had done with a fraternity brother Ken Brier. With help of other friends, Ken persuaded me to go to ride with him to University Hospital and have my stomach pumped out. It was humiliating but worth it.

My second attempt happened a couple of months later and was even more pathetic. It involved another girl whom I had dated exactly once. I saw her at a dance with someone else. They were walking out of the dance hall. I tried to get her attention, and she ignored me. In that same situation, I would have done the same thing she did, but on that spring night in 1971, I was beyond reason.

I went home and swallowed a bottle of Benadryl. I think they were prescription drugs to help my mom sleep. That is what they helped me do a few years later, but they also make you feel better. In slang, one would call them "uppers." They didn't put me under at all. I woke up in the middle of the night with an excess of energy. It was Saturday morning, but I guess the time concept went out the window. I happily showered, dressed for an interview scheduled for the following Monday morning, and sat in the living room, talking loudly and enthusiastically, completely bewildering my mother. Eventually, I went back to sleep and the pills must have worn out.

My mother noticed the pills were gone and knew I had tried to hurt myself. She woke me up and asked me if I felt okay. I said, "Yes" in complete surprise, and it was never discussed again. I had gotten lucky again. But in some ways, my mother was just as socially clueless as me. I obviously needed help. Both of us were too embarrassed to consider my seeing a therapist. But it was 1971, and that was not as cool as it is today.

My third time was the day after Mary's birthday in 1999. We separated in 1997, but for a short while in the winter of 1999, we tried to reconcile. I didn't see it working and backed out. Yet, I felt that there would never be anyone else, and after talking to her on her birthday, I just ran out of hope again. I also hated my job and saw no way out of that. Neither assumption was realistic but suicide is never a sane act. I tried the sleeping pill routine, wrote a goodbye note to all, crawled into bed with my large whale pillow and woke the next morning, still alive. At least it was creative that time but still, fortunately, a failure.

So, that's how I wound up in the Hall of Fame of Suicide Incompetence, along with the infamous kamikaze pilot who flew ten missions. I have finally learned, and am lucky to have learned this: nothing is so bad that you can't go on. And I mean nothing. It is easy now for me to say, but if you are in the suicidal frame of mind, it doesn't feel that way at all.

Feelings are the reason that people take their lives. They let their feelings about failures, disappointments, guilt and other crap mushroom and take over rationality. If you have survived enough pain to read this far, good, because knowing this can save you from making an eternally bad decision: Feelings are only feelings. No matter how intense or painful they are, your feelings come from you and are not reality. Even if the feelings are about things that happened, and they usually are, they are still magnified totally out of proportion to reality.

In my case, there was simply nothing that I couldn't live with. I could look for other work. I could get off my rear end, clean up the apartment and try dating someone. I had blown it all out of proportion. If you ever feel like you can't go on, just take a look at things in a practical perspective, and you will see that you can.

I have actually had a brush with suicide five times. The other two times, it involved someone else. In December of 1997, I woke up and dressed for work. I was almost out of the door before I walked into Mary's room to say goodbye to her. Our marriage was already in bad shape, and we did not usually sleep together. I looked into our second floor "bird room," where she lay, totally oblivious to my movements. Something did not seem right.

It wasn't. I noticed that all of her bottles of medication were empty. Then, I noticed a note, a suicide note. She was still breathing, barely. Things were so bad that I almost went to work without a word, so as not to bother her. I was lucky again.

It happened again in the fall of 1998, a year after we separated. Mary called me and asked me to come to Tucson and take the birds home with me. She was out of money and didn't think she could heat her house for them in the winter. I agreed, since I cared about the birds more than her at that point. I should have known something was up but was too angry to notice. When I arrived, she hadn't even prepared at all. I drove to a pet store and bought a net to catch most of the birds. I did this in a hurry.

Her place looked like hell. I wanted to leave as soon as I could. I put the birds in the car and looked at her. Her eyes were full of fear but my feeling was gone.

I drove away and within hours, she had attempted suicide, only to be found by a young woman who rented a room in Mary's house.

So if you wonder why this chapter is in the book, it is for a good reason. It is an important subject. So what if it isn't fun. You can't enjoy life if you aren't able to get by the pain that comes with it.

There are other reasons, I guess, why people take their lives. Let's take a look at them and understand why they really aren't reasons:

They think it will end their pain: How do we know? If there is eternal life for the "good" people, what is in store for those who kill themselves? What if you had to spend your eternity in a room with Ted Bundy or Timothy McVeigh? What if you had a nice little pad and even a TV, but the only thing to watch was "Kathie Lee's Greatest Hits?"

Worse yet, what if you had to spend eternity at a meeting of the Autism Society of America, watching a group of "normal" parents and professionals acting worse than you or I could imagine? Talk about a fate worse than death....

The point is: you don't know if it will be any easier if you are dead. So why take the chance? Why not take a

deep breath, walk around the block, and slowly make some sense out of the life that you know, no matter how bad it seems right now?

They want to punish the people who have hurt them and make them regret what they did: This was part of my thinking in my first attempt. Upon recollection after the attempt failed, I realized that I had made a real fool of myself. She never did anything wrong. I was the one who couldn't accept the reality, chasing this poor girl all over the campus. I don't think she would have enjoyed hearing about my demise, but there would have been no reason for her to regret anything and there usually isn't when people commit suicide to get a "pity" response. If anything, others might say "Good riddance!!

They judge themselves too harshly: This is common in people who are victims of violent crimes like rape. They often feel that somehow they could have avoided the situation and are responsible for what was done to them. It also happens to people in abusive marriages and relationships with partners whose demands are impossible to meet. If the person's self-image is wrapped up in having that relationship and he can't meet its demands, then suicide seems easier than the alternative, getting out of the relationship.

These seem to be the most popular bad reasons for suicide. I am sure there are others, but as I say, I am incompetent at this. If I was a real expert, I might know all of the reasons. If that was the case, I might have found a reason that "worked" for me and be too dead to write this chapter.

I think these are the most common reasons. Let's assume by now that you recognize that suicide is not a high functioning option. It helps to notice, ahead of time, if you or a friend is heading on that road. There are certain signs that a person's attitude towards life has retreated in a dangerous way:

1. An unkempt appearance, especially at work or in social situations where the person usually knows better.

2. Consistent trouble sleeping, indicated by unusual yawning and fatigue at one's workplace.

3. More than the usual clutter in a person's car, work space or living quarters. A decline in the usual extent of personal organization.

4. Irritability. Does the person get upset more easily than usual?

5. Isolation. The person is not doing the normal things he does that involve contact with people. He is no longer at the gym, golfing or doing his usual social activities.

6. Lethargy or the reverse. Does the person lack interest in any dialogue more than usual or has his interest become uncomfortably intense when someone pays attention to him at all?

7. New, unhealthy habits. Has the person started drinking noticeably or smoking; is there evidence of newly initiated drug use?

8. Actual statement of an intent to harm oneself and/or others, or even a speculative statement about what it would be like to do, witness or be part of such an action.

If any of these signs are true about you or a loved one, take a good look at yourself and ask why, because none of these are positive indicators. In one or more ways, a downward change in your self-esteem must be addressed before it gets any worse. If you notice this in somebody you live with, care for, or know, then you can help that person. Here's how:

a. Privately, share with that person what you have noticed. Ask the person to examine what is going on and why. Offer to help if needed. Tell the person that you can be called if there is something that he really needs to talk about.

b. If the person indicates that indeed, suicide has been on his mind, or shares any other self-destructive thinking, help that person find the nearest suicide hot line in your area. Ask the person to promise to talk to you before any action is taken that can harm him. Have the person promise to talk to somebody before ever doing anything drastic.

c. If there is a particular issue, like divorce, rape, spousal abuse, etc., there may be specific support groups available. Encourage the person to get in such a group. Even offer to go to the first meeting with him if that is allowed. If the person has counseling available to him, paid for by his health insurance, certainly encourage him to begin therapy immediately

d. If the person is despondent over a dead-end situation at work, see if he can get some time off to look at other options. It is possible to get a leave of absence from many employers and this can give a person breathing room to get better mentally and spiritually.

e. One warning on this: If the person does take a fixed leave, he must make a plan of what he will do with that free time. He can't stay in bed. He should come up with a list of other workplaces to visit and other alternatives to his present job. If he doesn't do that, his time off will be wasted, and he will return to work in the same mental condition that he had before.

The important thing is to let the person at risk know that he is not isolated. If you are the one at risk, then you need to avail yourself of the local support at your disposal, NOW. The road to self-destruction is rarely an overnight path. It takes time to sink that far and will take time and help to rebuild your self-esteem and confidence.

Before going on, I want to draw special attention to warning signal number seven. This has particular application at our schools, where some sick, isolated people are not only killing themselves, but are killing others, too. In almost every case, the criminals talked about what they wished to do or said threatening things that were ignored.

Duh!!! I know that none of you young people want to be known as a snitch, but if you hear a fellow student say something like, "I am so tired of the way this rotten school has treated me that I am going to get even someday," you are a fool if you don't tell a teacher or principal about this. That is a sick thing to say, and the person who said it needs help, big time. He might get mad at you and say he didn't really mean it, but what if he does, you say nothing and he carries out his words? How will you feel then? I'd rather take the chance and "rat" on him. I'd rather be unpopular for a reason than dead for no reason.

The school-rage pattern is too sad and consistent by now. The killers aren't the biggest kids. They are the ones usually getting bullied, teased and ridiculed. In the eyes of their peers, they are such "creeps' and "nerds" that nothing they say is taken seriously until it's too late. Sound familiar? That description could easily fit a lot of middle-schoolers with autism and other developmental disabilities.

No, I don't enjoy sharing this, but if you were looking for a "happy talk" book, this isn't it. This book is about reality and it isn't always a picnic.

I hope that none of my peers goes nuts and pulls the trigger on his classmates. But if he does, I don't want some lawyer offering a diagnosis of autism or any other condition as an excuse. I really don't care what your handicap is. You are still responsible for your actions, and if that means that you lose control, hurt or kill your fellow students and live, you deserve the same penalty as anyone else who does such a sick thing. You do the crime, you can do the time or worse.

That sounds extreme. It sure is. But this a big country, almost three hundred million of us now. It is big enough that somewhere, almost every extreme can and will happen. Being aware of how you and/or others can send signals of dangerous imbalance is very important.

In most cases, with detection and being enough of a friend to be a "good snitch," you can save lives and help someone who really needs it.

In addition to getting therapy and support, you can try a great new approach called Cognitive Behavior Therapy. My good Australian friend, Tony Attwood, author of the (over 100,000) bestseller "Asperger's Syndrome," is a big proponent of this. I have used it. Friends of mine, like Ken Brewer from my AGUA support group, have also gotten great benefit from it.

The basic goal of cognitive behavior therapy is to understand how your feelings affect the way that you view the world and often distort what is really there. Take depression, for example. That is a feeling, or usually the sum of a lot of negative feelings, about yourself and what you can do with your life. Depression really is a big negative curtain that your brain allows to fall in front of your eyes.

In other words, that depression is not the way the world really is. It is only the way that it seems. If you are depressed, that curtain that drops in front of your eyes and clouds your judgment can be lifted. Once you understand the distorting effect of your negative feelings, you will lift that curtain and see that the world that looked so bad now looks just as good as it ever did!

This is not a technique that you can learn in a day. It takes practice and self-examination and is well worth it. One great resource is "The Feel Good Handbook" by David Burnes. In this book you or your friend, preferably with the help of a therapist, can learn how to understand your feelings and stop them from ruining your life. In fact, you can learn how to let your feelings help you instead of hurt you! That book is the best resource that I know.

For example, even before you get that book, here is something you can start doing every night: Difficulty sleeping (and excessive yawning at work, as a result) is another warning signal. Try this when you are in bed:

Remind yourself of at least five good things that you did today. How about....

- You got up.
- You really didn't want to go to work, but you did.
- You did some task that you hated, but it had to be done.
- You fed your pets.

- Maybe you went shopping for something you needed.

- Or, even though you are feeling low, you didn't crawl into bed the minute you got home.

- You at least watched TV for a couple of hours.

If you are really depressed, five might seem like a big number. But if you look hard, you can find five good things that you did, every day. Reminding yourself of those things will help you sleep better.

Another thing you can do to battle morning lethargy and depression is this:

Plan tomorrow before you go to bed. Put all of the activities down on a piece of paper or on your computer calendar so you can immediately see it in the morning. Lay out the clothes you will wear. Make sure that what you need to take to work, your car keys, briefcase, etc., are in a consistent place that is easy to remember.

Depression can keep people from getting up. They think that by lying in bed, making up a dumb excuse, and calling in sick when they are just down, the day will be easier. Instead, they just wake up the next morning having missed a day of work and income, inconveniencing their co-workers and accomplishing nothing. If you have your day planned and waiting for you when you awake, it will be easier to fight the morning blues and get on with things.

The more times that you can fight back and stop depression from beating you, the easier it will be to keep fighting it until depression gives up on you and retreats to some other victim.

Let's review what I have shared in this chapter. After all, this could save your life or that of a friend.

1. Be aware of the warning signals, in others and yourself, that point to self-destruction.

2. When those appear, help that person find therapy and support making sure that he/she is not isolated. Make that person promise to reach out when all hope is lost.

3. Follow through. Make sure that support, contact and therapy continue until no risk appears.

4. Expose the person or yourself to self-improvement options like Cognitive Behavior Therapy.

In conclusion, let me remind you that barring reincarnation, we are all dead most of the time universally.

Suppose you could compact the entire history of the universe into one century. That's about 3.15 billion seconds or about one second for every five years that we know of. Your life will probably be twelve to twenty seconds out of that time. That is not very much time. Why make it shorter?

YOUR LIFE IS NOT A LABEL

"Baseball is ninety percent pitching. The other half is hitting."
Yogi Berra, Hall of Fame Catcher

An Ounce of Humor Beats a Pound of Prozac

I am often accused of having a sense of humor. What there is of it is not a savant skill at all. I have acquired some understanding of what humor is and how to invent some of it but it was not a natural talent. It is something that helps me get through life and should be part of everyone's life. One of the most self-defeating aspects of disabled people is that they are so often teased and ridiculed that they try extra hard to do right and avoid more of that. They wind up taking themselves too seriously and being too unforgiving of themselves.

My early memory is that I often felt that I was only moments away from the next time that I would say or do something that landed me in a sea of laughter, treading water when another unpredictable wave of life knocked me off any iceberg of understanding I clung to and back into an unpredictable ocean of life. Humor originally scared me. My first conscious exposure was the Dean Martin/Jerry Lewis frantic, whining movie. I found this and the tantrums of Donald Duck unbearable. Maybe I identified with these situations. But even though I was afraid of such unpredictable, over-stimulated humor, I was learning something very important to me.

I learned that people who make other people laugh are liked. I wanted to be liked, even when five. That is not always so with autistic people and I think it is evidence that I was never as autistic in some ways as the average one is. I hated accidental physical contact. I lacked social awareness. I had no tact. I could stick on a subject until nobody wanted to be around me. But I wanted to be liked. Humor became something I studied until I became good at it. At first, it meant watching all of the TV

269

"funny men," Jack Parr, Ernie Kovacs, Spike Jones, George Burns, Milton Berle and the leading ladies of comedy, Lucille Ball and Gracie Allen.

My visual instinct loved to watch these people and I had two older brothers and a father who loved comedy. I began to appreciate how people could move in a funny way, by making exaggerated movements or just plain surprising you.

One time, Ernie Kovacs played a marvelous joke on his audience. For weeks, he built up the appearance of a group, the Nairobi Trio, but every week, there was a different reason why they cancelled. Finally, the great moment came. The curtain lifted and there were three people in gorilla suits, playing instruments and singing a song that consisted entirely of the words, do, re, mi, fa, etc. in perfect synchrony to whatever note was sung. My brothers and I laughed uncontrollably. It was such a cool bond to share that hopelessly funny moment with them.

I learned other things from watching cartoons. There was the way that animal body language got exaggerated in the Disney animal cartoons. There was that nose of Pinocchio and the ears of Dumbo. My favorite was an improbable tale called "Willy, The Operatic Whale," about a sperm whale, who sang in three different voices, all by Nelson Eddy. By third grade, I understood the visual value of exaggeration and surprise as a great adjunct to humor, not only from what I have already shared but from the flourishes of Ernie Kovacs and Spike Jones when they made you laugh without a word.

There was the Lucille Ball scene with Harpo Marx, both acting as if the other was a mirror image, and her battle with the desserts on an assembly line. But I couldn't use this knowledge in my schoolyard attempts at humor. However, I began to invent my own jokes, usually way too long to justify waiting.

Here is an example of my second grade humor:

Long ago in Egypt, the Pharaoh had some slaves with no work to do. A country on the border needed them, so the Pharaoh let the other country have a few hundred slaves for a year. The King returned the slaves but understood that they were all a year older and worn out a little, so he also gave the Pharaoh ten more slaves. And that, was the start.......of...... human interest!!!

Made sense to me. I knew what interest was and could calculate it in my head. But imagine yourself on a school bus in elementary school, hearing that joke being said in a nervous, monotone voice by someone who obviously wants you to laugh because he's putting so much effort into it.

Obviously, I needed more training. It came from Gracie Allen, Bob Newhart and Allan Sherman. From Gracie, I finally learned that if you say something funny but don't act as if it is funny, you get a lot more response. From albums of the other two, I noticed how they said the funniest things in a voice that gave no indication that they thought they were funny. Also, their humor was a lot quicker than mine.

I also learned from watching how regular, non-comedian people often wound up very funny without planning. There was a Timex watch commercial in which John Cameron Swayze put a Timex watch on the propeller of a small boat engine and let it run in some water. Later, he stopped the engine and spent a minute, fumbling around for the watch. Then he held up the watch and said "We found it, and it is still ticking!" What made it really funny was the calm way he looked for it and never raised his voice, exuding full confidence in the wonderful watch that was in the water somewhere. I loved live commercials. Classic real-life humor.

There was another deeper benefit to my humor hobby. I was exploring what is called "Theory of Mind." Autistic people are said to have difficulty with TOM; we have a hard time imagining how other people think in a given scenario. By asking myself, "what do I say to make ---- laugh?", I developed TOM in a humor plane. I knew, if I say -----, then ----- will laugh because he expects me to say ------." That is theory of mind in humor.

The negative part was that I learned to lie. I learned that a lie could alter another person's view of reality. If that benefited me, a lie might be worth a risk. Even a lie is a mixed blessing because it still shows that the liar has enough social awareness to know that a lie might work. But it is not a habit to be encouraged. It is, however, not a totally bad thing to discover a lie told by an autistic child. But back to humor 101 and how I graduated from that to post Ph.D. humor.

I have a penchant for structure, also autistic. I began to notice how some humor had a linguistic pattern. I called it a "funny form." The general form could be, "It was so-----, that -- ---- happened." A specific example could be "It was so hot today, I saw birds hitchhiking on the New Jersey Turnpike!" I saw the humor of surprise comments. Almost forty years later, I amused friends with my imitation of Rodney Dangerfield. My version of him: "I can't get no respect. I went back to college and took a class in communicating with the dead. Now, I get phone messages from Jerry Garcia!"

John and Jim, my older brothers, both have a great sense of humor. They were cartoonists for the Islip High School student newspaper. My father took us all to the Brooklyn office of <u>Mad Magazine</u>, where we met Bill Gaines and some of the other geniuses of cartoon humor. Jim once drew a hilarious cartoon/ editorial about a gym teacher who was not exactly a paragon of fitness. As a matter of fact, sharing a brew with this teacher at the local bowling alley bar was a great rite of passage for high school men when they became legal or had a phony ID. My father intercepted Jim's cartoon before it was published.

So, by junior high school I was another class clown wannabe. But when you have two teachers as parents, your efforts get noticed a lot faster and discouraged.

One day we had a new music teacher. He was a professional trumpet player on the side and had a beatnik level mustache. I immediately began using every hip expression that I had gleaned from sneaking into my college brother John's room. This earned me a quick trip to the principal and by that night, a lecture from my father. He met the new teacher at lunch hour. That kind of grapevine choked off most of my high school humor activities. But the humor helped me laugh at myself. It took a long time, but I finally could share the laughter when I imagined how silly I once looked in a ballroom dance class.

I became interested in voices. One of my favorites was that of whoever played Al Capone. Of course, "The Untouchables" was my favorite TV series. I was born an untouchable!!

In my early forties, Jack Nicholson starred in "Batman." I worked at a college bookstore at the time and students kept calling me "Jack," saying I looked like him. I wound up imitating "The Joker" for Ron Smith Celebrity Look-alikes. It was fun. Once, I played the Joker at a birthday party for Lionel Ritchie's niece at a Bel Air home. It was a great party with a huge chocolate cake in the shape of the Batmobile.

Lionel Ritchie showed me something about spontaneous humor. At the end of the party, they handed out little souvenir bags to the children. Some of the adults, including me, decided to grab a bag and get Lionel's autograph.

I went up to him for my prize. A little child looked up at me and said, "Hey, Joker, he should be asking for your autograph!" Without hesitation, Lionel Ritchie handed me a bag to sign, which I did. Now, that is what makes a showman *a showman*. But as I found out, to make a lot of money imitating a celebrity, you have to do a lot more than just look like him. I just wasn't up to that in 1989 so my career as the Joker was short-lived.

Humor became part of me and remains today. It is a saving grace but does not come without a price. It can be overdone. I have noticed that one or two jokes may be appreciated in social settings, but a whole string of them shows how insecure you are in the situation. That took me a long time to learn. My humor hobby led to eventual obsessive speculation about what everyone I knew thought of me, especially girls. Elaborate charts and analysis got me nowhere in my constant campaign to impress someone into a lifelong state of marital adoration. That was way too much of a good thing but at least I was not in a social shell.

I notice other autistic people want to impress people with something; humor, knowledge, or prowess on the athletic field. What none of us understand is that people don't want to hear of it endlessly and be overwhelmed. Being pleased with our accomplishments is good, but we overdo it and don't get the attention we crave.

Even as an adult, I sometimes let humor get the better of me. Some people commented, after my first year of public presentations on autism, that I used humor too much. They were right. I learned to balance it with the need for information and now I think I use it just enough for it to help.

Some of my humor is not easy for others. I like to read billboards backwards. The words sound very funny that way but not everyone wants to hear that. Mary did and that is one of the reasons I quickly wanted her as a partner. It was like I was a radio that could play a few stations really well and the rest were static, with her being the only one who wanted that kind of radio.

Humor is important to me and I think it should work for you, too. It is impossible to always be right. It is a lot easier to relax and laugh, even if the joke is on you. I think that one of the best things about the support groups that I belong to, in person or on the Internet, is that we get to laugh among friends. I will never forget the time that one perpetual sob sister got his comeuppance. A fellow autistic man walked up to him and said, "You'd be a great guy if you weren't so autistic!"

Now, he could get away with that as a fellow autistic person. I am lucky to note that I learned that some humor is only allowed "within the family." Like the joke I heard at a People First conference, for all kinds of disabled people:

What do you do if a guy has a seizure in your bathtub? Answer: Throw in the laundry!

That is the kind of joke some people in a group can tell about each other, only. It is like understanding that you can hear family members whine about each other but if you are not part of that family, just listen and don't knock anyone because they will all unite against you.

I remember one day, I played basketball at a local college. The other nine players were all black. Every time one of them missed a shot or a pass, he got called a "nigger." I ran up and down, fortunately too winded to talk at all, while I pondered this scene.

These guys would have made a KKK meeting look tolerant. I figured out that it was an inside joke and I did not join in the trash talk. Finally, I threw a beautiful pass to one of them. He had made a cut to the basket, in the same situation, several times and I knew that this 9.6 hundred yard dash sprinter would do it again. He was so amazed at my perfect pass that he dropped it. The game came to a halt while the ball was retrieved and one of the other players looked at me and said., "It's okay, Jerry, call him a Nigger!!" I didn't, but it was fun for us to see the irony of it all.

That is just one example of the socializing impact of appropriate humor. It is not the only benefit. Humor is something very beneficial to the spirit. I think many of my peers do appreciate it and have read that we prefer teachers who have a sense of humor. It can be so much fun that it can be overdone and there is also a need to learn when and where it is not appropriate.

This has not been a long chapter and it need not be. Humor is not all of my life but I thought it important to include it. But like most good jokes, I think a chapter on humor can be short and sweet, too.

"A child born in 2001 has about a twenty-five percent chance of reaching the age of eighteen with his natural parents. A record percentage of children are born out of wedlock."

Recent official statistic

You Will Outlive Them

I had it a lot easier than you. I always had less of Asperger's Syndrome than many peers. I also grew up when this was a healthier and happier place to be young in many ways. I wish I could turn back the clock for all of you but I can't.

I am not just writing to talk about how good things used to be. I want to share what I took for granted and never should have. Most of the best things that ever happen to you will not happen because of money; they happen because the right people are there for you when you need them. That has not changed.

For one thing, there was the stability of life. Once my family settled down in Islip, New York, we never moved. I was in the same school district from first grade through my senior year. When I accepted my diploma, second out of 180, in June of 1966, many of the people on that stage were in the same boat as I was. They had the same parents as when they were born. They lived and went to school in one school system most of their lives. The crime rate was low. Interest rates were even lower and people walked the streets whenever they wanted to. It was that kind of town. Islip was incredibly corny and patriotic. They had a parade for everything. One of my high school friends said of it, "Islip is the kind of little town you could make fun of, but you can't because you live there."

It was easier, back then, for people to make it who might have joined the ranks of the Asperger's or even autistic population if

277

born today. After all, our world as a whole didn't require nearly as much adjustment to constant change, crowding and generally aggressive, hostile and abusive mass social interaction.

Look about you. Compared to forty or fifty years ago, every negative measure of life quality is worse: crime, divorce, suicide, child abuse, bullying, schoolyard massacres, pollution. It's all worse.

But you have to find a life in this world that keeps spinning faster and faster, pushing into new frontiers of self-indulgence with every new TV channel and Internet option. The world is not going to slow down and seek sanity, at least not yet, just because an increasing number of children find it harder to live in a hostile place that demands so much on the senses and offers so little in return.

You aren't going to get through this alone, even if you are the most normal child on the planet. That's why I remind you that you need to appreciate the people who are there, because your parents probably have a harder time being there for you than the parents of my generation did. In most families of my time, Mom stayed at home and Dad worked. My family was that way until I was in second grade. Mom went back to work teaching because she wanted to, not because she had to.

So, you can see why I feel lucky. I not only had the same two parents, I had more of their time. It is harder for families today. To have a home, car, college educations and all of the toys of this day, a family today can't do it on one income. And in some families, one person is the only one around. I don't have to tell a lot of you that!

It was different for me. My parents were not the warmest folks on the block, but they were as loyal as any Green Beret ever could be. I never had the feeling that I couldn't call them when I screwed up and get some good advice. They used to say, "home is the one place where if nobody else will let you in, they will." I had that kind of home as long as I needed it.

I never got to thank my father for his efforts. In my youth I was, like many of you, a distant child. My father made an extra effort to reach out. He took me on trips, and my brothers may have wondered why he did this. I know. He wanted me out of a shell, and he also wanted me to accept him as a father. I never got to that point, and he died when I was in college.

I hope that doesn't happen to you, with either parent. If you know how to say, "I love you, Dad (or Mom), remember to say it because it is music to their ears. You can't put a price on what it means to have anyone who you care about, say that to you. You can't make the mistake I did. I used to see where some kid got a late model car or some other toy and I would complain if my car didn't look as good or my clothes didn't match up. I remember once I even called my dad "cheap." Later, I felt ashamed when my mother suggested that my brothers and I buy him a new suit for Christmas because he had put off buying one for years, so he could buy things for us.

Money is not what makes our lives complete. Time, given and shared by family, friends and responsible community members, is what has a value beyond price and should be appreciated at every opportunity.

The time that my dad took me on a walk in the woods in upstate New York was magical. He never needed a map to go anywhere if he had been there before. This was a summer weekend, and my friends on the local Little League All-Star team were at the State Finals in Waverly, New York. We went up to watch them win the State title, but the walk in the woods with Dad had true championship quality.

We visited a forest where he had been several decades ago. He was curious. Once a tree fell in a storm. The tree was a big, old one. It had many rings, rings that showed which years had a lot of rain and which didn't. My father wondered if that fallen tree was still there. The trail, used by my father in the thirties, was still there in 1960. So was that fallen tree.

He showed it to me. I immediately sat down and studied it. My father took a happy, solitary walk and came back an hour or so later, knowing I would not have moved. I learned a lot from that afternoon. It explained why my father loved to spend time in our garden at home. It explained why he loved our pets and all animals. I also learned how a dead tree could teach me so much about history. It was on that day that I realized the real path to immortality: do something that outlives you. Leave the world a book, an organization, a tree, something. That is the way to immortality, not getting A's on the report card of whatever Easter Bunny you believe in.

≈

Time is far more valuable than money. If you want to thank your mom, dad or other special people in your life, thank them for the time they spend. Any idiot can pull out a checkbook. Only a real parent can spend time. There are always other things they can do with their time. There is never enough time when you grow up to do all that you wish to do. It is particularly important to thank your fathers. I say that because in general, fathers are not involved with us as much as they should be. Forget the ones who flaked out, got a divorce and just send child support, ...maybe.

The ones who are still around have a hard time relating to us. Most of us, after all, are boys. Whatever fantasy they had of a son is quickly smashed. My father was a lot more involved with my life than most of yours, but I can even remember him sometimes looking at me or thinking about some silly thing I had done and wondering if the stork had the wrong address. How could someone who looked so much like him do something so completely off the wall!

I am not saying this to make you feel bad about yourself. I am saying it to help you understand what may go on in your family. You can't live up to anyone else's fantasy. That is true for all children. You have to do your best. That might involve something that your parents also liked doing. I know some very athletic autistic people. They are usually in individual sports like track, gymnastics, martial arts or even ballet. I also know some families where Dad, Mom and Son are all "computer nerds." That kind of family bond is wonderful in any healthy form.

I was luckier with my mother, sharing her last two years in her apartment in Santa Monica. I needed a fresh start from a decade of aimless taxi-driving. She needed somebody to shop for her, take her to the doctor, and talk sometimes. It was a great chance for me and I hope it worked for her. The best thing is that my brothers and I all had a chance to thank her before she died. We knew it was going to happen. I was the last to see her alive. We spent her last evening watching her favorite show "Wheel of Fortune."

Parents are not the only special people although they have a unique place in anyone's life. There have been and still are other unforgettable people.

My best boyhood friend was a handsome first grade classmate named Johnny Aichoth. We spent hours doing everything: playing baseball, catching frogs, water-skiing and growing up, until he died of a mysterious illness in 1964, when I was fifteen. That was very hard to take.

I knew others who had short but great lives. One of the people who inspired me to join a fraternity at Michigan was a reporter on the college newspaper, the Michigan Daily. Less than two years later, Larry Meadow died of leukemia.

To think of such fine people as Johnny and Larry makes me feel very lucky to be alive and over fifty. A life is only once and is not a thing to waste. There isn't enough space here to thank my teachers. One deserving special mention is Mr. Harvey Egan, whose love of music carried an entire band through at least a thousand rehearsals that I witnessed. He produced an incredible number of all-state musicians. Another is my college math professor Tom Storer, a brilliant and humane friend, one of the giants in the field of combinatorics.

The important message of this chapter is simple: be grateful to all of the people who come into your life and add to it. They don't always know what to do or even why they are there, but your life is better because of all of them. I feel very lucky today, lucky that I still have two brothers, John and Jim, with whom to share memories and present good tidings. After my parents were gone, they were there when needed, and I hope to be there for them if necessary.

There also have been many friends, too many to list. Ironically, several of my best friends were all "Stephens:" Berry, Lazzaro and Ferguson. There must be some martyrdom involved in being a good friend of mine.

There have been a couple of Mike's: Novak and Simon, and three Ken's: Brewer, Weinman and Brier.

It was my fraternity little brother Ken Brier who gave me a great piece of advice, "Jerry, when you get to California, think of strangers as friends you haven't met yet." He added, "If you move too quickly, you catch misfortune. If you move too slowly, it catches you."

How does one thank a list of people that would fill another book? The best way is to recognize the value of unconditional parenting, friendship and teaching. If I had a dime for every piece of wisdom, stroke of encouragement and genuine act of love I received, I might be richer than Bill Gates!

It all started with Mom and Dad. I had thanked Mom, but I never thanked Dad in person. In 1998 I had an opportunity to visit their final resting place in upper New York state. It is a beautiful old cemetery that is shared with a local Indian tribe. I sat in front of their plots, and this time I got in the last word! I shared with them how my brothers and I were closer together, and I thanked them both for all they had done. Then, there were no more words to say on that autumn day that had begun with a trip to a favorite old place, the Baseball Hall of Fame in nearby Cooperstown.

I got up, walked to where I could kneel between their headstones, touch them both, and look at the beautiful tree behind them. The tears, tears of longing and gratitude that they never saw in life, said it all. I will never forget them and what they did as long as I live. It is said that people like me lack empathy. Not at all. It just takes some of us longer to express it. I hope it doesn't take as long for you to thank the people who make a difference in your life. In too many cases, you will outlive them.

"I did it my way" - Frank Sinatra

A Good Life is Not an Accident

Now, that's a way to go out. Old Blue Eyes couldn't have said it any better. He had remarkable talent and intensity. When he sang, every woman in the audience felt like it was a personal serenade. But even he had a final song as all of us, swans and singers alike, will.

What interested me about Frank Sinatra is what many don't know: he never read music. He just sang by ear. His more obvious negative was his temper, as documented by at least one ex-wife. It seemed that no matter how sweet his song was, you felt a creative tension, or perhaps the rattle of a snake about to go off and bite you if you offended it.

But this is about facing our mortality, and my wish that all of us end up living life in our way.

That last day is not always a day that we can plan. Some of us will die by accident. But most of us probably will know when that time has arrived. I don't think it should be a terrible day. It is scary now, to think of the end of my life, now that I really enjoy it, but less than it used to be. No, I don't look forward to it, but I think that I will feel better about the life I have lived. I want that last day to pass with dignity. I want to leave everyone who knows me feeling good about the life that I was lucky to live and share with them.

Lucky? Yes, lucky. Sure, it is no picnic to have any kind of challenge that makes you feel as if you don't have an equal chance with the rest of humanity. But at least you and I have lives as part of that human race. Look up at a night sky and you can see millions, if not billions of stars. How many of them are just full of countless tons of matter, all of which, no matter how impressive or beautiful, will never, even an atom of them, know what you and I know, what it is like to be alive.

That's why I feel lucky. I know where I want to spend that last day. Mary and I have a place where we can sleep with all of our parrots. There, not some hospital, is where I want to be. I see no sense in making you and every other taxpayer or medical insurance policyholder fork over more money to keep the elaborate machinery going that prolongs a life that should be over, for a few extra days, weeks or even months. I want to leave this earth as I entered, a human being connected to no tubes or artificial devices, only connected to others by contact like the hug my mom gave me when I was born.

But when I leave, I will be able to accept a hug from my wife. I won't mind a bit if the parrots want to sit on me and even take a little friendly nibble. I won't need a lot of people around. Just Mary and my parrots will be enough. I will remember the things I tried to do and be happy that I did at least some of them and tried my best to do the rest. I will also, probably, remember things that I can't tell you now. They will come as that time, once in a lifetime, comes to us all.

> "I know you don't understand me now, but someday you will."
> *Kevin Spacey, from "American Beauty"*

He was right, I am sure. I think that when a body and soul know that it is time to move on, there should be a tremendous amount of relaxation, of resolution, in preparation for the next journey. I think that in me, it will mean not only the freedom to remember the big events, but the little things that I took for granted at the time and meant so much more.

There was the time I was in second grade and my family went Christmas shopping in New York. It was such a big deal that we got a hotel room before going shopping for the evening. I forget the name of the store, but somehow, I got lost from my family. I guess I was just too naive to be concerned.

I looked around and saw nobody, Mom, Dad, John or Jim. I guess I should have found a store employee and asked for help, but I had some money in my pocket and just walked outside, hailed a taxi and in triumph, climbed into the back seat saying to the driver, "Take me to the Hotel Piccadilly!" He did. I bounded out of the taxi, gave the driver a tip and was sitting in the hotel lobby reading a paper when my family returned.

They were shocked and relieved to see me. I learned then that my brothers actually cared about me. While Mom and Dad fussed, Jim drew a sketch of me for an NYPD officer while John prepared to battle the gangs that must have captured me. I was in total disbelief. I hadn't felt threatened at all. In fact, on the way to the hotel, I had the taxi driver go through a parking structure where I entertained him by factoring license plate numbers on parked autos!

That is possibly the kind of memory, until recently forgotten, that may come up on my last day. But more than anything else, I work and plan now to make sure that when I leave the rest of you living folks, I will do it with dignity and a great feeling of satisfaction and gratitude for the opportunity to live and to be loved, touched and inspired by so many of you.

My last day should also involve some forgiveness. Certainly, I will have to forgive myself for all that is left undone. I must accept, for example, that I never resolved my relationship with my dedicated, but clueless, father who died thinking that I hated him. I can rejoice, however, that my mother did not go out like that.

More importantly, I have to forgive those who passed on before me for anything they did that hurt me and do the same for the people who I will leave behind.

Take those two young lost souls, probably kicked out of Navy boot camp, who walked by a laundromat in Ocean Beach, California, on Labor Day weekend in 1983, saw me alone, and mugged me. I remember their eyes, crazy. They must have been on PCP or some other crap. They weren't exactly professionals. They hit me with a billy club, but I was too hard-headed to pass out. When I turned around and confronted them with their incompetence, they ran. I said to them, "You try to mug me, you can't even knock me out, and now you want me to pay you for the privilege?"

So, I staggered down to a liquor store and asked the cashier for a quarter to call "911." He laughed and so did everyone in the store. I thought they were laughing at my bleeding state. I fought depression for months until I understood why they laughed: Why would I borrow a quarter to call "911?" It's a free call!

I imagine the muggers found karma sooner or later. Maybe they were lucky and got smart. Heck, they're probably born-again whatevers now with model families. I know that wasting time, hating them for what they did to me, in their drugged-out condition, does no good.

I can hate the sin but not the sinner.

My last day, I hope, will include a chance to peek at some of the math problems that I never solved and enjoy reading the solutions. I once wanted to always be right. Then I visited the Widener library on a tour of Harvard in 1965. Fourteen million books, I think it had. I knew that nobody could ever know all of that. In fact, if you take the IQ of a complete idiot, zero, and compare it to what you get when you divide all available knowledge in the Universe into the capacity of the smartest person, say a ratio of .0000000000001, we are all idiots by comparison to what's out there to be known. I have lived long enough to discover that every person I ever met could show me something that I didn't know.

Maybe it might take more than one day to die. There's a lot to finish up, it seems.

Dying, in a way, is like a final exam. If you haven't done your homework during the school year, there is no sense studying all night, just before that test. If you want your last day in this world to be a good one, positive, triumphant and inspiring to all who witness it, then you must work now like me to make that a certainty, barring accidents.

How do you do that? As I have said many times in this book, planning is your greatest friend. I don't care what age you are. Even if you are only ten, you have to accept the fact that you won't live forever. You always need to have a plan. You need to decide what experiences are ones that you really want and can have. This is not for impossible dreams. There are things within your reach that you can achieve, but not unless you take the long view of life.

That is very hard for people with autism. We get so caught up in the distress of the moment that every pothole in the street seems to swallow us up because we never see far enough ahead to avoid them. As one with over fifty years of experience, I can tell you that if you really try, your life will make more sense and you will have more control over it as you get older and wiser.

I have lists for my future: lists of books I want to read, places that I want to visit, sports I haven't learned to play, foods I want to know how to cook, all kinds of lists. It doesn't matter if I never have time to do all of them. In fact, those lists, when I get a chance to review them, change as I change. The important thing is that I will never, ever look at life as a finished business until forces far greater than me make that obvious.

This is not how I always felt. For most of my life, like a lot of you, I felt overwhelmed by all of the things I had to do. The world just wanted too much from me. I just wanted to reach a point where for the rest of my life, all of the problems would be solved. I would have no worries about my work, friends, health or anything else. Everyday, I would just wake up and go forth into a stress-free, no-problem, no-surprise, "perfectly solved" life.

That day hasn't come yet, but something better has. What has been given to me by good influences and won by me by my own efforts is the confidence that I can sail the ship of my life on this planet's oceans and take the waves, big and small. Some will rock the boat, but it won't sink. I will always do my best, learn from my failures and always, always move on.

That was not easy to acquire, but to me, it is more precious than any jewel you will ever see; to know that I am, like you, unique and born to a life that is meant to be lived with vigor, resolve and self respect. I know I was born different and so were you, but so what? That is not an excuse. It is a challenge to all of us to live as fully as we can, every hour of every day.

I have written long enough. It is up to you to take what I shared and use it as you see fit, for the rest of your life. I don't know all of the answers. I can't guarantee you a life any freer from disappointment than mine, but I can promise you that if you totally devote yourself to being your own best friend and respect that by always doing your best, then your last day of life will be a good one.

You too, will know that you did, for yourself and those who are dear to you, the most important things. You will know that the people in your life who were there for you, know you appreciated them. You will remember, like I will, some things that you may have forgotten as well as the greatest days like the one, possibly still ahead of you, when you stop demeaning yourself for not being what you think you should be, and instead love yourself as you are and make the best of that.

I sincerely want that day to come for you and hope that I have helped make it happen sooner. You must always remember that no matter how difficult things seem at the moment, life is a long road, and there is always time to recover from the bumps. There has never been someone exactly like you before, and if you give yourself a shot, you will grow and get wiser, more confident and happier.

When your last day comes, if you take charge now and take responsibility for your actions and review occasionally where you are growing and going, you should also remember other good days.

You will remember the first friend you ever made and how good that felt.

You will remember the first time that you finally said, "no" and stopped letting someone hurt you in the name of being a friend, teacher or anything else.

You will also remember the first time you decided to do something for yourself something that you had fallen in the habit of letting someone else do, and how empowered that made you feel.

It is never too late. I was into my fifties before much of this book became a daily part of my life. It doesn't matter. I know that my life now is as good as it can be and will continue to be that way because I love myself enough to guarantee that. Your life and the passion that you bring to it will inspire others. Thanks for the honor of your attention.

You are now free to roam about the universe as you find your destiny ...without a label.

APPENDIX

YOUR LIFE IS NOT A LABEL

How To Start a Support Group in your Area

When Mary Preble (ASA-Long Beach) and Kitty Rivet (ASA-San Gabriel Valley) decided to try setting up an adult support group, they had no idea if it could be done. One the other hand, they knew that they had nothing to lose by trying. But, they were successful.

Here's how it happened:

1. **Don't kill the idea before you give it a chance to work.**

2. **Plan an adult-centered event to attract possible members:**
   You need enough lead time, at least a couple of months, to identify people to contact about a meeting. Plan at least aa two-hour meeting at a convenient time and location. Send an uncluttered notice with a map if needed. Simply invite anyone who is a potential support group member, staff person, friend or parent to attend and help start a new support group for persons of the population you choose. (This can work just as well for conditions other than autism.)

3. **The Big Job: Identifying potential members:**
   Besides any ASA lists, you should contact therapists and service providers. The more people who show up at the start, the easier it will be to continue.

4. **Regularity and Flexibility:**
   You may find that the group, like AGUA, wants little more support than help with mailings, meeting places and transportation. On the other hand, they may want someone, like a post Ph.D. student, to moderate the meetings. Parents

and interested staff should be willing to help where needed without taking over.

It is best to have a regular time of month for meetings, and to use nametags until not needed. It is also best to have maps and clear directions and phone numbers to call for last-minute directions. Notices should be clear and concise, and mailing and phone lists should be updated and distributed regularly. Please ask each member if he wants to be on such lists. Females may not want phone numbers generally distributed.

5. **Participation**:
The more verbal adults can dominate meetings. What a surprise! This is why we often benefit from the company of friends or parents who help diplomatically assure that all in attendance get a chance to say something.

Organizations and Other Resources:

- ALUT (Autism Society of Israel):
  ihf.net/projects/autism/010118autism.org
- Autism Society of America: 1-800-3AUTISM
  www.autism-society.org
- Autism Society of Los Angeles (Largest individual chapter and conference in the world)   Phone: 818-953-3855
  www.autismsocietyla/org
- National Autism Society (Great Britain):
  www.oneworld.org/autism_uk/ or e-mail nas@nas.org.uk
- Asperger's Syndrome Coalition of America: 304-947-5639
  www.asperger.org
- Asperger's Association of New England: www.aane.org
- Autism Network International (Peer Run Information and Internet Support): www.ani.ac
- FEAT (Families for Early Autism Treatment): www.feat.org
- Geneva Centre for Autism (Canada, resources and huge convention) www.autism.net
- Homes for Independence (Non-profit organization to help autistic adults find affordable housing):
  www.homesforindependence.org
  E-mail: wholphin18@hotmail.com
- MAAP (More Advanced Autistic Persons) -
  Newsletter and Conferences: Fax: 219-662-0638
  www.maapservices.org   E-Mail: chart@netnitco.net
- NICHCY (National Information Hotline for Children and Youth with Handicaps) www.kidsource.com/NICHCY/index
- Partners in Policymaking (Federally funded advocacy training for parents and consumers):
  www.partnersinpolicymaking.com
- O. A. S. I. S. (On Line Asperger's Syndrome Information and Support): www.udel.edu/bkirby/asperger/index

Research Oriented Organizations:

- Autism Research Foundation www.ladders.org
- Autism Research Institute Phone: 619-281-7165,
  Fax: 619-563-6840 www.autism.com/ari
- CAN (Cure Autism Now): www.canfoundation.org
- DAN (Defeat Autism Now): www.autism.com/ari/dan.
- NAAR (National Alliance for Autism Research):
  www.naar.org
- Unicorn Children's Foundation: www.saveachild.com
- Unlocking Autism: www.unlockingautism.org

General Information Books/Articles

- *Asperger's Syndrome* - Tony Attwood, Ph.D. -
  (Jessica Kingsley Ltd.)*
- *Asperger's Syndrome-- Solving the Relationship Puzzle* -
  Stephen Gutstein (Future Horizons, Inc.)*
- *Autism Guide for Parents and Professionals* -
  Michael D. Powers (Future Horizons, Inc.)*
- *Discovering "Aspie"* - (*Morning News* article) -
  Tony Attwood, Carol Gray (Jenison Schools)*
- *Gray's Guide to Bullying, Parts One and Two (Morning
  News)* – Carol Gray (Jenison Schools)*
- *Understanding Autism and Asperger's Syndrome* -
  Gary Mesibov (TEACCH)
- *Martian in the Playground* -
  Claire Sainsbury (Lucky Duck Publishing Ltd.)
- *Asperger's—What Does It Mean To Me?* –
  Cathy Faherty (Future Horizons, Inc.)*
- *The Feeling Good Handbook* (Cognitive Behavior Therapy) -
  David D. Burns, M.D., Revised Edition (Plume Publishing Co.)

- *The Americans With Disabilities Act: Analysis and Implications of A Second-Generation Civil Rights Statute* - Robert L. Burgdorf, Jr., Harvard Civil Rights-Civil Liberties Law Review Vol. 26, pp. 413-522, 1991
- *The Americans With Disabilities Act: Questions and Answers* - U.S. Department of Justice, Civil Rights Division, Disability Rights Section, P.O. Box 66738, Washington, D.C. 20035-6738 or call 800-514-0301 (Voice) or 800-514-0383 (TDD)
- *Supportive Living* - Connie Lyle O'Brien and John O'Brien (Autism Society of Los Angeles)
- *Don't Mourn For Us* - Jim Sinclair (members.xoom.com/JimSinclair/dontmourn)
- *Tips for Running a Social Group* - Nancy Alar, MAAP Quarterly, Volume Two, 2001
- *We Overcame... The Story of Civil Rights for Disabled People* - Richard Bryant Treanor, Library of Congress No.: 92-083770, Regal Direct Pub., P.O. Box 8225, Falls Church, VA 22041

Personal Accounts Books:
(Listed in order of author's preference)

- *Beyond the Wall* - Stephen Shore (Autism Asperger Publ.)*
- *Pretending to Be Normal* - Liane Holliday Willey *
- *Emergence, Labeled Autistic* - Temple Grandin *
- *Thinking in Pictures* - Temple Grandin *
- *My Autobiography* - David Medzianik
- *Soon Will Come The Light* - Tom McKean (Future Horizons)*
- *My Autobiography* - (Autism Society of North Carolina)

*Available through Future Horizons, Inc.

YOUR LIFE IS NOT A LABEL

Newport's Emergency Guide to Fast Money

1. <u>Jobs that generate "Clean Green"</u> (Tips that you don't pay taxes on until you report them)

- Taxi Driving
- Pizza Delivery
- Waiter
- Carhop
- Bellhop
- Floral Delivery
- Shine Shoes
- Sell beer, food at ballparks and special events (contact stadiums and sports arenas for job connections)

2. <u>Pawnshops</u>
Keep the receipt! You will probably want to buy back the item at a later date.

3. <u>Sell anything recyclable</u>:

- Newspapers
- Glass
- Cans
- Plastic Bottles
- Cardboard

If you have a car, you can find a lot of this stuff in trash bins, behind supermarkets. Don't ever take stuff from an area that says to keep your hands off.

4. <u>Temporary Jobs</u>:
Sign up at agencies in whatever skill you have.

5. <u>Sell Blood/Plasma</u>:
   You can't be on any medication. You should drink plenty of liquids and no alcohol or dairy products, the day before you donate. You can usually do this twice a week in most cities and make 20 to 30 dollars each time for about two hours. Look in the yellow pages for Plasma Centers.

6. <u>Garage Sales</u>:
   Don't sell anything that you will regret selling, but if you put up some signs, this can raise some money.

7. <u>Experiment subjects</u>:
   Check bulletin boards at campuses for researchers looking for subjects. You usually get paid cash on the spot.

8. <u>Trash hauling or gardening</u>:
   If you see a place with an obvious need for either removal of trash or gardening, leave a note on the door with your number. If you get a call, make a deal and do it. Again, generally you will be paid in cash.

Top Priority Issues in
Autism and Asperger's Syndrome

1. <u>Lack of knowledge of life-span options</u>: Too much emphasis is still placed on "cures" and early intervention. The adolescent phase is about ten percent of a life span. It is not enough to dump people in group homes and walk away.

2. <u>Lack of training</u>: The people who need training the most, get the least. Every parent needs immediate access to information about best practices, as closely tailored to what is known about that particular child. For God's sake, we live in a computer age. Why is every family forced to reinvent the wheel? Not only that, but consider this: everyone on whom a parent relies for help gets training. But, there are no classes in the essential role of parenting.

    People with autism should be taught about peers who have gone on to live meaningful lives, and about people with other challenges who live full lives. There is a great need for books by autistic people, for their peers, on "how to do" anything from survive in college to get a date to how to make it as an independent servicer of vending machines. We need to share what we know.

3. <u>Lack of peer support</u>: Autistic people at all ages need time and space to share experiences and learn from their autistic peers and people with other disabilities. It is not hard to do. The problem has been a lack of will and interest from a community that harps on cures, early interventions and fantasizes its children won't need adult peer support groups. Wake up, parents and professionals. They will.

4. <u>Need for better assistance technology</u>: We must enable nonverbal auties to communicate by independent typing on devices that talk for them. This is far more preferable to picture exchange or FC, which is too prone to manipulation by the facilitator. The ability to communicate, while having complete personal control of that communication, must be a basic right.

5. "<u>Taxation without representation</u>:" Policies on research and services are made by public advisory boards, fundraising organizations, lobbies, ASA chapters, etc. who have systematically excluded autistic people from participation. Token appointments, as advisors who are there to be "seen and not heard," are the rule rather than exception. This will only end when enough auties step forward to be involved and when organizations respond with outreach efforts to identify and train peer leaders and advocates.

6. <u>Overmedication</u>: Too much medication is excessively prescribed because more natural approaches, diet, exercise, sensory integration, peer-support, counseling, etc. have not been thoroughly used. I understand that parents, especially single ones, are under great pressure because they have less time to give to all children. However, the one thing all children need from their parents is quality time with them. That, not medication, is the best answer. We have to find ways to help our parents give children what they need. Fight for more and better in-home assistance and tax credits for families with disabled children, not more meds.

7. <u>Inappropriate and abusive use of aversives</u>: Use of pain-inflicting intervention is abusive when applied to stop people from doing things that may be distracting to others but are not harmful. Such activities include rocking, hand-flapping, humming, gazing at hands, body parts or inanimate objects.

These activities are comforting to many people. They are not self-injurious. They are a matter of personal choice and may be nervous ticks somewhat, but aversives are not needed nor a moral option. I did many of those behaviors once and rarely do now, thanks to exercise, better self-esteem and an overall feeling of integration with my world.

Even in the case of self-injury, most people respond more to attempts to increase their self-esteem. Also, many people who engage in self-injury feel no or little pain, so an aversive that causes pain in a normal person might even be pleasurable.

Some aversives will not go away. They are relatively mild ones like spanking. But pepper spray, hair tugs, pinching, a loud "no" and shock applied to any human or animal have no place in civilized society.

The Newport "Common Sense" Checklist for Autistic Personalities

This is a <u>tongue-in-cheek</u>, somewhat humorous attempt to translate clinical babble into English. It is based on the theory that if "It looks like a duck, talks like a duck, walks like a duck, feels like a duck and smells like a duck, it is probably a duck." <u>This is not to be used in place of a real evaluation.</u>

It is only an attempt to identify possibly autistic behavior in a way that does not flush the subject down a developmental toilet.

For all statements, rate as how you disagree or agree, from -5 to 5. A zero means a neutral position or the statement does not apply. A five means total agreement. A minus five means total disagreement. Enjoy!

1. Your child loves "Big Mouth Billy Bass."

2. Your child thinks he's a Tele-Tubby.

3. Your child thinks Al Gore moves and talks normal and everyone else doesn't.

4. Your child puts the hamster on the record player.

5. Your child would rather turn a bicycle upside down, push the pedals and watch the wheels, than ride it.

6. (In England only) Your child thinks "Free Willy" was a documentary about sex offenders.

7. Your child thinks "Hominy Grits" (heard as "How many grits?") is a southern breakfast to be counted and eaten as fast as possible.

8. Your child wants to be an extra on "Jerry Springer."

9. Your child believes the WWF is real.

10. Your teenager, asked to "rotate the stock" at his job at a supermarket, is found spinning cans of food on the floor.

11. Your adult, trying to use a debit card, becomes a pickpocket when the ATM says, "please swipe card for service."

12. Your child never got the "Who's on First" routine.

13. Your child can either eat or talk, but not do both, at meals, without either leaving food uneaten or eating before the rest of you.

14. Your child could hum, "Louie, Louie" during Mass and not even know people hear him.

15. Your child thinks "Spin City" is a show about an autistic community.

16. Your child wants to cure you.

17. Your child walks by the TV, while "Third Rock From the Sun" is on and thinks the TV is a mirror.

18. Your child, on good days, can juggle one orange.

19. Your child prefers the family parrot to his speech therapist.

20. Your child's favorite kitchen utensil is the egg beater.

21. Your child loves to stop washing machines, dryers and put his finger as close to moving fan blades as he can without getting hurt.

22. Your child can not walk and chew gum at the same time.

23. Your child would rather arrange poker cards in order by suit and rank than actually play poker.

24. Your child can't read or run a bluff.

25. Your child would rather count the number of different cracks in the playground pavement than play with peers.

26. Your child just can't stop staring at pretty people or the mole on Cindy Crawford's cheek.

27. Your child can eat the same food for more days than you care to remember.

28. If you say something to your child, he may as well be on Mars, but if you show him a picture of what you are talking about, he will remember that, two years later, and ask you about it in a completely unrelated situation.

29. Your child always loses in "Simon says."

30. Your child thinks Judge Judy should mellow out and let the people talk whenever they want.

31. Your child thinks more tennis players should behave like John McEnroe.

32. Your child doesn't understand why Anna Kournikova is still on the tour.

33. Your child wore the same underpants for seven years without washing.

34. Your child may think the bathroom is a fecal art studio.

35. Your child thinks Bill Gates is cool.

37. Your child hates the school bus.

38. Your child hates team sports.

39. Your child can pickup either a melody or lyrics to lots of songs but only one track at a time.

40. Your child thinks a spelling bee is a very smart flying insect.

41. Your child is lost when an operator asks him to "hold a moment." He has no idea what a moment looks like, let alone how to hold it.

42. Your child's favorite movie is "Groundhog Day."

43. Your child never understands fairy tales when read to him, but remembers every cartoon.

44. Your child was impressed by the nose-growing scene in "Pinocchio."

45. Your child, when shown a parakeet, asks "Where is the other keet?"

46. Your child mistook the final scene of "Spartacus" for an autism parent's support group meeting.

47. Your child thinks "Caesar Salad" means to steal lettuce from his sister's plate.

48. Your child couldn't catch a fly ball if his life was at stake.

49. Your child thinks firemen are pyromaniacs.

50. Your child thinks "one way" is the name of his favorite street.

Total Scores will range from -250 to 250 in England and −245 to 245 elsewhere.

If total is above eighty-four, you may have a winner. This places your child in approximately the most unique .4% of the expected range. However, even if you eventually discover that your child is a winner, remember that all of this was couched in human terms and that is the way you must always love him/her. There is only one label that really fits all of us: human.

YOUR LIFE IS NOT A LABEL

So You Think You Are One of Us?

Perhaps this book makes you think that you have Asperger's Syndrome or some other form of autism. You are not the first to think so. Maybe you think your child is in that category. Either way, here is some friendly advice.

1. **Don't read any more personal accounts.** The more you read, the more you are likely to unconsciously skew your memory to remember what appears to fit with a diagnosis that seems to fit you.

2. **Do homework:** Get all available data, school and medical records, test results, etc. Identify people who knew you or the child in question, at as early an age as possible, who have reliable memories. Collect anything, photos, videos, written parental anecdotes that can help someone evaluate this situation.

3. **Find someone competent to evaluate you or the child:** The cheapest places are Regional Centers, but their people are sometimes not very competent. Call a local Chapter of Autism Society of America or whatever is the lead advocacy organization in your nation. You may want to attend a local parent support group and ask for good referrals.

   A good evaluation is not cheap, but a good one beats the heck out of a cheap, bad one.

The more homework, evidence and supporting observers you can provide, the better your chance of an evaluation that is accurate and helpful.

4. **If more than one diagnosis is possible, seek the one that qualifies you or the child for the services needed.** This depends where you live. In most areas I know of, a diagnosis of Asperger's Syndrome does not entitle one to as much assistance as one of High Functioning Autism or Autism. There is a lot of debate anyway, over whether there really is a difference between these two conditions, so don't let your insistence on the "exact" label cost you or a child vital services. You may know he's a "duck", but if the geese get more services and he can pass as a "goose", let him be diagnosed as a "goose."

Other Conditions Frequently Observed in Association with Autism or Asperger's Syndrome

NPD: Normal Personality Disorder occurs in about 9500 out of every 10,000 people. Its usual most prominent symptom is an incurable ability to walk and chew gum at the same time. NPD also may exhibit three or more of the following symptoms.

1. Inability to see that others may think differently.

2. An obsession with curing those who think or behave differently.

3. Use of gestures or expressions even when not felt (social lying for advantage). Offensive gestures such as assuming other people desire to shake hands, hug or have direct eye contact. Further intensified by introduction of noxious fragrances for a "pleasing" affect.

4. Insistence on multiple options in routine or other facets of life even when unnecessary, as in collections of shoes, clothing, cars, other toys and sexual partners.

5. Pathological Insincerity: Rigid adherence to ritualistic gatherings, birthday parties, reunions of class and family, church services, etc. for appearances, long after actual association with other attendees or participation is obviously useless.

6. Unnecessary communication: Expressions such as "I really can relate...,"exaggerated frowns, giggles and smiles when nothing needs to be expressed.

PPD: Professional Personality Disorder is a higher functioning part of the PPD spectrum. Sufferers of PPD have delusions of superior knowledge. They often speak to adult audiences like second grade school teachers.

PPD manifests itself in highly contradictory displays, as in use of PowerPoint presentations to describe highly visual thinkers while never showing a picture of anything or writing books in the same style. PPD also expresses itself through perseverative name-dropping; superficial justification of dubious theories by association with other PPD sufferers.

Some PPD cases have developed to the point where they take airplane trips, make hotel reservations and keep track of honoraria with no assistance.

APHID Syndrome, Version One: Autistic Parent, Heavily in Denial is expressed by a parent of an autistic child who can talk endlessly of the child's autism while standing next to a mirror and neither recognize nor admit recognition of any autism in himself.

APHID Syndrome, Version Two: Autistic/Asperger's Partner, Heavily in Denial is expressed by the partner of a spouse who is autistic in any sense and who views all problems of the relationship as a product of the spouse's condition. The best remedy for APHID Syndrome, Version Two is a regular mental enema. Failing that, sufferers of this version of APHID Syndrome make remarkable progress in peer support groups. (This is not to suggest at all, that an autistic spouse is a picnic!!)

APHID Syndrome, Version Three: Autistic Person, Heavily in Denial

This version of APHID symptomatology is expressed by autistic people who see their condition as a pedestal, an excuse to insist on total accommodation by the other 99.8% of humanity. Extreme cases of this manifest in the collecting of public disability assistance while insisting that one is not disabled.

Milder expressions of APHID Syndrome Version Three include:

1. Blanket discrediting of any statement made about autism or autistic people, by people who are not autistic.

2. Insistence on conditions so extreme that eliminates the possibility of any compromise that exposes the sufferer to work or any socially responsible action.

3. Insistence on having a definite and complete answer to any question posed on autism, which is above criticism because the APHID-V3 sufferer is autistic and you aren't.

YOUR LIFE IS NOT A LABEL